November 4, 1991

For Archbishop Rembert Weakland —

    With admiration and respect
for all you're endeavoring to achieve
— including the goals of this book.

        David Riener

# The
# PRISONERS
# of
# WELFARE

# The
# PRISONERS
# of
# WELFARE

## Liberating America's Poor from Unemployment and Low Wages

### David Raphael Riemer

PRAEGER

New York
Westport, Connecticut
London

**Library of Congress Cataloging-in-Publication Data**

Riemer, David R.
  The prisoners of welfare : liberating America's poor from
unemployment and low wages / David R. Riemer.
    p.  cm.
  Bibliography: p.
  Includes index.
  ISBN 0–275–92705–9 (alk. paper)
  1. Economic assistance, Domestic—United States.  2. Poor—
Government policy—United States.  3. Public welfare—United
States.  4. Job vacancies—United States.  5. Public service
employment—United States.  6. Income maintenance programs—United
States.    I. Title.
HC110.P63R49  1988
362.5'8'0973—dc19        88–3926

Library of Congress Catalog Card Number: 88–3926
ISBN: 0–275–92705–9

First published in 1988

Praeger Publishers, One Madison Avenue, New York, NY 10010
A division of Greenwood Press, Inc.

Printed in the United States of America

The paper used in this book complies with the
Permanent Paper Standard issued by the National
Information Standards Organization (Z39.48–1984).

10  9  8  7  6  5  4  3  2

To my father, Neal Riemer, with love and gratitude.

# Contents

# Tables and Figures

**TABLES**

# Preface

This book rests on eight assumptions, which some readers may not share and which others may share without fully appreciating the foundation they lay for the book's argument. In fairness to all readers, I would like to state these assumptions at the outset.

First, when I refer to the poor, I usually mean poor adults. Children under 18 constitute over one-third of the poor population in the United States, but virtually all such children live with impoverished adults—typically with one or both of their parents. The poverty of children and the poverty of their adult caretakers are, in fact, mutually dependent. Children are poor because the adults upon whom they rely for food, shelter, clothing, and so on have incomes below the poverty line. At the same time, the presence of children may cause a family with a low income, and thus the family's adult or adults, to fall below the poverty line (which rises with increasing family size). The principal reason I generally equate the poor with poor adults, however, is that this is a book about public policy, that is, how best to eliminate poverty in the United States. Since any plausible short-term effort to lift all of the poor—both children and adults—out of poverty must necessarily focus on the adults, it makes sense, for the purposes of this book, to define the poor in most cases as poor adults.

Second, I generally use the term welfare to mean the Aid to Families with Dependent Children (AFDC) program. When citizens, newspaper editors, and politicians speak of welfare, they usually mean AFDC. I follow the common usage, although I recognize that it would be technically more precise to define welfare as the entire network of cash-transfer programs, cash-substitute programs (such as Food Stamps), in-kind benefit programs (such as Medicaid), and service programs that are offered to poor persons by federal, state, and local governments. From time to time I speak of those other welfare programs, but when I do I usually refer to them by their unique labels.

Third, I make the assumption in this book that, on balance, the wisest policy is to require poor single parents with small children (as well as other poor persons) to work in order to obtain an income. There are some good reasons for just giving such parents money without requiring them to work. There are also good reasons for insisting that such parents work for their income, like most of the rest of us. The issue is a complicated one. It serves no purpose for the advocates of the opposing viewpoints to mock each other ("giveaways," "forced labor," etc.). Whatever your position happens to be, the opposite viewpoint is a legitimate one and deserves respect. On balance, I believe that the reasons for permitting a poor single parent with small children to receive money without working are less numerous and less powerful than the arguments for insisting that those parents should work for their income.

Unfortunately, it would double the size of this book to lay out fully all the factors that add up to this conclusion. Since only the conclusion itself is necessary for the rest of the book to proceed, I have decided simply to postulate the conclusion as an assumption. You may disagree, or you may agree, but since this is such a critical issue—an issue, regrettably, permitting little compromise—I feel that the best course is to lay out my position from the start.

Fourth, this book assumes that while the trends that are occurring within the poor population of the United States are of great interest to demographers and academicians, the changes that have taken place within at least the last decade do not offer much guidance when it comes to formulating short-term policies for eliminating poverty, which is the principal concern of this book. For this reason, while some data on trends are presented, this book generally contents itself with presenting a single year's data (usually for 1984, sometimes for 1985 or 1986) about whatever facet of poverty, welfare, or public policy is under discussion.

The same goes for the debate about trends occurring within the labor market—for example, the much-heralded shift from a manufacturing economy to a service economy and the much-debated increase in the relative proportion of low-wage jobs. Again, these trends and the debates surrounding them are of great interest. I assume in this book, however, that, whatever the trends happen to be, they offer little help in figuring out short-term solutions to getting the poor out of poverty.

Fifth, I assume that readers will both grasp and accept the double sense in which I use such expressions as "the poor will remain poor" or "the poor will get out of poverty." Sometimes I am referring to members (or the entirety) of the poor population at any one point in time; and thus, when I speak about eliminating poverty, I am speaking about the extent to which those individuals will (or will not) get out of poverty as the result of a given change in public policy. Sometimes, though, I am referring to the continuing poor population, which over time consists of different individuals with the common characteristic of poverty; and then when I speak about eliminating poverty, I mean the extent to which the overall incidence or rate of poverty will (or will not) be reduced as a result of a particular new policy. In context, the distinction should be clear. If the reader is having trouble with one meaning, try the other.

Sixth, I assume here that, whatever cultural differences divide the poor in this country (including, but not limited to, the black, urban underclass) from the rest of us, those differences are not so profound that they would prohibit the poor from getting out of poverty, if the right public policies were adopted by the U.S. government. Indeed, one of the most important premises of this book—stated or implied from time to time throughout the book, but whose centrality to the main argument of the book justifies its mention at the very beginning—is that the poor generally share the same values and attitudes about work that the rest of us possess. The poor need to work. The poor want to work. The poor, as will be pointed out, generally do work. They seek from work not only a decent income but the status of worker—a status that translates into social respectability and legitimizes participation in community life. There are always exceptions, but as a rule the poor's "culture"—if it exists, and whatever it might be—is not a major cause of their poverty.

Seventh, I assume that poverty in the United States—and the job shortage and abundance of low-wage jobs that constitute its primary causes, as will be argued—are neither the intended goals of any group within American society nor the inevitable consequence of the American system. Poverty can fairly be blamed on a number of specific features of our culture, economy, and government. Fixing the blame takes up much of this book. Poverty is not, however, the aim of business, or government, or any other segment of the United States. Neither is poverty ineluctable. I make the assumption throughout this book that poverty in the United States can be eliminated, notwithstanding its deep roots in our system, by building on potentially more powerful features of American culture, economy, and government.

My eighth and final assumption is that eliminating poverty remains an urgent—and an achievable—goal, one that we should seek to meet by the end of this century. It will take an extraordinary effort of organization and advocacy to accomplish the task. Yet it can be achieved, through peaceful means and normal democratic processes, *if* we begin by understanding the real causes of poverty, *if* we are willing to make some very tough fiscal and political choices. Vision and leadership will be the key. It is surely worth the try.

It is my hope that a mixed audience of "just plain" citizens, journalists, academic experts, and government officials will read this book. To accommodate such a diverse set of readers, I have perhaps included more information than any one group may care or need to absorb in order to follow my basic argument. Nonexperts may wish to skip or skim Chapter 1, if they are willing to accept the official poverty line as a satisfactory demarcation between want and sufficiency. Experts may wish to pass over Chapter 2, if they are already familiar with the census data linking poverty and work. Policymakers may wish to avoid the lengthy Chapter 9, if they are already convinced that the poor now have no legal right not to be poor, but ought to acquire such a right through legislation. Readers who agree that low-income workers need subsidized day care and health insurance, but do not particularly care about the details, may wish to ignore Chapter 11.

I would encourage all readers to read all of the other chapters. The Overview provides a road map to the entire book. Chapters 3, 4, 6, and 7 form the empirical core of this book. Unless you read them, you will have trouble making much sense of anything that follows. Chapters 5 and 8 present the key theoretical argument. Chapters 10 and 12 attempt to answer those twin bedeviling questions, What do you propose to do? and, What will it cost? The Conclusion argues that, like it or not, our options are limited, only a few of them will eliminate poverty in the United States, and only a choice akin to the one advocated here will solve the problem in a fiscally and politically acceptable manner.

# Acknowledgments

*The Prisoners of Welfare* has been a long time aborning. It may have begun to take shape in 1963 when my father, Neal Riemer, returned to central Pennsylvania from the great March on Washington with a giant button he had worn during the demonstration. The button pictured two hands (one black, one white) clasping in the midst of the words "March on Washington for Jobs & Freedom." I understood the freedom, but why the jobs? What was the connection? Could not anybody who wanted a job get a job? Were there not enough jobs? I was 14 at the time, and for the subsequent quarter of a century I have kept that button near me as a reminder of questions I knew were important but did not know how to answer.

The actual research that led to this book did not begin until nine years later, in 1972. I was assigned to take a look at the effectiveness of federal manpower programs (as they were then still called) by my boss Edgar Cahn, who headed a small (now defunct) public-interest law firm called the Citizens Advocate Center. I reviewed all the evaluations I could locate of MDTA (Manpower Development and Training Act of 1962) programs, the Job Corps, the Neighborhood Youth Corps, the JOBS (Job Opportunities in the Business Sector) program, CEP (Concentrated Employment Program), WIN (Work Incentive Program), and others and concluded "that, on the whole, poor manpower enrollees frequently obtain no skills at all, and at best obtain crude, unprofitable skills." As a result, I said, "average enrollee post-training earnings are so slight—usually just over the poverty line, never close to the BLS [lower living standard]—that it is clear that manpower programs . . .

have failed to provide most enrollees with jobs which afford a decent standard of living."

In preparing this report, which I completed in 1973 and called *Recycling the Poor: The Failure of Federal Manpower Programs*, I began to poke around in the Census Bureau reports on poverty and earnings. That research was the real beginning of this book, for in that research I began to understand how many of the poor in the United States wanted to work but remained unemployed, even in times of relatively low "official" unemployment and, just as significant, how many remained poor notwithstanding the full-time, year-round work they did. The conclusion I came to—logical enough, but empirically unsubstantiated at the time—was that there was a job shortage and an abundance of low-wage jobs. Even if manpower programs had been successful, I wrote, their potential impact on poverty was limited by what I then called an "undersupply" of both low- and high-wage jobs. It was not a bad piece of work, and I was surprised it never saw the light of day, but since my assertions about a job shortage and an abundance of low-wage jobs rested on thin ice, it was just as well.

The following year, at Harvard Law School, I returned to the theme in a paper for Professor Lance Liebman, entitled "A New Look at the Low-Income Population: Hard-Working People, Low-Paying Jobs." Again, I used Census Bureau data about poverty and earnings to conclude that poverty was primarily the result of a job shortage and too many low-wage jobs. The concluding paragraph, which I could have written yesterday, is worth quoting:

> But for millions of low-income workers [i.e., people who are capable of working, whether they hold jobs or not] who either can be expected to work full-time and year-round, or who already do so, *neither* income *nor* services are appropriate. To provide these people with welfare payments or in-kind help is both insulting and senseless. These people want—and should have—steady work and good wages. They have low income now precisely because, though they are strongly attached to the labor market, that market does not provide them with enough work and wages. Their path out of low income therefore leads to the creation of an expanded supply of stable, well-paying jobs.

Not very graceful prose, but essentially on the mark. Yet I still had no direct evidence of a job shortage or an abundance of low-wage jobs.

From 1974 until 1982 I kept thinking about the subject of this book and doing more research. In 1982 I finally came across the data I had been looking for: Katharine Abraham's study of the relationship between unemployed jobseekers and available jobs, which demonstrates the existence of a continuing (though varying) job shortage in the United States.

Because this book has been so long in the making, there are many to thank for the help they have provided me in writing it. I probably have not remembered them all. If anyone who should be mentioned here is left out, I hope my apologies will be accepted.

I want to begin by thanking my father, Neal Riemer, Andrew V. Stout Professor of Political Philosophy at Drew University. An extraordinary teacher, a fine scholar, a loving and compassionate man, husband, and father, he has given me support and encouragement at every stage of my life. His commitment to this book and his assistance in its completion are the single greatest reason that it has seen the light of day. It is dedicated to him with great appreciation, respect, and affection.

My mother, Ruby Riemer, a distinguished poet and teacher, also provided much support and encouragement, as well as editorial assistance. I wish to thank her as well.

The Time Insurance Foundation, by making available a generous grant to Congress For a Working America, paid for much of the research that I relied on in preparing the book. Funded by this grant, Dan Willett, a staff member of Congress For a Working America, did a fine job in tracking down data I needed and preparing clear summaries. Mark Mader, a law student at the University of Wisconsin-Madison, provided me with the excellent legal research upon which Chapter 9 is based.

Throughout the years, the staff and members of Congress For a Working America have provided both moral and intellectual support to the effort that culminated in this book. I particularly wish to thank Ed Bobinchak, Cindy Brown, John Gardner, Doris Jeffrey, Mary Jimmerson, Sharon Kalemkiarian, Julie Kerksick, Crosby Milne, Andy Moss, Ron Ottinger, Warren Sazama, S. J., Beth Schulman, Chuck Turner, Eden Weinmann, and Dan Willett for their help.

Much of what I know about poverty, welfare, and public policy I have learned from practitioners: the men and women who fashion public policy and write the laws. Several past and present staff members of the Wisconsin Legislative Fiscal Bureau and Wisconsin Legislative Council have been especially helpful: Judy Collins, Susan Goodwin, Ken Johnson, John Sauer, Dick Sweet, and Susan Robillard. A number of former or current legislative aides have also been of great assistance: Michael Youngman and Stephanie Case in Wisconsin, Rachel Block in New York.

My greatest debt in this area is to the dedicated and skillful Wisconsin legislators (past and present) with whom I have had the luck to work: Lynn Adelman, Dennis Conta, Dick Flintrop, Mary Lou Munts, Joe Strohl, Peter Tropman, and Rebecca Young. I have also learned much from several other state legislators with whom my work for the National Conference of State Legislatures brought me into contact: Marilyn Goldwater, Maryland; Mary Marshall, Virginia; and Paul Starnes, Tennessee.

Four other legislators I would like to single out for special thanks: Tom Loftus, Speaker of the Wisconsin Assembly; John Norquist, former Assistant Majority Leader of the Wisconsin Senate; Paul Offner, former Assistant Majority Leader of the Wisconsin Senate; and Jim Tallon, Majority Leader of the New York Assembly. Many of their insights into the U.S. welfare system and the U.S. health-care system are reflected in this book. I owe them each a great personal—as well as a great intellectual—debt. I also wish to express my gratitude to two of this country's most distinguished elected officials who, by letting me work for them, allowed me to learn most of what I know about what is wrong and what is right with government: Wisconsin's former governor, Patrick Lucey, and Senator Edward Kennedy.

Many individuals have helped me shape the concepts that eventually came together in this book. They may not all have realized that was what they were doing, and many of them will disagree with parts of what I have written, but I would nonetheless like to thank Steve Andrews, Richard Bartholomew, Bill Bechtel, Dan Borque, John Bryson, Scott Bunton, Barbara Crosby, Rick Curtis, Leo Friedel, Richard Froh, Peter Goldberg, Bob Greenstein, Bob Gris, Bill Hagan, Lesley Keegan, Steve Kelman, Peter Kramer, John Krick, Phil Lerman, Sue Manes, Dick Merritt, Carl Milofsky, Kathryn Morrison, Jay Noren, Mark Petri, Rick Phelps, Beth Perry, John Pittenger, Jeremiah Riemer, Seth Riemer, Hannah Rosenthal, Eliot Stanley, Amy Shapiro, Stuart Shapiro, Mike Soika, Kathy Sykes, Mindy Taranto, Kathy Brennan Wiggins, Gail Wilensky, Ken Willis, Joy Johnson Wilson, and Bob Wise.

Katharine Abraham, of the Brookings Institution and the University of Maryland, whose research is part of the foundation of this book, has over the years provided me with copies of her articles; she also furnished an update of her work to one of my researchers during the preparation of this book; I wish to extend special thanks to Dr. Abraham for her generous assistance. Also, during the final push to complete this book, a number of individuals provided me with additional information and insights. I particularly want to thank Ralph Andreano (University of Wisconsin-Madison), Charles Brown (University of Michigan), Deborah Chollet (Employee Benefits Research Institute), Irwin Garfinkel (University of Wisconsin-Madison), Daniel Horowitz (Claremont College), Frank Levy (University of Maryland), James Medoff (Harvard University), and Charles O'Connor (Bureau of Labor Statistics).

Several individuals reviewed the last draft of this book before it went to the publisher and provided helpful comments, both large and small.

My thanks again to several people already mentioned—my parents, Neal Riemer and Ruby Riemer, John Gardner, Mark Mader, Mark Petri, and Dan Willett.

I also wish to express my appreciation to Praeger and the fine editors assigned to me, Susan Pazourek and Karen O'Brien, for their confidence and support.

Finally, I want to thank my wife, Ellie Graan, for her sustenance and help. This book was written in time stolen from her and our newborn son Daniel. Her understanding and support can never be adequately described in words or appreciated enough.

# The
# PRISONERS
# of
# WELFARE

# Overview: Reshaping the Debate

This book seeks to reshape the current debate between conservatives and liberals about the cause of poverty in the United States, the role of the welfare system in perpetuating poverty, and the direction public policy should take in order to eliminate poverty.

The debate has often been presented as a clash between conservatives who blame the poor for their own poverty and liberals who blame external forces, such as the education system, racial and sexual discrimination, or the economy. While there is some truth in this formulation, it represents more a caricature of both sides than an accurate portrayal of their respective positions. Both conservatives and liberals offer analyses that ultimately lay the blame for poverty on external forces. They simply blame different external factors.

The basic conservative posture, articulated most forcefully by Charles Murray in *Losing Ground*, is that poverty—not historically, but today—is largely the result of the welfare system. Poverty in the United States was declining, Murray points out, before the welfare system was enriched by higher benefits and enlarged by an expanded array of cash substitutes and in-kind services in the mid–1960s. The subsequent dramatic rise in the black, urban underclass and the failure of poverty to drop further in the 1970s and 1980s, Murray contends, is the result of the welfare system's expansion. To restore the preexisting trend toward a reduction in poverty, Murray argues, Congress should simply eliminate the welfare system.[1]

Most conservatives shy away from taking so extreme a position, but they do typically advocate either a cut in welfare payments, or holding the line on payment levels (which means a cut in real dollars, because of inflation), or requiring all or most welfare recipients to work for their benefits ("workfare"). The common thread running through these conservative positions is the conviction that helping the poor get out of poverty requires, if not the elimination of welfare itself, at least the elimination of welfare's attractiveness as an alternative to work.

Liberal critics have until recently focused on challenging Murray's data and rebutting his assertions. The worst flaw in Murray's argument, they maintain, is his reliance on the logical fallacy of *post hoc, ergo propter hoc*—after this, therefore because of this. The fact that the rapid growth of the black, urban underclass and the halt in the poverty rate's decline both followed Congress's expansion of the welfare system does not prove that those specific effects were the result of that specific cause. The real causes lie elsewhere.

Perhaps the most forceful liberal exponent of this critique has been William Julius Wilson in his recent book *The Truly Disadvantaged*.[2] Wilson not only assails the sufficiency of Murray's data and the adequacy of Murray's logic, but offers his own, countervailing explanation of why the black, urban underclass has grown so rapidly and why efforts to reduce poverty have stagnated. The heart of the problem, Wilson argues, is the shrinking pool of marriageable black men, which has resulted from an extraordinary rise in black male joblessness. This pattern of joblessness, in turn, stems from profound structural changes in the U.S. economy, particularly the disappearance of unskilled, entry-level, low-wage jobs in manufacturing. The solution, Wilson maintains, is not to eliminate welfare but to establish a comprehensive program of economic and social reform. Such a program would not focus on the black, urban underclass *per se* or the welfare population *per se*. Rather, it would emphasize more "universal" policies, which the rest of the population might more readily embrace. The core of the program would be a national macroeconomic policy designed to create a tight labor market.

Just as Murray's proposed solution is too radical for most conservatives, Wilson's proposed solution is probably too radical for most liberals. As in the past, the dominant liberal view continues to be that if the poor received adequate education and training, did not confront racial and sexual discrimination, and (especially in the case of welfare recipients) could obtain affordable day care and health insurance, they could be expected to get out of poverty by getting into jobs—jobs that, presumptively, provided an adequate income. Wilson does not entirely disagree with this solution. He emphasizes, for instance, the importance of training. He in no way argues against affirmative action. The core of Wilson's solution, however, is one that some liberals will either refrain from embracing or hesitate to identify as the *primary* solution, that is, national macroeconomic policies designed to create a tight labor market.

This book addresses the same large concerns—poverty, welfare, and public policy—that conservatives like Murray and liberals like Wilson address, but the specific questions this book seeks to answer are different. This recasting of the questions is not a matter of style or ego. It has been done because of a conviction that the questions usually asked tend to distort the way we perceive U.S. poverty, the welfare system, and the choices available to makers of public policy. By redefining the inquiry, we can get a clearer understanding of why the poor are poor, why welfare perpetuates poverty, and how public policy should proceed.

None of this is to say that Murray, Wilson, and hundreds of other U.S. poverty experts are wholly wrong about poverty, welfare, and public policy. Their analysis and insights have contributed enormously to the debate. Many of their conclusions and recommendations show up in this book—for example, the conservatives' emphasis on the welfare system's perverse incentives to refrain from taking low-wage jobs and the reasonableness of expecting work in return for money, the liberals' emphasis on the poor's desire to work and the importance of affordable day care and health insurance. This book echoes, in particular, William Julius Wilson's insistence that liberals must look beyond enhancing the job-readiness of the poor to increasing the supply of jobs. Yet, notwithstanding the great debt owed to both conservative and liberal analysts, one of this book's dominant themes is that both the conservative and the liberal modes of analysis—including Murray's and Wilson's—have tended to limit the debate in ways that get in the way of our understanding poverty as a whole, the role of the welfare system, and the options available to policymakers.

How, then, does this book refocus the debate? What are the different, more clarifying, more helpful questions asked here?

First, this book looks at the entire poor population of the United States and asks, Why do all the poor remain poor? Most commentators—conservative and liberal alike—have tended to focus on discrete segments of the poor population: the black, urban underclass; blacks in general; racial and ethnic minorities; women; welfare families; the physically handicapped; the mentally handicapped; the working poor; and so on. Murray (implicitly) and Wilson (explicitly) focus on the black, urban underclass and welfare families, which have always been the most studied subgroups. This book looks at the poor as a whole—black and white, underclass and working poor, welfare families and nonwelfare families. There is no reason why subsets of the poor, whose poverty seems most intractable, should not receive special attention, but for both practical and political reasons the widest possible focus makes the most sense. As a practical matter, notwithstanding the evidence about "intergenerational poverty" and "intergenerational welfare," there is enormous movement from one subgroup to another, just as there is enormous movement in and out of poverty. Thus, to deal effectively with the subgroups that pose the toughest problems (the black, urban underclass and welfare families) it is necessary to focus not only on those subgroups as they now exist but on all the other subgroups of the poor population from which many have come and to which many will return. From a political perspective it is difficult to devise solutions that provide real help to the subgroups most in trouble, if those solutions leave them substantially better off economically than the remaining subgroups of the poor population or reduce the other subgroups' access to jobs. Yet, lifting up the black, urban underclass and welfare families to the relative—and sometimes actual—disadvantage of the remaining poor is precisely what will happen unless all the poor are lifted up simultaneously. The only way to finesse the practical and political problems that arise from focusing on subgroups of the poor is to focus from the beginning on all America's poor.

Second, this book concentrates on the missing link in the entire debate about poverty, welfare, and public policy by asking, What is the relationship between poverty and the job market? If the poor are to be lifted out of poverty by working, are there enough jobs available, and do those jobs pay wages that are high enough? Most commentators—conservative and liberal alike—have tended to avoid this issue, though in different ways.

Conservatives tend to duck the question altogether. Murray, for instance, does not seriously inquire as to whether, if the welfare system were eliminated, there would be enough jobs; he assumes, without offering any evidence, that the jobs will be there. (Conservative politicians are only slightly less sophisticated. When asked if there are enough jobs, Ronald Reagan's classic response has been simply to wave the Sunday help-wanted ads.) With somewhat greater candor, conservatives will typically acknowledge that many poor persons cannot get jobs that get them over the poverty line. They seem to imply, however, that this does not represent a problem. Remaining poor while working full-time and year-round is either assumed to be a satisfactory state of affairs, an assumption that is seldom made explicit and almost never argued, or a temporary stage on the way to higher-paying jobs, an assumption that is never proved.

Liberals, by contrast, often assert that there are not enough jobs to go around, but they seldom offer any proof. Wilson, for instance, grounds much of his argument on the phenomenon of widespread black male joblessness, and he asserts on a number of occasions that this joblessness is the result of an aggregate shortage of jobs. Indeed, unless Wilson postulated a shortage of jobs, his recommendation that the U.S. government embrace macroeconomic policies that promote a tight labor market would not make sense. Yet nowhere in *The Truly Disadvantaged* is there any evidence that, compared to the number of unemployed seeking work (however defined), the number of available jobs (however defined) is smaller; that is, that there is an actual job shortage. Liberal scholars have similarly failed to explore in depth the connection between the poor who do hold jobs and the wage structure of the U.S. economy. Unlike conservatives, liberals are far more inclined to note that many poor people who hold jobs on a full-time, year-round basis still end up below the poverty line. The liberal consensus is that this is clearly an unacceptable state of affairs, in part because liberals perceive that for many such workers poverty will remain a long-term if not a permanent condition. It is therefore surprising that liberal scholars have been satisfied to assume, rather than demonstrate empirically, a strong connection between poverty and the wages U.S. employers pay.

This book delves into this largely unexplored region. It attempts to address squarely the question of whether the poor as a whole can get out of poverty, if the supply of jobs and the structure of wages remain the same.

Third, building on the first two questions, this book revisits the question, Is there really much connection between poverty and welfare? To what extent can poverty as a whole really be increased or reduced by the welfare system, whether unreformed or reformed? Most commentators—conservative and liberal alike—have addressed this question, and they have tended to draw a strong link between poverty and welfare. Conservatives, adhering to Murray's basic thesis, have argued that much of poverty can be explained by welfare, and thus much of poverty could be eliminated by eliminating welfare or at least curtailing benefit levels and imposing a work requirement. Liberals have seldom blamed poverty on welfare, but they have argued that much of poverty could be eliminated by "doing welfare right," that is, giving recipients more education and training, combating racial and sexual discrimination more effectively, and providing subsidized day care and extending Medicaid. Wilson, somewhat unique among liberals, argues against these welfare-specific solutions, but he nonetheless favors pursuing some of the same approaches (particularly training programs) on a broader basis. The conservatives' and liberals' particular prescriptions for attacking poverty by modifying welfare differ sharply, but the general prescription is the same: You can do something about poverty if you change the welfare system.

This book seeks to reexamine the connection between poverty and welfare in the light of the evidence presented about the availability of jobs and the structure of wages in the U.S. economy. The same questions explored by both conservatives and liberals—What is the connection between poverty and welfare? Can poverty be reduced, if not eliminated, by altering the welfare system?—are examined again, not so much in greater depth as in a new context. The old familiar question thus becomes, Is there really much connection at all between poverty and welfare—and between poverty's elimination and welfare's reform—in view of the fundamental, underlying link between poverty and the structure of the U.S. economy?

The fourth and final question this book asks is, To the extent poverty in the United States is largely the result of a shortage of jobs and a plethora of low-wage jobs, what can be done in the short term to get the poor out of poverty by providing the unemployed poor with jobs and by providing the working poor with higher remuneration? This inquiry—and the solutions it implies—are not unique. Its points of departure from other approaches, however, should be highlighted.

To begin with, this question rests on the conviction that the only equitable and effective way to eliminate poverty in this country is by means of a jobs solution—and only a jobs solution. Both conservatives and liberals have at times advocated dealing with poverty by making all poor persons eligible for cash payments. As will be discussed elsewhere in this book, the cash solution fails at almost every level: It fails to give unemployed poor the jobs they want; it is unfair to the rest of us, who pay the bill; it would be (if it truly eliminated poverty) extremely costly; and it is politically unacceptable. Those who are seriously committed to eliminating poverty in this country should no longer bother to ask themselves whether a cash solution or a jobs solution is preferable. Only a jobs solution gives the poor what they want, can be accomplished at a reasonable price, and stands a chance of commanding broad political support. The question should be, What kind of jobs solution works best?

The final question this book asks is also somewhat unique in its emphasis on a short-term solution. The question is, What can we do *now* to provide the unemployed poor with jobs and the working poor with adequate remuneration? There is no mystery about the need for prompt action. Poverty is a terrible thing, and we should seek to end it right away. The real reason for underscoring the need for a short-term solution, however, is to suggest that there is also a need for a long-term solution and that such a long-term solution may well be (and probably should be) very different.

This book, in seeking to develop short-term measures for providing the unemployed poor with jobs and providing the working poor with higher remuneration, should in no way be construed as advocating that we do not need a permanent solution to the problem of ensuring every American who wants to work a steady job that provides a decent income. On the contrary, we desperately need a long-term solution. Nor should this book, in advocating the creation of community-service jobs and the expansion of the current federal wage-supplement program, be construed as supporting those particular measures as part of the long-term solution. They may or may not be part of the long-term answer. For a host of reasons, this book does not tackle the long-term inquiry, but that decision should not be misunderstood as downplaying the need for a long-term solution or recommending what the long-term solution ought to be.

In the normal course of events, outlining the frame of reference for a book—in this case, the ways in which this book seeks to refocus the current debate about poverty, welfare, and public policy—should be a sufficient introduction, especially where the basic thesis of the book is fairly simple. Yet, though this book's thesis is simple, it contradicts the conventional wisdom about the causes of poverty in the United States, the role of the welfare system, and the best way to lift the poor above the poverty line. A brief overview may therefore be useful in avoiding both confusion and dismay.

Millions of poor Americans—constituting the vast majority of the poor—are poor for three reasons:[3]

1. They cannot work, or old age exempts them from work, yet their unearned income is below the poverty line.
2. They can work, but they cannot find jobs, and their joblessness either leaves them without any income or with an income from other sources that is too low to get them above the poverty line.
3. They are working, but their wages are low, so low that, whether or not combined with other sources of income, they fall below the poverty line.

The conventional explanations of poverty in this country are largely incorrect. The poor's lack of motivation, their lack of education and training, their victimization in many instances by racial and sexual discrimination, and their difficulty in obtaining affordable day care and health insurance have little to do with why poverty persists in the United States. Rather, poverty in the United States is primarily the result of an inadequate system of social-insurance payments, an imbalance between the number of unemployed jobseekers and the number of available jobs, and an even greater imbalance between what workers in this country want—jobs that afford them enough income to maintain a decent standard of living—and the number of such middle-to-high-wage jobs available in the nation's economy.

The conventional wisdom does help to explain why any *particular* individual ends up being poor. A worker who is unmotivated, inadequately educated or improperly trained, a black or a woman, or someone who has trouble finding day care or health insurance will, indeed, have a much tougher time landing a job, moving up to high-paying employment, and getting out of poverty in the United States than a worker without those deficiencies or handicaps. This is because the characteristics of workers are the easiest device on hand for rationing a scarce supply of jobs and a scarcer supply of good jobs. To the less-committed, less-prepared, less-favored, less-flexible workers go no jobs or low-wage jobs (or, at least, a disproportionate share thereof). To the more-committed, more-prepared, more-favored, more-flexible workers go the middle-to-high-wage jobs (or, at least, a disproportionate share thereof). There is nothing novel about this way of rationing scarce goods. The "worse" competitors generally end up with the worst prizes—and the "better" competitors generally end up with the best prizes—in any contest in which there is a limit on the number of prizes awarded. Divvying up prizes in this fashion also has the virtue of simplicity. Finally, this approach seems fair. Except for its arbitrary classification of blacks and women as worse competitors and whites and men as better competitors (which some contend is either no longer occurring or not significant, but which others view as a profoundly distorting factor), assigning the worse competitors the worst prizes and the better competitors the best prizes rewards individuals for behavior and attributes (motivation, education, training, etc.) over which they have some measure of personal control.

The conventional wisdom fails to explain, however, why the poor as a *group* end up poor—that is, why poverty persists in the United States. The full explanation can be found only in the shortage of jobs and the plethora of low-wage jobs. In short, poverty refuses to disappear in this country primarily because there just are not enough jobs—especially good jobs—to go around.

The welfare system does not cause poverty, but by its design it fails to eliminate poverty. The poor who get full welfare benefits receive too little in cash and other assistance to get out of poverty. Most of the poor get only limited help (e.g., Food Stamps) or no help at all from the welfare system. America's poor are the prisoners of welfare, not because their poverty is initially created by welfare, and not because their poverty is perpetuated by welfare, but because their escape from poverty is neither the principal object nor the ultimate outcome of most of the welfare programs our society has created. Escape is, indeed, impossible as long as the welfare system retains its current structure.

The poor are not the only prisoners of welfare. The rest of us are its prisoners as well. Resentful of welfare cheaters; frustrated by the perverse incentives welfare offers to the poor not to form families and not to work; angry that welfare recipients receive benefits that other equally poor individuals cannot obtain; embittered by the apparent failure of a seemingly endless battery of government programs to make a dent in the welfare rolls; dismayed by the stinginess of elected politicians who refuse to give the poor enough to live on, while they subsidize the middle class and the well-to-do—we, the majority, have allowed ourselves to be distracted from engaging in a reexamination of the basic assumptions on which the welfare system is based. Above all, we have failed to inquire seriously as to whether welfare's most fundamental assumption is correct: that just beyond the borders of welfare there is available a sufficient number of jobs that provide decent pay. We ourselves are the prisoners of welfare in the sense that we have failed to disenthrall ourselves from our own bitterness and fictions about the system and our unspoken panic about the possibility of alternatives. Yet, until we surmount these barriers of feeling and thought, we cannot begin to build the system anew—or, rather, we cannot start to construct a fundamentally different system for meeting our obligation to the poor.

An outline of what such a different system would look like concludes this book. Since poverty cannot be ended by the current welfare system, rather than reform welfare we should scrap it entirely. Since poverty is primarily the result of an inadequate social insurance system, a shortage of jobs, and a surfeit of low-wage jobs, the solution proposed is to

- Provide the poor who cannot work, or whom we do not expect to work, with cash payments that are sufficient to get them above the poverty line;
- Offer the poor who can work community-service jobs;
- Provide the poor who are working with wage supplements sufficient to get them above the poverty line.

This approach will still leave many of the once-poor—as well as many of the never-poor but near-poor—with genuine day-care and health-insurance needs, and therefore various solutions to those problems are also presented. The penultimate chapter seeks to answer the questions, What will this cost, and how do we pay the bill?

Samuel Johnson said two centuries ago, "A decent provision for the poor is the true test of civilization."[4] For decades we have failed to meet the test. This book is an effort to explain why.

The poor themselves are not the problem. They, like the rest of us, need and want to work. Most of them do work. Cruelty and selfishness on the part of the nonpoor are not the problem, either. Americans on the whole are kindly and generous people. There is no conscious or subconscious desire to keep the poor in poverty on the part of the business community, the government, or any other "interest" in the United States. Lack of resources is also not the problem. The federal budget has been horribly mismanaged, but the cost of eliminating poverty is not so great that our society cannot afford to pay the price, preferably by reallocating current expenditures, if necessary by raising taxes.

Rather, the main reason we have failed to make "a decent provision for the poor" is that we have simultaneously failed to understand poverty's causes and allowed ourselves to become obsessed with the welfare system (some falsely blaming it as the cause of poverty, others falsely hoping to reduce or eliminate poverty by reforming an unreformable system). A new and accurate understanding of poverty's causes is urgently needed. We must liberate not only the poor but ourselves from the welfare prison. An entirely different framework for eliminating poverty is required. That framework should be based on hiring the unemployed poor and raising the income of the working poor. Whether the specific short-term proposals suggested here are the right ones or whether others would be better, we should establish as a firm goal the elimination of poverty in this rich land by the year 2000. As the United States enters the twenty-first century, we should have passed the "true test of civilization."

## NOTES

1. Charles Murray, *Losing Ground: American Social Policy, 1950–1980* (New York: Basic Books, 1984).

2. William Julius Wilson, *The Truly Disadvantaged: The Inner City, the Underclass, and Public Policy* (Chicago: University of Chicago Press, 1987).

3. There are a relatively small number of people in the United States who are poor for reasons other than those listed, for example, imprisonment following conviction for a crime, or a personal preference for uncompensated or low-paying employment. These impoverished individuals are not the concern of this book. In any case, they constitute only a small fraction of the poor in the United States.

4. James Boswell, *Life of Samuel Johnson* (Chicago: Scott, Foresman and Company, 1923), p. 169.

# PART ONE
## WHY THE POOR ARE POOR

# 1
# Who Are the Poor?

A person is counted as poor by the U.S. Bureau of the Census if she or he belongs in a family unit—either a one-person "unrelated individual" or a multi-person "family"—whose total family cash income falls below a specified dollar threshold. The threshold is commonly called the poverty level or poverty line. Depending on the characteristics of the family unit (e.g., the age of the unit's head or householder, or the number of related persons in the unit), the poverty line varies.[1] Table 1 sets forth the poverty line for 1985.[2]

The poverty line changes from year to year to reflect changes in the cost of living. Table 2 shows, for a family of four, the changes in the poverty line between 1960 and 1985.[3]

The poverty line is a concept so ingrained in the thinking of the U.S. public—so widely used by academicians and editors, so taken for granted by bureaucrats and legislators—that it has become endowed with a kind of sanctity. Nonetheless, its legitimacy is periodically challenged by both the Left and the Right. Liberals have sought to demonstrate that the poverty line is too low, and that large numbers of those whose income rises above it are nonetheless really poor, in the sense that they earn too little to maintain a "decent" standard of living. Conservatives have sought to undermine the poverty line from another direction. Many officially poor people, they point out, receive income substitutes like Food Stamps and in-kind benefits like Medicaid. If the poor's income were recalculated to include the cash value of these benefits, many officially poor people would have real incomes above the poverty line. Use of a poverty line that measures only cash income

**Table 1**
**Poverty Line, 1985**

| Family Size | Poverty Threshold | |
|---|---|---|
| One person  (unrelated individual) | $ 5,469 | |
| Under 65 years | | 5,593 |
| 65 years and over | | 5,156 |
| Two persons | 6,998 | |
| Householder under 65 years | | 7,231 |
| Householder 65 years and over | | 6,503 |
| Three persons | 8,573 | |
| Four persons | 10,989 | |
| Five persons | 13,007 | |
| Six persons | 14,696 | |
| Seven persons | 16,656 | |
| Eight persons | 18,512 | |
| Nine persons or more | 22,083 | |

**Table 2**
**Poverty Line for a Family of Four, 1960–85**

| Year | Poverty Line |
|---|---|
| 1960 | $ 3,022 |
| 1961 | 3,054 |
| 1962 | 3,089 |
| 1963 | 3,128 |
| 1964 | 3,169 |
| 1965 | 3,223 |
| 1966 | 3,317 |
| 1967 | 3,410 |
| 1968 | 3,553 |
| 1969 | 3,743 |
| 1970 | 3,968 |
| 1971 | 4,137 |
| 1972 | 4,275 |
| 1973 | 4,540 |
| 1974 | 5,038 |
| 1975 | 5,500 |
| 1976 | 5,815 |
| 1977 | 6,191 |
| 1978 | 6,662 |
| 1979 | 7,412 |
| 1980 | 8,414 |
| 1981 | 9,287 |
| 1982 | 9,862 |
| 1983 | 10,178 |
| 1984 | 10,609 |
| 1985 | 10,989 |

inevitably overestimates true poverty in this country, conservatives assert, because it ignores the cash value of a host of noncash benefits.

The number and percentage of poor people would indeed vary substantially, if income other than all cash income were counted. In 1985, the official number of poor in the United States was 33.1 million or 14 percent of the population. That number would rise to 50.5 million or 21.3 percent of the population, if government cash-transfer payments of all kinds (i.e., Social Security, unemployment compensation, Aid to Families with Dependent Children, etc.) were excluded. The tally declines to 35.2 million or 14.9 percent of the population, once Social Security and other social insurance payments are included; declines further to the official level, once means-tested cash transfers are added; and declines below the official level to 29.5 million or 12.5 percent of the population, once the cash value of food and housing benefits are taken into account. The number would rise again to 31.8 million or 13.5 percent of the population, if federal taxes were subtracted, but would decline again if the cash value of Medicare, Medicaid, and other in-kind benefits were included.[4]

The usefulness of the poverty line as a satisfactory boundary between want and sufficiency goes unchallenged, however, by these alternative tallies of how many Americans are really poor. The alternatives say nothing about the poverty line itself, that is, about its suitableness as a measurement of how much income is (and is not) enough to maintain a decent standard of living in the United States; rather, they criticize the way in which income is defined for the purpose of deciding whether a person or family is (or is not) poor. The distinction between, How much is enough? and How much do you have? may seem at times a subtle one, but it is important to keep the two questions (and their answers, and the answers' criticisms) separate.

The assaults launched on the poverty line have, in any event, failed to dislodge the sway it holds over U.S. public opinion. The main effect has been to spur scholars and policymakers to devise a broader array of instruments for distinguishing want from sufficiency, allocating public benefits, and measuring the low-income population. The Census Bureau now regularly reports on the population below 125 percent of the poverty level.[5] Measures such as 125 percent, 150 percent, and 175 percent of the poverty line—as well as the "lower living standard" of the Bureau of Labor Statistics—have been incorporated into the eligibility standards of a variety of state and federal benefit programs.[6] Paralleling its reports on the officially poor, the Census Bureau and other government organs also periodically publish estimates of what the poor population would look like if noncash benefits were taken into account.[7]

The preeminence of the official poverty line in defining who is in want in the United States should, of course, not shut off debate about its validity. The story of how the poverty line came into being only reinforces the value of ongoing scrutiny. It is a tale worth retelling— a classic American yarn of nimbleness and absurdity—one Mark Twain would have relished, had he lived in our time.

The story begins with the Department of Agriculture's development in the 1950s and early 1960s of a series of food plans for U.S. families. The least costly of these, the economy food plan, was "designed for short-term use when funds are extremely low."[8]

> The over-all economy plan cost per person, assuming four to a household, was estimated at $4.60 a week for January, 1964. [Based on the annual average Consumer Price Index (CPI), this would equal $15.94 for 1985.] For an average four-person family . . . the food costs . . . came to 70 cents a person per day, or 23 cents a meal. [Adjusted for the CPI, this would equal $2.43 per person per day or 80 cents a meal for 1985.] . . . No allowance was made for any meals away from home, for between-meal snacks, or food for guests.[9]

How was the economy food-plan amount chosen? It appears to have been arbitrarily pegged at 80 percent of the department's low-cost plan, which had "long been used as a guide for families who must watch food expenses."[10] According to the Department of Agriculture's 1955 survey of food consumption, only one out of ten nonfarm families spent less for food than the economy food plan called for, and by 1965 it was estimated that the number of families spending less for food than the plan assumed was even lower.[11]

The economy food plan could, in theory, provide adequate nutrition, but from the start it was understood that many families spending so little on food would end up with nutritional deficiencies. "If a family follows this plan exactly, adequate nutrition is attainable, but in practice nearly half the families that spent so little fell far short: of families spending at this rate in 1955, over 40 percent had diets that provided less than two-thirds the minimum requirements of one or more nutrients."[12]

Notwithstanding the inherent defects of the economy food plan as a basis for determining how much money real families needed in the real world to achieve a nutritionally adequate diet, by the early 1960s it was imperative to define poverty officially in order to know how much of it there was to fight.

> In 1964 no official estimates of the nature or extent of poverty in the United States existed, nor was poverty a focus of government studies or programs. In the aftermath of the Great Depression of the 1930s, poverty commanded little academic attention and few legislative initiatives ex-

plicitly designed to aid the poor were proposed. The situation changed dramatically in the 1960s. John Kennedy, influenced by the poverty he observed while campaigning in West Virginia and by contemporary accounts of the plight of the poor . . . directed his Council of Economic Advisers to study the problem. After Kennedy's assassination, Lyndon Johnson accelerated the work of the Council and, in his first State of the Union speech in January 1964, declared war on poverty. Shortly thereafter he announced a set of companion programs designed to enhance the general welfare and create the Great Society.[13]

Scrambling to keep pace with events, the Council of Economic Advisers decided that poverty was an income of under $1,500 for a person living alone and under $3,000 for a family. It shortly became clear that the council's definition would not work, since the poverty line was too high for small families and too small for large ones.[14] The Social Security Administration was asked to develop alternatives, and submitted two measures of need.

> It remained for the Office of Economic Opportunity and the Council of Economic Advisers to select the lower of the two measures and decide they would use it as the working tool. The best you can say for the measure is that at a time when it seemed useful, it was there. It is interesting that few outside the Social Security Administration ever wanted to talk about the higher measure. Everybody wanted to talk about the lower one, labeled the "poverty line." . . . [15]

What exactly did the Social Security Administration do in 1964 in order to construct the poverty line? In brief, it took the economy food plan and multiplied it by three. No independent calculations were made of the dollar amounts actually required to meet minimal shelter, clothing, transportation, and other needs. Rather,

> It was determined from the Department of Agriculture's 1955 survey of food consumption that families of three or more persons spent approximately one-third of their income on food; the poverty level for these families was, therefore, set at three times the cost of the economy food plan. For smaller families and persons living alone, the cost of the economy food plan was multiplied by factors that were slightly higher in order to compensate for the relatively larger fixed expenses of these smaller households.[16]

At the time—1964—when this calculation of the poverty line was introduced, it was already known that the multiplier might be unwarranted. U.S. families in the mid–1950s spent an average of one-third of their income for food, but poorer and richer families spent different percentages. "Poorer families generally devoted more than one-third of income to food, and those better off used less of their income in this way."[17]

The poverty line is thus the product—literally, the mathematical product—of two assumptions about the poor, neither of which is clearly true. First, it rests on the assumption that families spending the amount prescribed by the economy food plan can maintain a nutritionally adequate diet, yet the evidence suggests that many of them cannot do so. Second, it rests on the assumption that the poor's food spending constitutes one-third of their total spending, yet the evidence indicates that poor people generally allocate more than one-third of their budgets to food.

However convoluted the poverty line's origin may be, its adjustment to changing times has been fairly straightforward. Through 1968, the economy food plan was adjusted annually for inflation, and the result was then multiplied by three. Beginning in 1969, the entire threshold was adjusted annually for changes in the entire Consumer Price Index.[18]

The question of whether the official government poverty line is a sound measure of what it takes to maintain a decent standard of living in the United States, or whether some other measure should be substituted, thus remains an open one. That the current poverty line's greatest virtue was its availability ("The best you can say for the measure is that at a time when it seemed useful, it was there") is surely faint praise. At the same time, the issue of the poverty line's validity should not be blown out of proportion. It is not an issue that requires a resolution satisfactory to all in order for public policy toward the poor to go forward. Whether the poverty line should stay the same, should go up, should go down, or should be adjusted in some other fashion, the goal of getting all Americans whose cash income is below the current poverty line to a cash-income level that at least equals the current poverty line is one that makes sense in view of what it costs normal people to live in the United States.

It is also a goal that comports with the judgment of the U.S. public about what a minimally decent standard of living costs in this country. For several decades the Gallup organization has been asking nonfarm Americans: "What is the smallest amount of money a family of four (husband, wife, and two children) needs each week to get along in this community?" As Figure 1 indicates, over the last quarter of a century the poverty line for a family of four has been consistently lower than the median annualized amount that Americans believe a family of four needs to "get along" in this country. A cash income equal to at least the poverty line thus represents a standard that the vast majority of the public can be expected to support.[19]

However comical the history, arbitrary the origin, or defective the

**Figure 1**
**Poverty Line versus U.S. Public Opinion of Smallest Amount of Money Needed to Get Along in Community for a Family of Four, 1959–84**

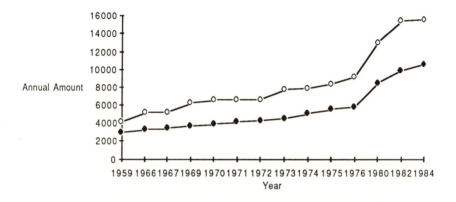

Key: Lower line = Poverty line for a family of four
Upper line = Gallup Poll median average weekly amount
(annualized) a family of four needs to "get along"

structure of the official poverty line, it seems reasonable to stick with it as a crude benchmark of who is poor in the United States, for the purpose of reexamining our policy toward the poor. The poverty line is a concept familiar to millions of Americans. Its demarcation between want and sufficiency is a given for most of this country's policymakers. While the flaws of the current poverty line may be obvious, it is far from clear that we can do any better. Finally, the poverty line is not perceived by the public as an unreasonably high boundary separating deprivation from adequacy: Most Americans believe that it takes an annual income substantially greater than the poverty line to make ends meet. It would be a great misfortune if honest disagreement among scholars about how poor is poor ended up thwarting the widespread agreement that prevails in this country about the acceptability of the official poverty line as a useful tool for measuring poverty and the desirability of raising the poor's cash income to the current poverty line.

## NOTES

1. The poverty line for each family unit is actually a weighted average. First, the Census Bureau establishes a separate poverty line for each of 48

cells, which vary by the number of persons in the cell, the age of the house-holder, and the number of related children under 18. Second, the bureau mul-tiplies each cell's unique poverty line by the number of actual families in the cell in the year in question. Third, for each family size the bureau adds the products of the prior calculation and then divides the sum by the total number of families. The Census Bureau notes, "Because family composition does not remain constant from year to year, the weighted average thresholds... will not reflect, identically, the change in the CPI...." Bureau of the Census, "Characteristics of the Population Below the Poverty Level: 1984," Series P–60, No. 152, June 1986, p. 122.

2. Bureau of the Census, "Money Income and Poverty Status of Families and Persons in the United States: 1985," Series P–60, No. 154, August 1986, p. 33.

3. Bureau of the Census, "Characteristics of the Population," p. 121; and "Money Income," p. 33.

4. U.S. Congress, House, Committee on Ways and Means, "Background Material and Data on Programs Within the Jurisdiction of the Committee on Ways and Means," March 6, 1987, Table 18, "Antipoverty Effectiveness of Cash and Noncash Transfers (Including Federal Income and Payroll Taxes) for All Families and Individuals, 1979–1985," pp. 641–42.

5. See, for example, Bureau of the Census, "Characteristics of the Popu-lation," pp. 8–10.

6. In Wisconsin, for instance, persons at 85 percent or less of the poverty line, at more than 85 percent but at 100 percent or less of the poverty line, at more than 100 percent but at 125 percent or less of the poverty line, and at more than 125 percent but at 150 percent or less of the poverty line receive different levels of financial assistance under the federally subsidized Low-Income Energy Assistance Program. Persons with income below 150 percent of the poverty line are eligible to receive federal surplus food. The legislature chose 175 percent of the poverty line as the cut-off for participation in a series of experimental health-insurance plans. The Bureau of Labor Statistics' lower-standard-of-living budget for a four-person family serves as the basis for cal-culating the state's payment standard under the Aid to Families with De-pendent Children program. See Susan Robillard, Wisconsin Legislative Fiscal Bureau, "Aid to Families With Dependent Children," January 1987, pp. 8, 28, 30; 1987 Wisconsin Act 27, §1840m, enacted and vetoed in part, August 1, 1987.

7. See, for example, Bureau of the Census, *Estimates of Poverty Including the Value of Noncash Benefits, 1985,* Technical Paper 56, Sept. 1986; and Committee on Ways and Means," *Background Material.*

8. Mollie Orshansky, "Measuring Poverty," in *The Social Welfare Forum: 1965* (New York: Columbia University Press, 1965), p. 216.

9. Ibid.

10. Mollie Orshansky, "Children of the Poor," *Social Security Bulletin,* Vol. 26, No. 7, July 1963, p. 8. In Orshansky, "Measuring Poverty," p. 215–16, the economy food plan is subsequently described as costing "about one-fourth less" than the low-cost plan.

11. Orshansky, "Measuring Poverty," p. 216.

12. Ibid.

13. Sheldon H. Danziger and Daniel H. Weinberg, eds., *Fighting Poverty: What Works and What Doesn't* (Cambridge: Harvard University Press, 1986), p. 1. The contemporary account referred to is Michael Harrington, *The Other America: Poverty in the United States* (New York: Macmillan, 1962).

14. Orshansky, "Measuring Poverty," p. 214.

15. Mollie Orshansky, "How Poverty Is Measured," *Monthly Labor Review*, Vol. 92, No. 2, February 1969, p. 38.

16. Bureau of the Census, "Characteristics of the Population," p. 121.

17. Orshansky, "Measuring Poverty," p. 214.

18. Bureau of the Census, "Characteristics of the Population," p. 122. See the Census Bureau's "Poverty Definition," p. 121, for a description of other technical changes made in the poverty line.

19. George Gallup, Jr., *The Gallup Poll: Public Opinion: 1985* (Wilmington, DE: Scholarly Resources, Inc., 1986), p. 49; and *The Gallup Poll: Public Opinion: 1972–1977* (Wilmington, DE: Scholarly Resources, Inc., 1978), pp. 1, 240–41, 416, 663–64.

# 2

# Poverty and Work

After years of obscurity, the poor in the United States have become a
common topic of popular discussion, academic analysis, and political
debate. The raw numbers depicting the overall size of the poor population, so startling when brought to light in the early 1960s, have lost
much of their shock value. We sometimes need to force ourselves to
recall that the presence of over 30 million poor Americans, nearly 14
percent of the population, in a land as rich as ours, is truly disturbing.

This chapter, after reviewing briefly the size and more commonly
discussed characteristics of the poor population, focuses on a portion
of the data that have received relatively less attention: the numbers
describing the poor's work experience. The story these numbers tell
may not initially seem alarming, but when properly understood, they
raise some of the most unsettling questions about the causes of poverty.

The number of poor in the United States declined from 39.9 million
in 1960 to 23.0 million in 1973, then rose again to 35.3 million in 1983,
before dipping again to 33.1 million in 1985. As a percentage of the
population, the poor dropped from 22.2 percent in 1960 to 11.1 percent
in 1973, then increased again to 15.2 percent in 1983, before tapering
off to 14.0 percent in 1985. Table 3 chronicles the decline and rise of
America's poor over the last quarter-century.[1]

For unrelated individuals, related children under 18, blacks, and
Hispanics, the percentages below the poverty line are consistently
greater than for the overall poor population. For family members other
than related children, householders, and whites, the percentages below
the poverty line are consistently smaller than for the overall poor
population. Persons 65 and over had a higher percentage below the

**Table 3**
**U.S. Population below the Poverty Line, 1960–85**

| Year | Number (millions) | Percent |
|------|-------------------|---------|
| 1960 | 39.9 | 22.2 |
| 1965 | 33.2 | 17.3 |
| 1968 | 25.4 | 12.8 |
| 1969 | 24.1 | 12.1 |
| 1970 | 25.4 | 12.6 |
| 1971 | 25.6 | 12.5 |
| 1972 | 24.5 | 11.9 |
| 1973 | 23.0 | 11.1 |
| 1974 | 23.4 | 11.2 |
| 1975 | 25.9 | 12.3 |
| 1976 | 25.0 | 11.8 |
| 1977 | 24.7 | 11.6 |
| 1978 | 24.5 | 11.4 |
| 1979 | 26.1 | 11.7 |
| 1980 | 29.3 | 13.0 |
| 1981 | 31.8 | 14.0 |
| 1982 | 34.4 | 15.0 |
| 1983 | 35.3 | 15.2 |
| 1984 | 33.7 | 14.4 |
| 1985 | 33.1 | 14.0 |

poverty line from 1960 to 1981, a lower percentage thereafter, compared to the overall poor population. For all groups, the trend over the last two and a half decades corresponded roughly to the overall trend: a decrease in poverty from 1960 to 1973 (or 1974), followed by an increase in poverty through 1983, and then a tapering off in the incidence of poverty through 1985 (although both the number and percentage of poor Hispanics and elderly bucked the trend and rose from 1984 to 1985).[2]

Many analyses and discussions of the U.S. poor focus on their age, sex, race, ethnic, and education characteristics. In passing over those ways of looking at the poor, this book does not seek to imply that there is nothing disturbing about the fact that the poor include disproportionate numbers of children, women, blacks and Hispanics, and persons who have received minimal education. The focus here, however, is on poverty as a whole and on the linkage between poverty and the job market. For the purposes of this book, therefore, the data that command the greatest attention are the intriguing data compiled by the Census Bureau that describe the poor's work experience.

The Census Bureau divides the poor into two broad groups for the purpose of presenting their work experience: not in the labor force[3] or in the labor force.[4] Those in the labor force are first segmented into those in the armed forces and those in the civilian labor force; persons in the civilian labor-force group are then counted as either unemployed[5] or employed.[6] Consistently, the data show that the poor are strongly connected to the labor force and form a major part of it. The data also consistently indicate that a large percentage of the poor in the labor force are employed at paying jobs and that impoverished workers represent a major share of all U.S. employees.

In 1984, for instance, the 33.7 million whom the Census Bureau classified as below the poverty line fell into two groups totaling 13.9 million units—6.6 million unrelated individuals and 7.3 million families—each headed by a householder. The Census Bureau estimated the labor-force participation of these unrelated individuals and family heads as of the date of its survey, March 1985. Most of the 6.6 million unrelated individuals did not fall in the civilian labor-force category, but 2.5 million or 38.4 percent did. These poor unrelated individuals constituted 13.6 percent of all (poor and nonpoor) unrelated individuals in the civilian labor force. A majority of the 7.3 million poor family householders, 3.7 million or 51.3 percent, were classified in the civilian labor force. They represented 8.0 percent of all (poor and nonpoor) householders in the civilian labor force.[7]

Of both the poor unrelated individuals and the poor family householders who were classified as belonging to the civilian labor force, the overwhelming majority were employed at the time of the Census Bureau survey. Of the 2.5 million poor unrelated individuals in the civilian labor force, 2.0 million or 78.1 percent were employed. These constituted 11.4 percent of all (poor and nonpoor) single individuals who indicated they were employed at the time of the survey. Of the 3.7 million poor family householders in the civilian labor force, 2.9 million or 76.4 percent were employed. They represented 6.5 percent of all (poor and nonpoor) family householders who said they were employed.[8]

The numbers provide a snapshot of America's poor at a single point in time. When the poor are asked about their work experience during an entire year, a similar pattern of labor-force participation emerges. Most of the poor who are not children, disabled, or retired engage in paid work.

In 1984, out of 33.7 million poor people, 22.2 million were 15 or over. Of these, 2.7 million were ill or disabled, and 2.1 million were retired, leaving 17.4 million or 78.3 percent who could and whom we might expect to work. Of this 17.4 million, 9.1 million or 52.2 percent did work. If the pool of potential workers is further diminished by subtracting from the 17.4 million 15-or-over, nondisabled, nonretired group the 2.3 million who indicated they were attending school, 15.1 million poor people remain who could and whom we might expect to work. The 9.1 million who did work would then constitute 60.1 percent.[9]

Let us now take a closer look at the 15.1 million 15-and-over, non-disabled, nonretired, nonstudent poor population. There are three main groups: (1) 4.6 million individuals who do not work because they were keeping house or for other unstated reasons; (2) 1.4 million persons who did not work because they were unable to find work; and (3) the 9.1 million workers already mentioned. If all of these individuals are classified (contrary to the official definition) as being in the labor force, then, of a poor labor force of 15.1 million, a total of 10.6 million or 69.7 percent either sought work but could not find any, or did, in fact, work. If the 4.6 million individuals whose housekeeping or other activities kept them from working are excluded from the labor force (consistent with the official definition) and only those who either sought but could not find work or who engaged in work are left, then of this redefined poor labor force of 10.6 million, virtually all—9.1 million, 86.2 percent—worked.[10]

The Census Bureau counts as work anything from a few hours in a few weeks to the standard 40 hours or more per week during the standard 52-week year. It is therefore useful to inquire how many of the 9.1 million poor workers in 1984 worked less than full-time or less than year-round during the year.[11] The answer is that a large number of the poor who worked, 3.7 million or 40.5 percent, worked part-time. Of the majority of 5.4 million who worked full-time, over half, 3.3 million or 61.4 percent, worked only part of the year. The mean number of weeks worked, however, was 31.3, and a significant proportion of the country's 9.1 million officially poor workers in 1984—2.1 million or 22.8 percent—worked both full-time and year-round.[12]

It is difficult to scan the data about the poor's work experience—especially the data indicating that nearly a quarter of poor workers did full-time and year-round work, yet remained poor—without raising a number of unsettling questions.

How can we let poor people who are ill or disabled, and who in general often cannot work, remain below the poverty line?

How can we allow poor people who have retired, and whose old age in most cases presumably justifies their retirement, remain below the poverty line?

Why can the poor in the labor force who are unemployed not find jobs? Are they lazy, are they so badly educated no one will hire them, are they subject to sexual or racial discrimination, can they not find day care, or are the jobs simply not there? Why do the partially employed poor not work full-time and year-round? Laziness? Lack of education? Discrimination? Inadequate day care? Job shortage?

Finally, why do the poor who work full-time and year-round not manage to get out of poverty? They are clearly not lazy; but is inferior education or discrimination keeping them from securing higher-paying work, or are their wages just too low?

The data about the poor that the Census Bureau regularly gathers, tabulates, and publishes, cannot fully answer these questions.[13] We must look elsewhere. In doing so, it is helpful to keep in mind that the poor whose poverty we are seeking to explain constitute a far larger population than the Census Bureau reports suggest, when viewed over a long period of time. The table that began this chapter indicated that, since the mid–1960s, the percentage of poor in the United States has fluctuated between roughly 11 percent and 15 percent of the total population; but the percentage who will end up being poor at some time in their lives is much greater. According to Greg Duncan of the University of Michigan's Survey Research Center, "In any ten-year period, one-third of Americans will see their standard of living drop by 50 percent or more, and one-quarter will live in poverty for at least one year." Duncan found not only that "family incomes are highly volatile" but that "a rapid rise or drop in living standards is closer to the rule than the exception." He also found that hard times are generally not predictable: "Eighty-six percent . . . who experienced a sharp drop in their standard of living had not expected it beforehand."[14] The poverty in the United States that this book seeks to explain is at any one time the poverty of a tenth of us, but over a decade it is the poverty of one out of every four.

## NOTES

1. Bureau of the Census, "Characteristics of the Population Below the Poverty Level: 1984," Series P–60, No. 152, June 1986, p. 5; and idem, "Money Income and Poverty Status of Families and Persons in the United States: 1985," Series P–60, No. 154, August 1986, p. 3.

2. Ibid.

3. "All civilians 15 years old and over who are not classified as employed or unemployed are defined as 'not in the labor force.' This group of persons who are neither employed nor seeking work includes those engaged only in own home housework, attending school, or unable to work because of long-term physical or mental illness; persons who are retired or too old to work; seasonable workers for whom the survey fell in an off season; and the voluntarily idle. Persons doing only unpaid family work (less than 15 hours during the survey week) are also classified as not in the labor force." Bureau of the Census, "Characteristics of the Population," p. 124.

4. "Persons are classified in the labor force if they were employed as civilians, unemployed, or in the Armed forces during the survey week." Ibid.

5. "Unemployed persons are those civilians who, during the survey week,

had no employment but were available for work and (1) had engaged in any specific job-seeking activity within the past 4 weeks, such as registering at a public or private employment office, meeting with prospective employers, checking with friends or relatives, placing or answering advertisements, writing letters of application, or being on a union or professional register; (2) were waiting to be called back to a job from which they had been laid off; or (3) were waiting to report to a new wage or salary job within 30 days." Ibid.

6. "Employed persons include (1) all civilians who, during the survey week, did any work at all as paid employees or in their own business or profession, or on their own farm, or who worked 15 hours or more as unpaid workers on a farm or in a business operated by a member of the family, and (2) all those who were not working but had jobs or businesses from which they were temporarily absent because of illness, bad weather, vacation, or labor-management dispute, or because they were taking time off for personal reasons, whether or not they were paid by their employers for time off, and whether or not they were seeking other jobs. Excluded from the employed group are persons whose only activity consisted of work around the house (such as own home housework, painting or repairing own home, etc.) or volunteer work for religious, charitable, and similar organizations." Ibid.

7. Ibid., p. 65.

8. Ibid.

9. Ibid., p. 37.

10. Ibid.

11. "A person is classified as having worked at part-time jobs during the preceding calendar year if he worked at civilian jobs which provided less than 35 hours of work per week in a majority of the weeks in which he worked during the year. He is classified as having worked at full-time jobs if he worked 35 hours or more per week during a majority of the weeks in which he worked.... A year-round, full-time worker is one who worked primarily at full-time civilian jobs (35 hours or more per week) 50 weeks or more during the preceding calendar year." Ibid., p. 125.

12. Ibid., p. 37.

13. The data cited in this chapter, considered without any context, suggest that as many as 44 percent of the poor—the 7 percent 15 and over who are attending school, the 12 percent who are keeping house, the 4 percent who are unable to find work, the 11 percent who worked part-time, and the 10 percent who worked full-time, but less than year-round—could theoretically be poor because they are lazy, that is, prefer leisure over available employment. It strains credulity, however, to believe that laziness explains more than a few percentage points of the poverty within these groups.

14. Greg J. Duncan, "On the Slippery Slope," *American Demographics*, Vol. 9, No. 5, May 1987, pp. 30–35.

# 3
# The Job Shortage

As the last chapter disclosed, at any given time huge numbers of people in the United States are both poor and unemployed. The present chapter seeks to explain why.

Let us briefly recapitulate the data linking poverty and unemployment. Of the 7.3 million family householders who were below the poverty line in 1984, 0.9 million (12.1 percent) were unemployed in March 1985, when the Bureau of the Census conducted its survey. As a percentage of the 3.7 million poor family householders in the civilian labor force, the unemployed represented nearly a quarter.[1]

Of the 6.6 million unrelated individuals below the poverty line, a smaller but substantial portion—0.6 million (8.4 percent)—were unemployed. Since nearly two-thirds of poor unrelated individuals are outside the labor force, however, the percentage of unrelated individuals in the labor force who are unemployed is much higher. Of the 2.5 million in the civilian labor force, the unemployed represented over a fifth.[2]

Why do the poor who are unemployed not find jobs? There are several possible answers.

1. They actually prefer to remain unemployed.
2. They are too poorly educated to obtain any employment.
3. They lack the specific skills needed to secure the particular jobs available.
4. They cannot get transportation to available employment.
5. They cannot find the day care or health insurance they need in order to accept available jobs.
6. There are not enough jobs available.

In addition to these across-the-board answers, there are several possible answers that pertain only to certain groups.

- Welfare recipients are unwilling to relinquish benefits to take jobs that leave them worse off, when wages, work expenses (especially day care), and the loss of Medicaid are taken into account.
- Blacks, Hispanics, and other minorities face racial or ethnic discrimination.
- Women face sexual discrimination.
- Handicapped individuals fear loss of Medicaid, face discrimination, or both.

The potential explanation that requires perhaps the most thorough investigation and analysis is the possibility that there are not enough jobs available. Do the poor who are unemployed belong to a general group of unemployed jobseekers whose aggregate number exceeds the aggregate number of unfilled jobs—or is the aggregate number of unfilled jobs greater? All the other possible reasons that poor jobseekers cannot secure employment hinge to some extent on this question's answer.

If there are not enough vacant jobs available, then regardless of any other obstacles that might also exist and regardless of individuals' or society's capacity to overcome those other barriers, some—perhaps most—of the poor unemployed are likely to remain poor and unemployed. Lack of education, training, transportation, and so forth, instead of proving to be primary and real barriers to employment, will turn out to be merely secondary and theoretical roadblocks to a job. The provision of "adequate" schooling, skills, access to work, and so forth will largely amount to an empty promise: a precancelled passport to employment.

If, on the other hand, there are enough jobs to go around, then the major barriers faced by poor unemployed individuals must, indeed, be a lack of education, training, transportation, and so forth. Getting the poor out of poverty by providing these services becomes not only a sensible but the only sensible strategy for policymakers to follow. Schooling, skills, and access to work will indeed constitute a passport to employment.

Which is it? A job shortage or a job surplus?

Amazingly, both government and the academic community have largely ignored this issue. Although many countries regularly collect data on job vacancies, Katharine G. Abraham has concluded that "there exists no comprehensive, consistent U.S. job vacancy series" of data.[3] The Bureau of Labor Statistics (BLS) conducted "pilot job vacancy projects" from 1964 to 1966, and on the basis of this experience, collected vacancy information for the U.S. manufacturing sector from 1969 through 1973. After BLS discontinued this effort, the states of

Minnesota and Wisconsin continued to collect vacancy data on their own for the periods 1972–81 and 1976–81, and BLS briefly revived its vacancy-data collection for the period 1979–80.[4] According to Abraham, "there have in fact been no new job vacancy data collected in the United States since 1981."[5] Perhaps because of the dearth of data, only a handful of scholars appear to have paid serious attention to the ratio between jobseekers and jobs in this country. The best work has been carried out by Abraham. As a graduate student at Harvard University, she prepared a doctoral dissertation on the subject. Subsequently, as assistant professor at the Massachusetts Institute of Technology and research associate at the Brookings Institution, she synthesized her work in articles published in the academic and popular press.[6]

Abraham's approach in her seminal article in the *American Economic Review* was a methodologically conservative one. She excluded from the unemployment rate not only so-called discouraged workers (i.e., persons convinced that no work is available and who have therefore given up active job search) but persons already attached to an employer (i.e., those on temporary layoff and those due to start a job within 30 days), and she made "very generous allowances" to correct downward bias in the BLS, Minnesota, and Wisconsin job-vacancy rates she used.[7] Nonetheless, "comparison of the two rates suggests that the number of persons seeking work has typically been much larger than the number of vacant jobs."[8] Abraham's central conclusion is as unequivocal as it is disturbing:

> If it could be assumed that the vacancy rate/unemployment rate relationships observed in the available survey data mirrored the vacancy rate/unemployment rate relationship prevailing in the United States over the same time period, reasonable estimates would be that there were roughly 2.5 unemployed persons for every vacant job during the middle 1960s, an average of close to 4.0 unemployed persons per vacant job during the early 1970s, and an average of 5.0 or more unemployed persons for every vacant job during the latter part of the 1970s. The number of persons counted as actively seeking work is somewhat smaller than the total number of unemployed persons, so that the comparable average job seeker-to-vacancy ratios would be 15 to 20 percent smaller.[9]

In the article she wrote for the *Washington Post* in 1982, Abraham projected her estimates of unemployed persons-to-vacancy ratios backward into the 1960s and forward into the early 1980s:

> During the last half of the 1960s, when the unemployment rate hovered within the 3.5 percent to 4.0 percent range, the number of job openings probably came close to equaling the number of unemployed persons. Labor markets have been less tight during the 1970s than during the

latter part of the 1960s. Between 1970 and 1980, a period that included three recessions and produced an average unemployment rate above 6.0 percent, there were probably an average of four or five unemployed persons per vacant job.

Today, with the unemployment rate at 9.0 percent, the number of unemployed persons almost certainly exceeds the number of open slots. A reasonable estimate, based on the historical relationship between the unemployment rate and the job vacancy rate, is that there are currently no more than 1 million jobs vacant in all sectors of our economy; that is, the number of unemployed persons most likely exceeds the number of vacant jobs by a factor of 10 or more. Even if every available vacant job could be filled instantaneously by an unemployed person, we would have achieved only a relatively small reduction in our unemployment count.[10]

Since 1982, unemployment rates have declined. "My best guess, then," Abraham has indicated, "would be that, at current unemployment rates between 6.0 and 6.5 percent, there are two to three times as many unemployed people as vacant jobs." Because the methodology she uses both somewhat underestimates the unemployment rate and is constructed to estimate vacancy rates on the high side, Abraham suggests that, if anything, the actual ratio of unemployed people to vacant jobs could be higher.[11]

Abraham was, of course, not the first academician to suggest that there are many more unemployed jobseekers than available jobs. Lester Thurow had earlier sounded the same theme: "Lack of jobs has been endemic in peace-time during the past fifty years of American history. ... we need to face the fact that our economy and our institutions will not provide jobs for everyone who wants to work. They have never done so, and as currently structured, they never will."[12] Many less illustrious critics of the U.S. economy have also made the point. Not until Abraham's careful and methodologically conservative research, however, has it been possible to demonstrate empirically and incontestably that in this country there are more unemployed looking for jobs than there are jobs to be filled.

Strangely, Abraham's findings appear to have been largely overlooked by her fellow academicians. Her research has been equally ignored by the popular press and government policymakers. Why this is so is unclear. It may be due in part to the highly technical nature of most of her work, though she spells out her conclusions in quite plain English. It may be due in part to the journals in which her research has been published, although the *American Economic Review* is hardly an obscure periodical, and she provided an excellent summary of her basic finding in nothing less than the *Washington Post*. The neglect of Abraham's research is particularly puzzling because, as pointed out at the beginning of this chapter, the issue she resolves is such a crucial one: that is, whether the poor who are unemployed do not have work primarily because of laziness, inadequate education, deficient skill training, lack of transportation, discrimination, or lack of day care or health insurance, or primarily because of a shortage of jobs. Abraham's research does not entirely dispose of the issue, but it does strongly suggest that the poor who are unemployed—like others who are unemployed—are more likely than not to be unemployed because the larger group of unemployed to which they belong substantially exceeds the supply of available jobs. The direct implication of her findings is that neither changing the unemployed poor themselves by motivating them to work, nor improving their education level or giving them skills, nor reducing such barriers as inadequate transportation to work, racial and sexual discrimination, or unaffordable day care or health insurance, will do much to get them into jobs—unless, of course, nonpoor unemployed jobseekers sit idly by or current jobholders give up their positions, neither of which is likely to occur. The only way to get most of the unemployed poor into jobs (without prohibiting nonpoor jobseekers from competing or displacing the incumbent jobholders), Abraham's research suggests, is to create large numbers of new jobs. In the conclusion of her article in the *American Economic Review* Abraham makes these points herself:

> What does my central finding that there are typically many more unemployed persons than job openings imply for macroeconomic theory and policy? It strongly suggests that measures such as training programs or increased job service funding designed to improve the process whereby unemployed workers are matched with available jobs, while perhaps a good idea for other reasons, cannot be expected to have any dramatic effect on the aggregate unemployment rate. If, for example, there are four unemployed persons for every vacant job, the aggregate unemployment rate would be only 25 percent lower, even if every available position could be filled *instantaneously* with an unemployed individual; the unemployment rate reduction which improvements in the matching process could *in fact* be expected to produce would be considerably smaller, since one cannot realistically hope to reduce the average duration of a vacancy to anywhere near zero. In most situations, large reductions in the aggregate unemployment rate will only be achieved if more jobs can be created.[13]

In her article in the *Washington Post*, Abraham is even more direct:

> The implications of these numbers for policymakers seem clear. The current situation cannot be blamed on the unemployed lacking interest in work. Gutting our social insurance programs will not lead to signif-

icant reductions in the unemployment rate. Nor is the central problem that the unemployed lack the skills required to fill available jobs, though this may explain the particular difficulties faced by certain groups. Training programs for the hard-core unemployed may be a good idea for other reasons, but we cannot hope for them to have any substantial effect on the aggregate unemployment rate.

The real problem we face today is that there simply are not enough jobs to go around. Any policy package designed to lower the unemployment rate must recognize this important fact.[14]

In short, the poor who are unemployed—together with their nonpoor competitors—face a massive job shortage. It may not be the only reason, but it is the primary reason, why such a substantial number of poor persons, as well as the great majority of unemployed persons, cannot find work. Until we acknowledge this fact, we will have great difficulty in getting unemployed persons—both poor and nonpoor—back to work.

## NOTES

1. Bureau of the Census, U.S. Department of Commerce, "Characteristics of the Population Below the Poverty Level: 1984," Series P–60, No. 152, June 1986, p. 65.

2. Ibid.

3. Katharine G. Abraham, "Help-Wanted Advertising, Job Vacancies, and Unemployment," *Brookings Papers on Economic Activity*, Washington, DC, 1987, p. 207.

4. Katharine G. Abraham, "Structural/Frictional vs. Deficient Demand Unemployment: Some New Evidence," *American Economic Review* 73, No. 4 (September 1983): 709–10; and idem, "Help-Wanted Advertising" pp. 212–13.

5. Letter from Katharine G. Abraham, Research Associate, Brookings Institution, to Dan Willett, Congress For a Working America, July 14, 1987.

6. See Katharine G. Abraham, "Vacancies, Unemployment and Wage Growth." Ph.D. dissertation, Harvard University, 1982; "Too Few Jobs," *Washington Post*, May 25, 1982, p. A–17; "Structural/Frictional Unemployment" and "Help-Wanted Advertising."

7. Abraham, "Structural/Frictional Unemployment" pp. 708, 714.

8. Ibid., pp. 708–9.

9. Ibid., p. 722.

10. Abraham, "Too Few Jobs."

11. Abraham, letter to Dan Willett.

12. Lester C. Thurow, *The Zero-Sum Society* (New York: Penguin, 1984), p. 203. Reprint of 1980 edition.

13. Abraham, "Structural/Frictional Unemployment" p. 722.

14. Abraham, "Too Few Jobs."

# 4
## Low-Wage Jobs

The preceding chapter examined the poor who are unemployed and concluded that a major cause of their predicament is a serious (though until recently undocumented), massive job shortage. This chapter looks at the poor who hold jobs. Since their poverty (except in the case of those employed less than full-time and year-round) cannot be logically attributed to a job shortage, we need to look at the jobs they hold.

During the history of the United States up until World War II, there was no equation between getting out of poverty and holding a job. The stories of millions of slaves, farmworkers, and factory workers make this clear. Work provided income, but whether it provided enough income to maintain a decent living standard depended on the specific job. Since the postwar economic boom, however, many have come to believe that getting out of poverty was the automatic consequence of getting a steady job—that is, full-time and year-round employment. Regrettably, such a belief has no basis in fact. If a job ever meant an escape from poverty in this country, it no longer does so.

According to Census Bureau data for 1984, 2.1 million of the poor in the United States, over a fifth of all the poor who worked, held full-time, year-round jobs, but still ended up below the poverty line.[1] Data from other sources tell the same story.

Using Census Bureau data, for example, the Bureau of Labor Statistics (BLS) reported that in 1983 66.8 million Americans 16 and over worked full-time and year-round.[2] Their personal earnings were as follows: for 1.6 million (2.5 percent of the total), under $3,000; for 2.8 million (4.2 percent of the total), between $3,000 and $6,699; for 6.5 million (9.8 percent of the total), between $6,700 and $9,999; for 14.0

**Table 4**
**Full-Time, Year-Round Workers: Personal Earnings and Poverty Status, 1983**

| Personal Earnings | Total Number (millions) | Below Poverty Level | |
|---|---|---|---|
| | | Number (millions) | Percent |
| Under $3,000 | 1.6 | 0.7 | 45.4 |
| $3,000--6,999 | 2.8 | 0.6 | 21.8 |
| $6,700--9,999 | 6.5 | 0.4 | 6.8 |
| $10,000--14,999 | 14.0 | 0.2 | 1.8 |
| $15,000 and over | 41.9 | - - - | --- |

million (21.0 percent of the total), between $10,000 and $14,999; and the balance, 41.9 million (62.6 percent of the total) had personal earnings of $15,000 and over.[3] As in the case of the Census Bureau's own report for 1984, the BLS report on the preceding year notes that 2.1 million full-time, year-round workers—3.1 percent of all such workers—ended up below the poverty line. Not surprisingly, as Table 4 indicates, the lower the full-time, year-round worker's personal earnings, the more likely the worker (if an unrelated individual) or the worker's family was to end up below the poverty line.[4]

Deborah Chollet, senior research associate at the Employee Benefit Research Institute, has sliced the pie in yet another way. Using Census Bureau data for 1985, she calculated how many workers aged 18–64 earned various average percentages of the minimum wage. Chollet notes that approximately 40 percent of all workers in the United States (workers in small establishments in particular industries, supervisory workers, and professional workers) hold jobs or have occupations that are not subject to the minimum wage.[5] Not all workers who are exempt from the minimum wage are actually paid less than the minimum wage, of course, but a substantial number are paid subminimum wages and large numbers are paid wages not greatly in excess of the minimum. Of 112.4 million workers (most but not all of whom worked full-time and year-round), 18.3 million (16.3 percent) had average hourly wages equaling 0–99 percent of the federal minimum of $3.35 per hour (which translates into $6,968, if the worker worked 40 hours per week and 52 weeks per year). Another 8.8 million (7.8 percent) earned, on average, between 100 and 124 percent of the minimum wage. And 24.5 million (21.8 percent) earned between 125 and 199 percent of the minimum. Finally, 40.6 million (36.1 percent) earned between 200 and 399 percent of the minimum, and the remaining 20.2 million (18.0 percent) earned 400 percent or more of the minimum.[6] As the preceding BLS figures should make obvious, not all those earning less than the min-

**Table 5**
**Usual Weekly Earnings of Full-Time Workers by Earnings Categories,**
**1986 Annual Averages**

| Weekly Earnings | Number (millions) | Percentage of Total |
|---|---|---|
| All earning levels | 78.7 | 100.0 |
| Under $100 | 0.4 | 0.5 |
| $100-149 | 3.4 | 4.3 |
| $150-199 | 6.8 | 8.7 |
| $200-249 | 10.1 | 12.8 |
| $250-299 | 8.2 | 10.4 |
| $300-349 | 8.4 | 10.7 |
| $350-399 | 6.2 | 7.8 |
| $400-499 | 12.1 | 15.3 |
| $500-599 | 8.6 | 10.9 |
| $600-749 | 7.0 | 8.9 |
| $750-998 | 4.4 | 5.6 |
| $999 or more | 3.1 | 4.0 |

imum wage ended up in poverty, but it would be reasonable to conclude that many earning so little—as well as a fair number earning just above $3.35 per hour—had families so large, or other sources of income so small, or both, that they did end up below the poverty line.

Finally, unpublished BLS tables on wage and salary workers "who usually work full-time" offer another dimension of the poor who work. Using Census Bureau data for 1986, BLS tabulated the "usual weekly earnings" of 78.7 million full-time workers, 16 years and over, by both earning (under $100 per week, $100–149 per week, etc.) and occupational categories. Table 5 shows the results by earning categories:[7]

The 0.4 million full-time workers whose usual weekly earnings amount to less than $100 per week ended up, if they were fortunate enough to work every week, with annual earnings of less than $5,200. The 3.4 million whose weekly earnings fell between $100 and $149 per week wound up, assuming they worked each week, with annual earnings of between $5,200 and $7,748; and so on. Again, it must be stressed that low earnings do not guarantee poverty: If you live alone or have a small family, or another family member has a job, or you have significant unearned income (interest, dividends, capital gains, etc.), your holding a job or jobs that afford low earnings can still get you above the poverty line. Given a normal distribution, however, it is inevitable that a large number—if not the majority—of the men and women whose earnings each week are low will end up officially poor.

The likelihood of ending up poor varies dramatically with the particular occupation a worker holds. According to the BLS, while the

78.7 million workers in 1986 who usually worked full-time had median weekly earnings of $358, the medians for specific occupations varied from a low of $91 per week for private child-care workers to a high of $721 per week for petroleum engineers. At $91 per week, a child-care worker who is employed for 52 weeks would earn $4,732 per year, an amount lower than any of the 1986 various poverty thresholds. At $147 per week, the median for private-household cleaners, a full year's worth of work earns $7,644, enough for a single person or two-person family to get above the 1986 poverty line, but not enough for three-person or larger families to escape from poverty. At $198 per week, the median for teacher aides, a full year's worth of work earns $10,296, enough for a single person or small family to rise out of poverty, but insufficient for a four-person or larger family. The median weekly earnings for waiters and waitresses is $172; for cooks (except short-order cooks), $196; for food-counter and fountain occupations, $152; for textile sewing-machine operators, $179; for pressing-machine operators, $199; for farm workers, $192. Altogether, 10.2 million U.S. workers who worked full-time had median earnings of under $200 per week, which during a 52-week years means an annual income of $10,348—not enough for a four-person or larger family to get out of poverty. Another 10.0 million workers had median earnings of $200–214 per week, still not enough at an annual income of $11,128 for a four-person family to get out of poverty.[8]

It must be remembered that these occupational weekly earnings amounts represent medians. Half of the workers in each occupational category had weekly earnings that were lower, the other half had weekly earnings that were higher. Fortunately, the BLS provides data on how the workers in each occupational category are distributed around the median. For example, there are 25,000 private-household cleaners, 15.9 percent of that category, whose weekly earnings were under $100 (as opposed to the median of $147), which translates into a maximum annual income of $5,200, an amount below any of the poverty thresholds. A total of 34,000 teacher aides, 18.9 percent of that category, had weekly earnings no greater than $149 (as opposed to the median of $198), which means a maximum annual income of $7,748, an amount sufficient for single people and two-person families to get out of poverty, but not enough for three-person or larger families to cross the poverty line.[9]

In short, no matter how you slice the U.S. demographic pie—whether you look at the poor and ask how many of them work full-time and year-round; whether you look at full-time, year-round workers, determine what they earn, and then inquire how many of the low earners are poor; whether you count the number working at or near the minimum wage, measure median weekly earnings, or examine the distribution of weekly earnings—you are forced to come to the same conclusion. Poverty is not divorced from the job market. Poverty is to a large degree a product of the job market. Millions of people in the United States, pursuing their own self-interest, work long and hard at the best jobs they can find, yet they end up poor. Lack of sufficient work—that is, part-time employment—is among the reasons the poor who work still end up poor. Another reason, of equal or greater importance, is the prevalence of low-wage jobs in the United States. Even working as long and as hard as can be reasonably expected in order to get out of poverty, millions of the poor nonetheless remain poor, because the jobs they hold pay wages that are very low.

Surprisingly (as surprising as the failure of the U.S. government to collect comprehensive and consistent data on job vacancies), the government does not systematically count how many low-wage jobs there are in the economy. The government does not measure the number of jobs by wage rates at all. The Census Bureau asks what workers *earn*— and on the basis of these earnings data it is possible to speculate about how many jobs provide what level of wages—but the correlation between earnings and wages is not precise enough to permit anything close to an equation of the two. A worker, for instance, may earn $10,000 per year, but does that represent one full-time, year-round job that pays $10,000? Or one full-time, year-round job that pays $8,000 and a part-time, part-year job paying $2,000? Or two part-time, part-year jobs paying $5,000? Until the U.S. government (or some other organization) actually surveys employers on a periodic basis and regularly reports on the wage structure of the economy, it will be impossible to know precisely the extent to which poverty in particular and low earnings in general are a function of the wages paid by the jobs themselves.

In the event that unrelated individuals who work or families with one or more workers do succeed in getting out of poverty, whether by virtue of a single job or a combination of jobs, they will still not necessarily be free to spend all of their income to achieve what getting out of poverty is meant to accomplish: maintaining a decent standard of living. How much disposable income they actually have depends on how much government lets them keep. From the mid–1970s to the mid–1980s, federal payroll and income taxes crept upward. By 1986, a single person at the poverty level had a combined tax of 11.3 percent of income; a two-person family's tax rate was 9.2 percent of income; three-, four-, and five-person families had tax rates of 6.3 percent, 10.4 percent, and 10.8 percent, respectively. The Tax Reform Act of 1986 lowered these rates (usually significantly) for all family units, although by 1989 it is estimated that a single person's combined federal tax will have crept back up to 10.3 percent of income; a two-person family's rate will be 7.5 percent; a three-person family will have a "negative" tax rate of −1.8 percent, presumably because of the operation of the Earned Income Tax Credit; but tax rates for four- and five-person families will be 2.2 percent and 4.5 percent.[10] Poor workers, like everyone else, also pay state and local sales and property taxes (the latter often indirectly through rent) and are subject to state income taxes in many jurisdictions. It is always preferable (all other things being equal) for a poor person to work at a job that pays more rather than less, but the extent to which poor workers and their families can, in effect, be taxed back into poverty—that is, left with an after-tax income that is well below the poverty line, even if their before-tax income is above the poverty line—needs to be appreciated.

As the preceding discussion should make clear, research into the area of low-wage jobs is in its infancy. We know a lot about earnings, but we know little about the wage structure of the U.S. economy—that is, how many jobs pay how much. We also need to understand more clearly the difference between the pretax income jobs initially appear to provide and actual disposable income.

Notwithstanding these gaps in our knowledge, the available data make it abundantly clear that one major reason the poor are poor in the United States is low-wage jobs. Assuming that we wish to continue permitting such low-wage jobs to be made available (a proposition that by no means commands a censensus in this country, as evidenced by various proposals to raise the federal minimum wage), we must begin to deal with the complex double consequence of such employment:

- First, low-wage jobs permit some unemployed persons to get jobs. In other words, if the low-wage feature of certain jobs were eliminated by requiring a higher minimum wage, some of the jobs (it is unclear how many) would be eliminated.

- Second, low-wage jobs, if relied on as a sole source of income, leave some single persons and small families, as well as many larger families, below the poverty line. Once taxes (and other unavoidable, albeit not legally mandated expenses, such as day care) are subtracted, low-wage jobs leave an even greater number of single persons and families with disposable income below poverty-line levels.

This much should be clear: Poverty cannot be eliminated in the United States unless something is done to raise the income of millions of individuals who work, often full-time and year-round, at subminimum-, minimum-, or just-above-minimum-wage jobs.

## NOTES

1. Bureau of the Census, "Characteristics of the Population Below the Poverty Level: 1984," Series P–60, No. 152, June 1986, p. 37.

2. "Respondents are asked how many hours they usually worked per week during the year. They are classified as having worked at full-time jobs if they worked 35 hours per week or more in a majority of the weeks employed during the year.... Year-round, full-time work is employment of 50 to 52 weeks during the year, usually at a full-time job." Bureau of Labor Statistics, "Linking Employment Problems to Economic Status," Bulletin 2222, March 1985, pp. 28–29.

3. Ibid., p. 42.

4. Ibid. Because of rounding, the number of full-time, year-round workers below the poverty line, shown in the various personal-earnings categories in the chart, do not add up to 2.1 million, the actual total.

5. Deborah J. Chollet, Employee Benefit Research Institute, "The Erosion of Health Insurance Coverage Among the Nonelderly Population: Public Policy Issues and Options." Statement before the U.S. Congress, House, Committee on Small Business, May 6, 1987, pp. 10, 35.

6. Ibid., at table following p. 10.

7. Bureau of Labor Statistics, "Usual Weekly Earnings of Employed Wage and Salary Workers Who Usually Work Full-Time by Detailed Occupation and Sex." 1986 annual averages, unpublished tabulations from the *Current Population Survey*. I wish to thank Charles M. O'Connor, Chief, Division of Occupational Pay and Employee Benefit Levels, for supplying this information. The total number of 78.7 million workers is probably lower than the 112.4 million that Deborah Chollet's paper discusses ("Erosion of Health Insurance Coverage"), primarily because only full-time workers are analyzed. The total number of workers is probably higher than the 66.8 million that the BLS paper discusses ("Linking Employment Problems"), primarily because the focus is not limited to full-time and year-round workers.

8. Bureau of Labor Statistics, "Median Weekly Earnings of Wage and Salary Workers Who Usually Work Full Time by Detailed (3-Digit Census Code) Occupation and Sex: 1986 Annual Averages." Unpublished tabulations from the *Current Population Survey*. These tables were also made available by Charles M. O'Connor (see n. 7).

9. Bureau of Labor Statistics, "Usual Weekly Earnings."

10. U.S. Congress, House, Committee on Ways and Means, "Background Material and Data on Programs Within the Jurisdiction of the Committee on Ways and Means," March 6, 1987, Table 27, pp. 656–58.

# 5
# The Long Queue

Facts ought to shape our public policy, but at best they play a supporting role. Images exercise a far greater influence in fashioning our government's conduct. One need recall only a few of the more powerful images that have influenced U.S. history—States' Rights, Union, Manifest Destiny, the Big Stick, the Arsenal of Democracy, the Iron Curtain, the New Frontier, the Evil Empire—to appreciate how simple images can stir and unleash popular feeling, define the issues, and set the basic course that government follows.

None of this is to say that facts are unimportant, or to assert that images are all-powerful. In the first place, facts—together with prejudice, self-interest, transcendent values, historical accident, and a multitude of other influences—determine what a society's governing images will be. In the second place, the images that channel the activity of government are usually multitudinous and conflicting, seldom few and uniform. Finally (a point hardly to be overlooked as we begin the third century of the U.S. Constitution), our government is structured to neutralize the sway of dominant images over the political process by dividing power—first between the states and the federal government, second (at each level of government), among a legislative branch, an executive branch, and a judicial branch—and by investing some of those who hold power (e.g., U.S. senators and federal judges) with lengthy or lifetime terms of office. By making it difficult for images that excite the public's enthusiasm to shape the exercise of governmental power, the U.S. system of government offers a greater chance for facts, values, and prudence to influence public policy. In order for a dominant image to be discarded or recast before it shapes public policy, however, there must be powerful groups in society or powerful officeholders in government who are willing to manipulate the levers made available by state and federal constitutions.

It sometimes occurs, therefore, that notwithstanding both the facts themselves and the constraints put in place by our governing structure, a false but potent image seizes the public's imagination, penetrates the thinking of policymakers at every level of society and government, and shapes public policy for decades. The facts that undermine the false but dominant image may simply not be known. Or there may be no organization or constituency capable of impressing the facts on the public's consciousness. Or the facts may be so repugnant to the dominant image that the public denies them and clings even more tenaciously to the image. Or, finally, the facts may be frightening or threatening to the views of the vast majority—requiring them to take unwanted steps, if they acknowledge the facts are correct and their original image was wrong—in which case the facts may be secretly or formally acknowledged, but their invalidation of the dominant image not accepted.

One need not stretch one's imagination to find examples in American history of facts that were repugnant to the dominant image. Native Americans, black Americans, and Hispanic Americans are equal to "white" Americans in any factual way that counts. Yet for over 300 years of colonial and postcolonial history, images of their inferiority as human beings and citizens of the United States deeply penetrated the thinking and feelings of the white majority that dominated our culture and held all the reins of power. These perceptions of inferiority quickly became imbedded in the nation's laws (including the U.S. Constitution itself). It required not merely the fact of equality but a civil war and the forceful advocacy of equality by thousands of individuals, groups, and officeholders to shatter the dominant image of white superiority and end that image's grip on our laws. A century after the movement for racial equality began, the effort to eliminate the image of white superiority has still far to go, and racial discrimination still remains a powerful social force.

Our history also includes many chapters in which facts were secretly or formally acknowledged, but their consequences avoided. The imprisonment of Japanese Americans in concentration camps after the outbreak of World War II is a good case in point. There was no evidence that these U.S. citizens were traitors, or even sympathetic to Japan, so as to justify their incarceration without trial—or even to justify accusing them. On the contrary, there was abundant evidence that they were loyal to the United States, willing to fight and die for their country. These facts were acknowledged, privately, by the people who ran the U.S. Justice Department. To acknowledge these facts publicly, however—and to act accordingly by allowing Japanese Americans to remain in their homes and businesses—was too frightening. So, even while accepting privately the truth of Japanese Americans' patriotism, the U.S. Justice Department locked them up in conformity with the absurd dominant image that all "Japs" were spies and fellow travelers.

Poverty in the United States presents another case of conflict between the facts and the dominant image. The facts have largely failed to shape the public's understanding of why the poor are poor. They have generally been ignored by the policymakers who fashioned the antipoverty programs of the last 25 years. Why?

For roughly that time period, Census Bureau and other data have consistently suggested that the poor are poor primarily because (1) they cannot work, or are exempted from work by old age, but receive inadequate social insurance payments; (2) they are unemployed or partially employed; or (3) they hold jobs, often full-time and year-round, that pay low wages. Such data have hardly gone without comment. Nearly a quarter of a century ago, the principal inventor of the poverty line, Mollie Orshansky, pointed out that "more than half of all poor families report that the head currently has a job." Indeed, "half of these employed family heads, representing almost 30 percent of all the families called poor, have been holding down a full-time job for a whole year."[1] Scholars have remarked on the same and related connections between poverty and work ever since. Nor has the imbalance between job-seekers and available jobs been hidden. Katharine Abraham, on the basis of her exhaustive work, announced in both the *American Economic Review* and the *Washington Post*[2] the existence of a long-standing and massive job shortage. Both before and after her authoritative study, others have noted—albeit with less definitive evidence—the existence of a job shortage.

The implication of these facts—the policies they dictate—are fairly straightforward. To get the poor out of poverty, we need to (1) provide those who cannot work, or who are exempt from work by virtue of old age, with higher social-insurance payments; (2) ensure that those who can work, but are unemployed in full or in part, have access to a roughly equal number of readily available full-time or part-time jobs, which means creating most of those jobs in some fashion, because too few existing jobs are available; and (3) guarantee that those who work full-time and year-round bring home more money, which in turn means either raising their wages or supplementing their wages. One can dispute at great length as to how these policies should be carried out. Facts that we have known for nearly a quarter of a century make it pretty clear, however, that lifting the poor out of poverty requires a tripartite strategy of higher social insurance payments, job creation, and wage augmentation.

Why has society not responded? Why have policymakers proceeded in a different direction? Why, since poverty was "discovered" in the early 1960s and "war on poverty" declared in the mid–1960s, has the principal U.S. response been to spend billions of dollars on education, training, housing, health care, and community action?

One important reason—though certainly not the only one—is that the facts about poverty and the implication of these facts for public policy run directly counter to a widely held and deeply engrained public image about why the poor are poor. Notwithstanding the facts, the dominant image Americans have is that the poor are poor because barriers impede their access to good jobs that are available. Knock down those barriers and the poor will move into good jobs, and poverty will be eliminated. The barriers are lack of motivation (due to laziness, alienation, or whatever), lack of education, lack of training, racial and sexual discrimination, inadequate day care and health insurance, and inadequate services of many other types. Provide motivation, education, training, affirmative action, day care and health insurance, and other services and the poor will climb up to the good jobs awaiting.

The barrier image is not without its virtues, nor is it entirely invalid. It is simple: All of us easily understand obstacles, hurdles, things that keep us from achieving the good things just beyond our grasp. The barrier image is also an emotionally intense image, deeply rooted in U.S. history, validated by the experience of the great majority of the population who are not poor, and strengthened by the experience of many of today's poor. Our ancestors and parents overcame barriers—the ocean, the frontier, the sweatshops—to rise out of poverty. Many of us, individually, overcame obstacles to achieve economic security. And it is indisputable that huge numbers of poor people—blacks, Hispanics, and Asian immigrants, as well as whites—are today climbing out of poverty by overcoming the obstacles that stand in their way.

The barrier image is indeed an excellent one for any individual—any one person—to use in seeking to rise out of poverty. It accurately portrays what that person must do to get ahead in the economic world.

The barrier image, however, is a woefully inaccurate image of why the poor population of the United States *as a whole* is poor. The economic status of those who cannot work or whose old age exempts them from work; the enormous and continuing imbalance between the aggregate number of jobseekers and jobs; the plight of millions of full-time, year-round workers who hold low-wage jobs—none of these facets of poverty in the United States is successfully explained by the barrier image. An entirely new and different image is needed to depict why the poor as a group remain poor.

In fairness both to the barrier image and any effort to develop a more accurate image, the problem of poverty among persons who cannot work (including those whose old age exempts them from work) should be dealt with outside the dominant barrier image or its successor. The poverty of these people—principally disabled or retired—is a simple matter. They cannot work, or we do not expect them to work. We have already decided that they should be paid sufficient cash in regular monthly installments, through social insurance programs like Supplemental Security Income (SSI) or Social Security, to maintain an adequate living standard. We just do not give them enough. The only relevant image to explain the poverty of this group—if image be needed—is that of a gap: the gap between the social insurance income they get from us and the social insurance income they *ought* to get from us to rise above the poverty line. It is for the vast majority of the poor—the nondisabled, non-retired, able-bodied unemployed, and workers as a group—that the barrier image is fundamentally flawed and a new image is required.

The image that the facts best support—the new portrait of U.S. poverty that is most consistent with the evidence—is that of the long queue. Queue comes from the Latin *cauda*, or tail, and is typically defined as "a line . . . of persons waiting to be served"[3] or a "file or line . . . of persons waiting their turn."[4] People stand in queues as they wait to get on a bus at a bus stop, or as they wait to get food in a cafeteria, or as they wait to buy tickets to a movie. The last to arrive joins the end of the queue, then moves up as the individuals at the head board the bus, take food, or buy tickets. A simple queue has two main features: one line, and "first come, first served." Not all queues, however, are so simple.

Some queues have multiple lines. At a baseball stadium or symphony concert, for instance, bleachers or balcony customers may be asked to stand in one line to get their cheaper tickets, while box-seat or orchestra-seat customers queue up separately to pick up their more expensive tickets. Price often, but not always, explains why separate queues form. The separate lines at supermarkets, custard stands, banks, and post offices are based on factors such as speed of service ("Six Items or Fewer"), type of purchase ("Cones Only"), or simply the vendor's efforts to allocate its personnel most efficiently.

First come/first served is the rule that governs the formation of most queues, but sometimes other rules supersede. A single line of passengers forms to board most airplanes, for instance, but it does not matter who arrived first at the airport or even who checked in first at the counter near the departure gate. Ticketed coach passengers who first walk up to the departure gate itself get to enter the plane first; they are preceded by first-class passengers, who in turn are preceded by families with young children; people in wheelchairs board ahead of everyone else.

Another breach of the first come/first served rule is hopping queues. To insert oneself in the middle or at the head of a line that has already formed is often considered the height of rudeness, but it happens all the time. A couple—arriving late at the movie theater—joins friends at the head of the line. A parent with a screaming baby is allowed (often encouraged!) to go to the head of the check-out line in a grocery store. The first come/first served rule rests on the principle of fairness, and it gives way when other values (friendship, quiet, etc.) seem to be of greater importance.

The simplicity or complexity of a queue is largely determined by the queue's purpose or objective. Each queue has an objective to which it is intimately related: the allocation of seats on a bus, the distribution of seats in a movie theater, the timing of entering an airplane, the timing of buying groceries, and so on. The characteristics of a queue directly reflect the characteristics of its objective. Traditional queue patterns (one line and first come, first served) will generally apply if the queue's objective is simple; those queue patterns will be replaced by more elaborate patterns (multiple lines, queue hopping) as the objective becomes increasingly complex. The queue for a movie theater is simple, because the objective is simple: Sell moviegoers tickets and let them take any available seat in the theater. By contrast, the queue for boarding an airplane is more complex, because the objective is more complex: Verify passengers' boarding passes and let them onto the plane; satisfy those passengers who have spent more for first-class tickets and expect special service in return; assist parents with children who will have difficulty maneuvering in a crowded airplane corridor; assist persons in wheelchairs who will have even greater difficulty maneuvering on a crowded plane. A kiss may be just a kiss, a sigh may be just a sigh, but a queue is not just a queue. The features of each queue mirror the features of its objective.

The evidence suggests that the poor are poor in this country primarily because they form part of a long queue of unemployed and working adults whose number far exceeds the number of good jobs available—that is, jobs that are steady and that pay a wage at least high enough to get the typical individual or family over the poverty line. It is important to understand that this queue is a complex and dynamic one. Its intricacies and transformations are exceeded only by the intricacies and transformations of the job market (both unfilled jobs and filled jobs) to which it relates. The queue is far from a single line. It is inaccurate to describe it even as a set of multiple lines. It is more like a giant web, an enormous tangle of unemployed and working persons, moving in various directions at various speeds in relationship to each other, in relationship to the job market as a whole, in relationship to good jobs in general, and in relationship to specific good

**Figure 2**
**The Ideal Balance of Workers and Good Jobs**

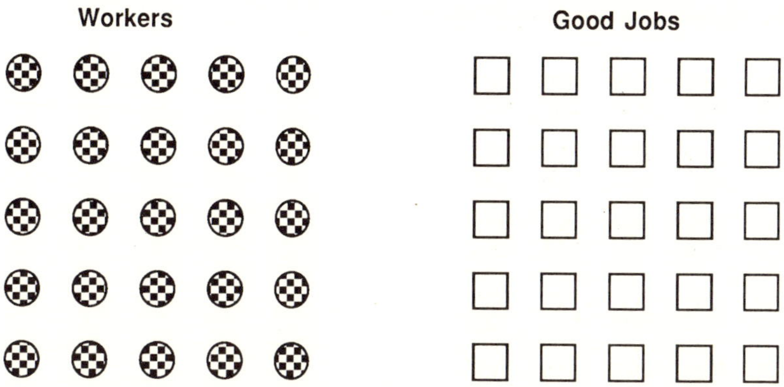

Workers                                    Good Jobs

jobs. The relative position of persons in this queue for good jobs—that is, their closeness to the head of the queue and thus their likelihood of getting a good job—can (and does) change frequently. Individuals can (and do) both join and leave the queue, as they either enter the potential labor force, lose a good job, get a good job, or leave the potential labor force through disability or retirement or death. The length of the queue can also (and does) change as the economy worsens or improves, as the number of good jobs shrinks or grows, but the long queue is always there.

In an ideal world there would be no queue for good jobs at all. In this economic Garden of Eden, there would be an equal number of qualified workers and good jobs. Each worker would receive a superb general education before going on to achieve mastery in a chosen field of expertise. Every job would be full-time, year-round, and well paid— providing both ample cash income and attractive fringe benefits. Figure 2 conveys the general idea.

In this economic Garden of Eden, every qualified worker would hold a good job, and every good job would be filled. Neither unemployment nor job vacancies would scourge the earth. The need of workers to be employed and the need of firms to have their positions filled would harmonize like the music of the spheres. Figure 3 depicts the perfect equilibrium.

Mankind, alas, has fallen from grace. With the expulsion of Adam and Eve from the Garden of Eden came not only war, pestilence, and famine but also unemployment and job vacancies. Humbly accepting our earthly fate, we have redefined our ideal—taken it down a peg or two—so that it looks like Figure 4. All workers remain qualified; all jobs count as good ones; the number of workers exactly equals the

**Figure 3**
**The Ideal Match of Workers and Good Jobs**

Workers Employed in Good Jobs

**Figure 4**
**The Near-Ideal Balance of Workers and Good Jobs**

Workers Employed
in Good Jobs

Unemployed
Workers

Unfilled
Jobs

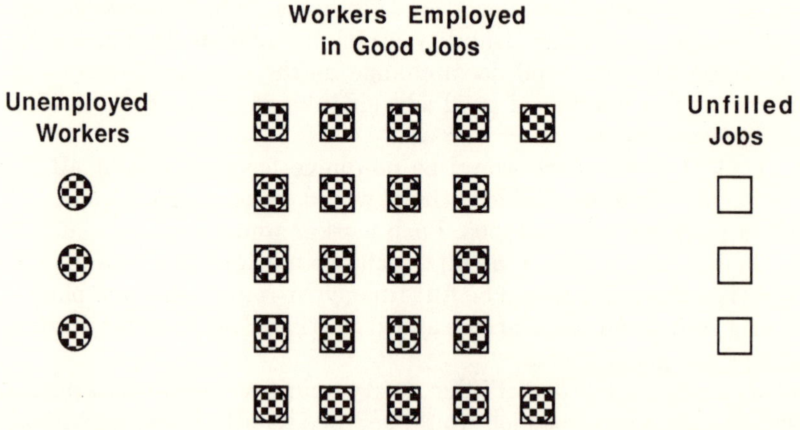

number of jobs; and the vast majority of workers are employed, just as the great majority of jobs are filled. The only glitch is that some of the workers have not found jobs, and some of the jobs remain vacant. In this redefined ideal, however, the queue of unemployed workers is not a problem. The jobs are there for the taking. It is only the workers' ignorance (they may not know that the jobs are available), or residence (they may not reside where the jobs are located), or lack of some very specialized technical training, or some other easily correctable obstacle that thwarts a perfect balance. The equilibrium between qualified

**Figure 5**
**The Workers and Jobs Continuums**

| Workers | Jobs |
|---|---|
| Unskilled ------- Skilled | Low Wage ------- High Wage |

workers and good jobs, if not entirely achieved, is in large part real and is entirely obtainable.

We all know, of course, that even this redefined ideal is still far from the truth. Workers are not all skilled: Some have bad skills (for example, the habit of showing up late for work); some we would consider unskilled (that is, lacking in any widely recognized technical expertise); some have the wrong skills (for instance, a mastery only of punching computer cards in an era of microchips); and some have the skills most sought after by employers. Similarly, not all jobs are good ones: Some provide only limited hours of work, some pay just the minimum wage, some offer no health insurance or other fringe benefits. Just as workers extend along a skill continuum, jobs extend along a wage continuum (wages, here, acting as a surrogate for all the features of a job). Figure 5 begins to paint the real world—the world we all know from our daily lives—of workers and jobs.

This map of the world of work, however, still leaves out much important detail. Slavery, segregation, and racism—nearly 500 years of racial oppression—have made it far more difficult for blacks to obtain training or to pursue good jobs. Women, once barred by law or custom from attaining certain skills, pursuing any paid employment, or seeking good jobs, continue to face sexist barriers. Partly as a result of these factors, blacks, Hispanics, and other ethnic minorities, as well as women, tend to concentrate toward the "unskilled" end of the worker continuum. Whites and men tend to concentrate toward the "skilled" end of the continuum. Figure 6 portrays the pattern.

**Figure 6**
**Discrimination-Based Version of the Workers and Jobs Continuums**

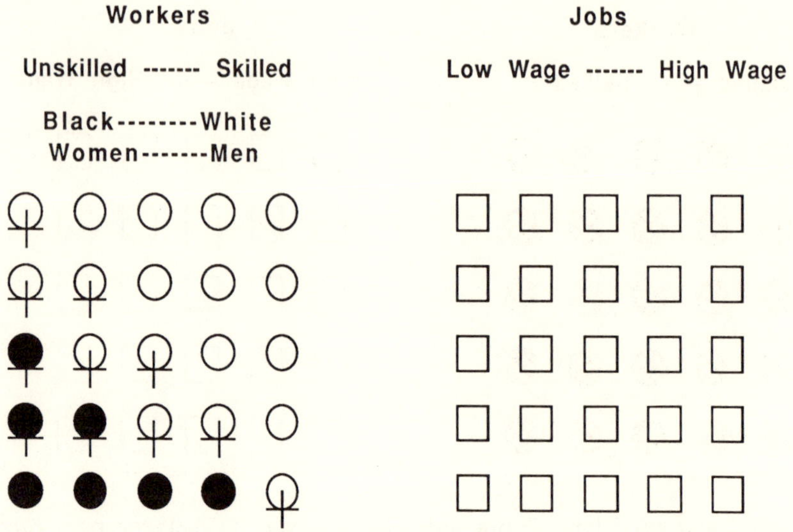

Workers                                                    Jobs

Unskilled ------- Skilled                    Low Wage ------- High Wage

Black--------White
Women-------Men

The continuum of workers (ranging from unskilled to skilled) and the continuum of jobs (ranging from low-wage to high-wage) are of course functionally connected. Workers from the unskilled end of the workers' continuum tend to get jobs at the low-wage end of the jobs continuum. Workers from the skilled end of their continuum tend to get jobs at the high-wage end of the jobs continuum. The connection is by no means neat and clean. The unskilled son of the company's boss may go straight to vice-president at $50,000 per year. The Ph.D. in physics may end up selling hot dogs in Central Park. These aberrations do not disprove the general linkage, however, between the skills a worker has and the probability that the worker will end up in a low-wage or high-wage job. The pattern, depicted in Figure 7, is too obvious to belabor.

In the less-than-perfect U.S. economy of which we speak—where too many workers lack skills and too many jobs are not good ones—one would hope that at least every worker had a job and every job was filled. During certain brief periods of modern U.S. history—World War I, World War II, the mid–1950s, the early 1960s, and perhaps others— such an equilibrium, shown in Figure 8, was nearly attained.

For most of U.S. history, however, full employment has not been a reality. Nonetheless, the dominant image of the economy is one in which the number of workers equals (roughly) the number of jobs. This view, described in Figure 9, holds that for every (or almost every) unemployed person there is a job waiting somewhere, and that full

**Figure 7**
**The General Process of Matching Workers and Jobs**

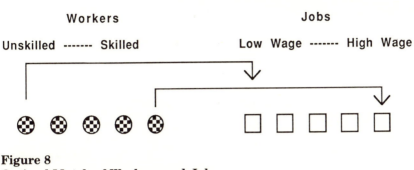

**Figure 8**
**Optimal Match of Workers and Jobs**

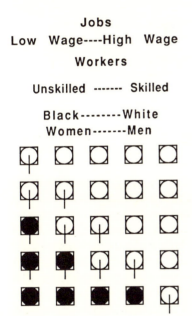

employment is a practical possibility. It is simply a matter of overcoming the barriers—lack of motivation, lack of general education, lack of specific training, discrimination, and so on, that stand between the worker and the job.

More realistic proponents of this view would acknowledge that many unemployed persons will have to settle for less-than-permanent, low-wage, low-benefit jobs. The unemployed cannot count on access to a better supply of good jobs than those already working; they may even have to accept disproportionately fewer good jobs, as persons already

**Figure 9**
**Equilibrium between Workers and Jobs**

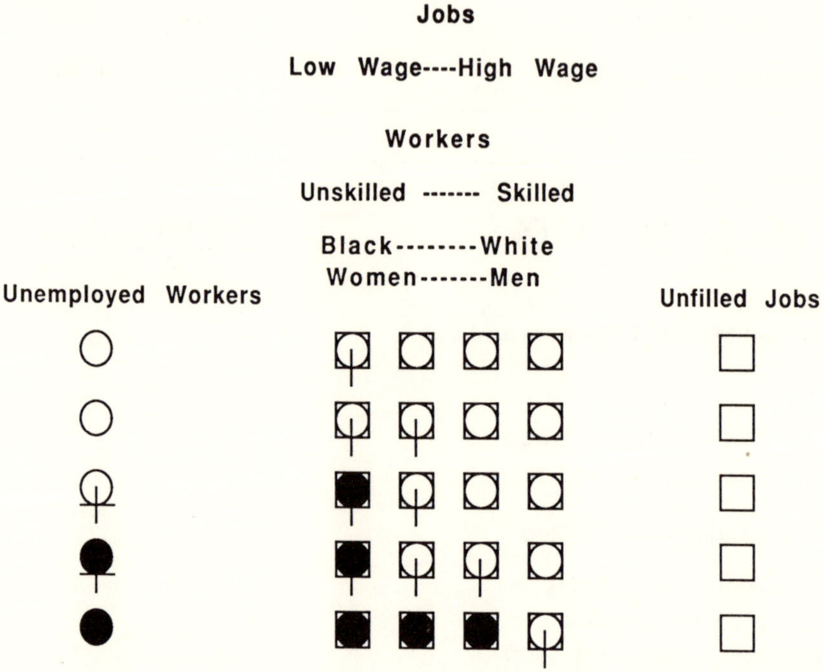

**Jobs**

**Low   Wage----High   Wage**

**Workers**

**Unskilled   -------   Skilled**

**Black--------White**
**Women-------Men**

**Unemployed   Workers**                                                    **Unfilled   Jobs**

at work in worse jobs move ahead of them into any new good jobs that open up; but at least the unemployed can get jobs. In this more realistic perspective, overcoming barriers still remains the key to employment. By modifying workers' motivation, education, training, and so forth, or by modifying prospective employers' discriminatory practices, all unemployed workers can still be fitted into existing jobs of one kind or another. Figure 10 depicts this interpretation of the economic world.

Remote as such a view is from the economic Garden of Eden, remote as such a view is from even the redefined ideal in which every worker (unemployed or employed) has access to a good job (unfilled or filled), how lucky we would be if even this sober view of the U.S. economy bore any relationship to reality. All the evidence, regrettably, suggests that this image simply does not fit the facts. The data that are available make clear that the number of unemployed jobseekers far exceeds the number of available jobs. The data also suggests that the combined number of unemployed jobseekers and workers in less-than-good jobs vastly exceeds the number of good jobs in the economy. The unpleasant truth, shown in Figure 11, is a long queue for good jobs.

Poverty in the United States, as Figure 11 helps to make graphically

**Figure 10**
**"Realistic" Equilibrium between Workers and Jobs**

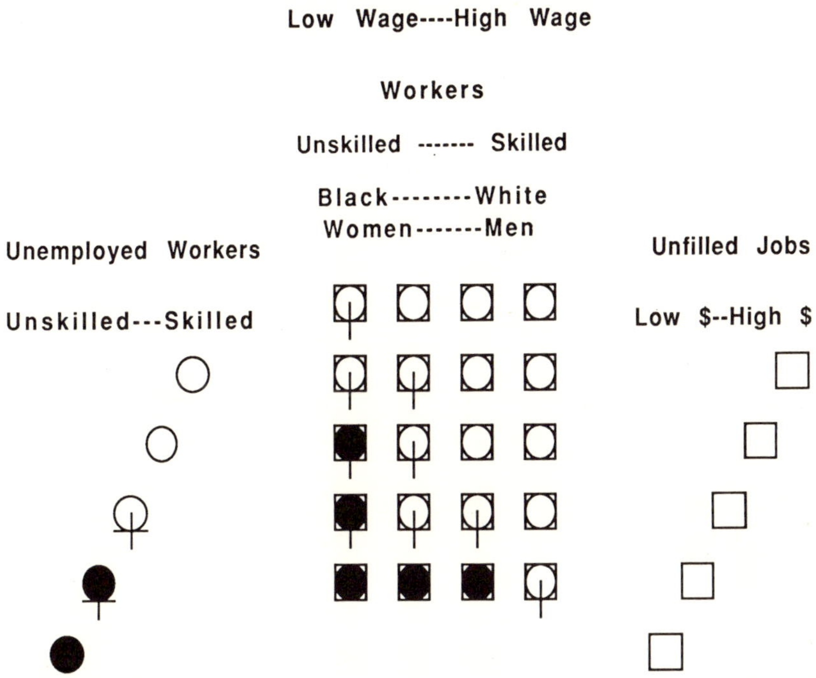

Low  Wage----High  Wage

Workers

Unskilled ------- Skilled

Black--------White
Women-------Men

Unemployed  Workers                                    Unfilled  Jobs

Unskilled---Skilled                                      Low  $--High  $

clear, is primarily caused by the fact that the long queue of unemployed jobseekers and workers in less-than-good jobs far exceeds the number of good jobs available. Unemployed workers and low-wage employees, like middle-wage employees and high-wage employees, all want good jobs, but there are just not enough good jobs to go around. Some of the unemployed workers and low-wage employees who do not get the good jobs—depending on both the exact amount of their own earnings and such factors as family size, the number and wages of other family earners, and unearned income—end up below the poverty line. Others make it across the poverty line. Their position in the long queue, combined with the other factors, decides which it will be: poverty or not.

Why the good jobs are not there is a question about which reasonable people may differ. What can and should be done to create new good jobs and to transform an even larger number of existing jobs into good jobs is also a legitimate subject of debate. The fact that poverty in the United States is largely the consequence of a long queue of unemployed and low-wage workers, who do not hold but who are seeking good jobs, should not be a serious matter of question or dispute. The old flawed image of poverty's causes—the image of barriers that block the poor's

**Figure 11**
**The Long Queue: Disequilibrium between Workers and Jobs**

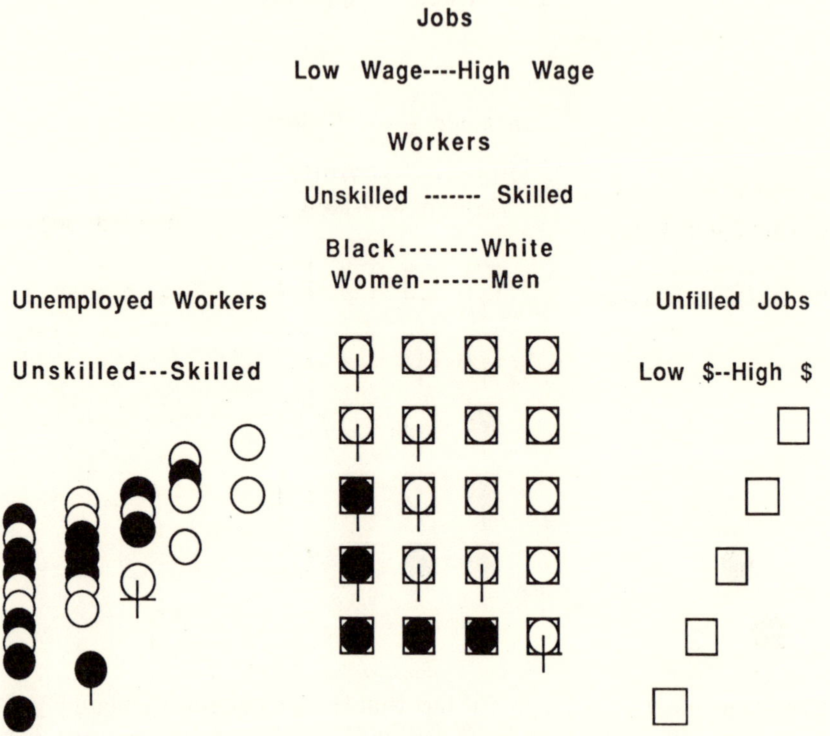

access to available good jobs—urgently needs to be replaced by this far more accurate image of the long queue in the minds of academicians, journalists, other opinionmolders and policyshapers, and elected officials. Only when those who control the direction of public policy get the image of poverty's causes "right" are we likely to be able to move forward to poverty's elimination.

## NOTES

1. Mollie Orshansky, "Counting the Poor: Another Look at the Poverty Profile," *Social Security Bulletin* Vol. 28, No. 1, January 1965, p. 5.

2. Katharine G. Abraham, "Structural/Frictional vs. Deficient Demand Unemployment: Some New Evidence," *American Economic Review* 73, No. 4, (September 1983): 708–724; and "Too Few Jobs," *Washington Post*, May 25, 1982, p. A–17.

3. *Webster's New World Dictionary*, revised pocket-size edition, 1973.

4. *Random House Dictionary of the English Language*, unabridged edition, 1966.

# PART TWO
# WHY WELFARE REFORM WILL FAIL

# 6
## Faulty Premises

The defects of the U.S. welfare system are so well known that they need only be briefly recapitulated here.[1] Payments that leave children far below the poverty line; perverse incentives to enter the system and avoid leaving it, compared to taking work when it is available; administrative complexity beyond belief—all this has been spoken of, over and over again, for decades. By contrast, the defective premises that underlie the debate about welfare reform have received little attention.

Much of the current debate about welfare and welfare reform hinges on the assumptions that the partisans in the debate make about the purposes of welfare, the legitimacy of expecting or requiring recipients to work, and the reasons why recipients initially enter the welfare system and subsequently remain on welfare instead of obtaining work. This is not the place to provide a detailed account and assessment of the conflicting assumptions, and the inevitably conflicting conclusions, of the main parties to the debate. A brief summary of the terms of the debate, however, is necessary in order to proceed.

The traditional liberal position has been that single parents with young children should be offered welfare so that they can maintain a decent living standard; that requiring single parents to work is unjustified, as they should have an unrestricted choice between receiving welfare or taking a job; and that welfare recipients do not find work, primarily, because of a lack of adequate education and training, racial or sexual discrimination, a lack of affordable day care, a lack of health-care coverage, or some combination of these barriers. The basic liberal position is surrounded by a variety of ultraliberal or neoliberal positions that depart from the central doctrine on key points. Ultraliberals have argued that not merely single parents with children but all poor people should be entitled to the whole range of welfare benefits; that even people with substantial employment, including full-time jobs, should be eligible for welfare in addition to (and, should they quit, in lieu of) working at the jobs they hold; and that benefits should be dramatically higher (at or above the poverty line). Neoliberals, by contrast, have asserted the legitimacy of requiring single parents with older children (defined variously as over 6 months, over 3 years, over 5 years, in school, etc.) to work for their benefits; have been warm to the concept of rewarding private-sector agencies that successfully place recipients in regular private-sector jobs; have at times strongly advocated the strengthening of child-support laws and enforcement, so as to reduce welfare caseloads and payments in proportion to the collection of additional dollars from noncustodial parents who fail to pay enough or pay at all; and have generally advocated shrinking the size and cost of the welfare system.

Notwithstanding the many differences within the liberal camp, however, certain central themes constantly reemerge: (1) the value and necessity of taking care of poor children whose parents (usually) have engaged in morally reprehensible behavior (e.g., sexual promiscuity), been irresponsible (e.g., failed to use birth-control methods), or simply had bad luck (spouses who deserted or died); (2) the conviction that, at least for some single parents who receive it, welfare is a legitimate alternative to working, especially at low-wage jobs; and (3) the belief that defects in the way welfare recipients are treated by our culture, economy, or policies (bad education, bad training, racism, sexism, no day care, no health care) are the principal reasons why recipients do not seek or obtain work.

The basic conservative position is that welfare is for short-term economic emergencies and should serve merely as a temporary bridge to work. However unpleasant it is to ask women with young children to work, a number of fundamental social values—promotion of self-reliance, instruction of children about the importance of work, fairness to similarly situated women who have chosen to work and now pay taxes, reduction of the tax burden—require that welfare recipients should immediately be required to seek private-sector employment. If that fails, they should then be required to work off their benefits in order to keep up their job readiness, give them an incentive to get off welfare should they find a job, and "repay" the taxpayers. It is the conservative position that, just as the initial reasons a woman gets welfare are personal (an out-of-wedlock baby, or desertion or death of a husband), the main reason welfare mothers do not find work are also personal—for example, greed, laziness, lack of motivation, or lack of effort.

The basic conservative position is also surrounded by a variety of "radical" conservative or ultraconservative positions that depart from the central doctrine on key points. Radical conservatives—concerned with the way in which different family categories are treated by the welfare system (single-parent families get help, dual-parent families usually do not; a nonworking parent gets help, a working parent often does not) and persuaded that this disparate treatment creates "perverse incentives" to form and maintain single-parent families headed by nonworkers—have advocated the replacement of welfare by guaranteed annual income schemes (such as the negative income tax), which, while providing admittedly low payments, counteract the system's perverse incentives by treating all family units alike. Ultraconservatives, on the other hand, have argued that the welfare system should simply be abolished, or should be limited to a brief period of time, or should be limited to noncash assistance. Single mothers need no or very little help, or, though they need help, they are more harmed than helped by welfare—so the system should basically be abolished.

In some respects, compared to the range of opinion within the liberal camp, the differences within the conservative camp are far more striking. Nonetheless, when welfare is criticized and as solutions are fashioned, certain constant themes appear: (1) welfare should be a temporary, short-term, transition to work; (2) for most if not all recipients, work should be expected (as part of the welfare system itself, if the recipient fails quickly to obtain a job outside the system); and (3) whether initial eligibility for welfare was the recipient's fault (as in the case of an out-of-wedlock child), someone else's fault (as in the case of desertion by a husband), or no one's fault (as in the case of the death of a husband), remaining on welfare after an initial emergency period is generally the recipient's fault and is more likely than not the result of a desire to get something for nothing, indolence, or of lack of ambition.

In recent years, as many observers have noted, the conventional liberal and conservative positions have tended to merge. The liberals have moved to the right with respect to expecting—sometimes requiring—welfare recipients to work. The conservatives have moved to the left by acknowledging that the reasons some recipients do not work include the failure of government to provide adequate education, training, day care, and health insurance. The following story from the *New York Times* typifies press accounts of the new, tentative, alliance on welfare between liberals and conservatives:

> In the last six months, studies cascading out of Government offices and private research centers have produced a new consensus on the need to overhaul the welfare system. This time around, work is perceived as the

solution to dependency, and training and job placement as the way for long-term welfare recipients to break out of the cycle....

In the Depression, there was a surplus of labor, so Congress saw no reason to compel women with young children to enter the labor force. Now, more than 50 percent of women with children under the age of 6 work. So the new consensus emphasizes the value of work as a source of dignity and self-respect, and the mutual obligation of welfare recipients and government agencies: Able-bodied parents have a responsibility to support their children, and government agencies are obliged to provide child care and other aid to help them do so.[2]

The new liberal–conservative alliance, as might be expected, has gathered enough steam to persuade large numbers of elected officials to attempt to convert the new amalgam of left-leaning and right-leaning welfare reform principles into law. In addition to considerable activity at the state level (the California and Massachusetts welfare reform experiments are perhaps the best known), action is afoot in Congress. Senator Daniel Patrick Moynihan, Democrat from New York, announced in September 1987 that 54 senators from both parties had signed up as cosponsors of his bill "to overhaul the nation's basic welfare program." The key ingredients include the following:

- Many welfare recipients would be required to work;
- States would be required to establish education and training programs;
- Coverage of two-parent families, now optional at the state level, would be mandated;
- Child-support payments would be automatically withheld from the wages of noncustodial parents.[3]

A similar bill, drafted by four committees of the House of Representatives and largely reflecting the perspective of the House's Democratic majority, was awaiting floor action as 1987 came to an end. The Moynihan proposal's estimated cost was $2.3 billion over a five-year period. House Democrats estimated that their proposal will cost $5.3 billion over five years, a price tag that their Republican colleagues disputed. In any case, both the Moynihan bill and the House Democratic bill were too costly for the Reagan administration. Whether either bill—or some hybrid or compromise that enjoys White House support—will become law in 1988 thus remains uncertain. Nonetheless, the mere fact that, on an issue that has so deeply divided Congress in the past, such a large measure of agreement has emerged bodes well for the passage of some sort of major welfare reform law within the next few years.[4]

It is heartening that, in the effort to remake the welfare system, so many U.S. liberals and conservatives have managed to find some common ground. What is disheartening—what is the seed of a political tragedy—is that the "new consensus" to redo welfare itself rests on fundamentally faulty premises about why welfare recipients do not seek or take jobs.

In the preconsensus era, notwithstanding their main differences, both liberals and conservatives shared the belief that if welfare recipients somehow became different people they would get jobs, become self-supporting, and no longer burden society. The liberal perspective was that there was nothing wrong with welfare recipients *per se*, but that they lacked certain "internal" assets—higher levels of knowledge, specific skills—which they needed to acquire to obtain employment. They also lacked certain "external" assets—enough cash to pay for day care, sufficient resources to buy health insurance—which they required in order to make regular employment feasible or acceptable. Change welfare recipients by building up their internal and external assets, and purify the job market by prohibiting *de jure* racism and sexism and by combatting *de facto* discrimination, and recipients will go forth and get jobs.

The conservative perspective is darker, but in the end similar enough. People who stayed on welfare beyond the short-term, emergency, adjustment period for which welfare was meant had personalities that—if not utterly manipulative, lacking in desire, or unwilling to exert effort—were at least sufficiently manipulative or indolent that they intentionally avoided pursuing employment. Nonetheless, built into the conservative approach is the belief that, by altering the incentives that welfare offers, compared to the incentives that work offers, recipients' personalities would generally adjust in a positive manner to the new environment by pursuing work. Cut or control welfare benefit levels, keeping them below the minimum wage, and recipients will see where their self-interest lies and pursue work. Require recipients to work for their welfare, and they will decide to pursue private-sector jobs instead. Eliminate (as the radical conservatives propose) the distinction between types of families (single-parent/dual-parent, nonworking/working) with respect to the provision of cash, and eligible persons will seek to form families and take jobs. Eliminate (as the ultraconservatives propose) the entire welfare system, and recipients will quickly respond to the new reality by finding income where it is available—that is, in the job market. In short, despite conservatives' traditional deep pessimism about the perfectibility of human beings, when it comes to welfare they seem to believe in the mutability of personality in response to a new environment of incentives.

The new consensus incorporates both the liberal and the conservative view that changing welfare recipients' themselves—transforming them into different people—is the key to getting them jobs. From the con-

servatives the new consensus borrows the belief that once welfare recipients are required to participate in work-related programs
(sometimes including "workfare" jobs) in order to get their benefits—
so that their choice becomes work for welfare or work for a regular
employer—their personalities will adjust to the new set of incentives
by pushing them out into the labor market to seek regular jobs. The
liberal contribution to the new consensus is the belief that once welfare
recipients' internal and external assets are strengthened by a heavy
dose of education, training, day care, and health insurance, they will
generally be able to secure employment. In brief, while the new consensus merges liberal and conservative attitudes commonly thought
to be antithetical, it also reinforces the underlying, jointly held liberal
and conservative belief that by changing welfare recipients—making
them different and better—they will get off the welfare rolls and into
jobs. Indeed, by combining two quite different theories about the possibility and value of improving welfare recipients so that they can go
out and get jobs, the new consensus makes personal improvement more
important than ever as the underlying solution to the problem.

There can be no doubt that improving welfare recipients—either by
providing them education, training, day care, or health insurance, or
by stimulating their desire to abandon welfare by imposing new work
requirements that are more onerous (or no less onerous) than the burdens of regular employment—will succeed to a limited extent in getting
recipients off welfare and into jobs. Since 1973 the number of families
(and thus the number of family caretakers) getting AFDC benefits has
ranged from 3.1 to 3.9 million, and projections suggest that the number
will climb toward (though not exceed) 4.0 million over the next several
years.[5] If any sizable percentage were required to participate in workfare and other work-related programs, and simultaneously afforded
additional education, training, day care, and so forth, it is probable
that thousands—perhaps tens of thousands—who would not otherwise
have found work will do so.

It is, however, a fantasy to believe that the majority of the welfare
population—the long-termers who normally remain on the rolls beyond
an initial 6-to-12-month period—whether they are "improved" as recommended by either the liberals, the conservatives, or the new consensus, will quickly move off the welfare rolls and into jobs.[6] As these
welfare recipients enter the labor market, they join the long queue
composed of other unemployed workers who are competing for a much
smaller number of unfilled (both low-wage and high-wage) jobs, plus
employed low-wage workers who are competing for the dramatically
smaller number of unfilled high-wage jobs. The going is rough for
everyone in the queue; far fewer than half of the unemployed queue
members (if Katharine Abraham's research is correct) can expect to

get jobs immediately, because that's all the immediate employment available; even fewer of the unemployed queue members can expect to get good jobs.

Because of the law of large numbers, some welfare recipients, regardless of or because of their improvement, will fare well in the competition, advance through the queue, and find jobs—sometimes good ones. The great majority of them, however, are in a bad competitive position before their improvement takes place. They are less educated than most of their competitors.[7] They have fewer marketable skills than most of their competitors. They have less work experience than most of their competitors. The welfare stigma will attach to them— and not to most of their competitors. The fact that they are disproportionately black or Hispanic will be a handicap in a job market in which racial discrimination remains a reality.[8] Because of these handicaps, the great majority of welfare recipients start off at the end of the queue and are likely to lose out to less-handicapped persons in the competition for scarce jobs. The different improvements favored by liberals, conservatives, and the new consensus will probably help some of the welfare recipients advance to higher positions in the queue (at the expense of others). It is doubtful, however, that most welfare recipients' profound handicaps in the competitive process can be sufficiently overcome by improvement to produce a dramatic advancement in their position in the queue. Welfare recipients—once improved by education, training, day care, health care, motivation, and so forth—may lose out relatively less in the competition for scarce jobs, but most can still be expected to lose out to better-qualified competitors.

Even if the welfare population's competitive disadvantage could be entirely eliminated (that is, even if as a group their motivation, education, training, etc. placed them in the queue in no worse or even better positions than unemployed non-welfare-recipients), the situation for welfare recipients would only marginally improve. A very high percentage of the persons in the queue are unemployed persons whose number far exceeds the number of available jobs. All of the people in the queue, by definition, lack good jobs. Were welfare recipients to distribute themselves equally throughout the unemployed portion of the queue, most of them would still end up unemployed in roughly the same proportion that the nonwelfare unemployed in the queue are unemployed; that is, as a group, they would generally remain unemployed in the short term and many would remain unemployed in the long term. Eventually, any given cohort of improved welfare recipients who join the unemployed portion of the queue will tend to filter into jobs as part of the normal competitive process, but the next (and the next) cohort of improved welfare recipients who join the unemployed portion of the queue will have to start the process all over again. The pattern is exactly the same for the nonwelfare unemployed in the queue. Most in the queue eventually filter into jobs, but new recruits (high-school dropouts, high-school graduates, college graduates, laid-off workers, women entering the workforce, immigrants, etc.) continue to replenish the unemployed segment of the queue.

Finally, even if the great majority of welfare recipients (much less all) somehow did manage, thanks to their improvement, to get jobs, and even if welfare recipients managed to secure good jobs (a further problem not discussed because of its obviousness), and even if this trend continued as year after year new waves of welfare recipients passed quickly through the queue into jobs that paid well—it must be clearly understood that this victory for welfare recipients would not be a victory for other unemployed and low-paid workers in the queue, and it would be at best a half-victory for society as a whole. If Barbara Booth, AFDC caretaker, gets education and training that position her to take a job, then Sally Smith, non-AFDC recipient who is also unemployed and who would otherwise have gotten the job, loses badly. Depending on Sally Smith's circumstances, she could take Barbara Booth's place on the welfare rolls. This is not to say that the realignment of individual positions in the queue is entirely a zero-sum game, but it has a substantial zero-sum element. Improving the competitive status of 3.5–4.0 million AFDC caretakers within the queue for good jobs will not necessarily mean that 3.5–4.0 million non-AFDC-recipients who are also in the queue will join the AFDC program. It is likely, however, that large numbers of the latter will be drawn into the welfare system. This obviously raises some tough ethical questions: Which non-AFDC-recipients should be displaced? Should they also get some improvement at public expense? Ethics aside, a massive swapping of positions in the queue—AFDC recipients getting off welfare and into such jobs as are available, some non-AFDC-recipients going onto welfare because their competitive ability to secure employment has so substantially worsened—is a very expensive proposition. We must pay for the improvement (i.e., the education, training, day care, health care, etc.) of the "regular" AFDC population, pay benefits to the "new" AFDC population that has displaced them in the queue, and perhaps pay for the improvement of the new AFDC population as well.[9]

In short, the premise of all three approaches to welfare reform, the liberal, the conservative, and the new-consensus—that changing the characteristics of welfare recipients will produce a substantial increase in their getting jobs—rests on three faulty premises. First, it rests on the premise, which is based on no demonstrated evidence, that when welfare recipients compete with millions of other jobseekers, they will succeed to a significant extent in beating out their competitors in the scramble for jobs. This assumption ignores the research of Katharine

Abraham, which indicates that the number of unemployed jobseekers already greatly exceeds the number of available jobs. It ignores the presence of the long queue of unemployed workers plus low-wage workers (many of whom are comparatively better educated and trained) who are already actively pursuing good jobs.

The second faulty premise that underlies the liberal, conservative and new-consensus approaches to welfare reform is the belief (often unstated, but always implicit) that when welfare recipients do get jobs, their living standard will improve. Compared to the assumption that most welfare recipients can—with improvement—compete effectively with other jobseekers, this assumption may be less important, but it plays a critical role in all theories of welfare reform. Most (not all) liberals appear to believe that, once enabled to obtain jobs (thanks to education, training, day care, etc.) most welfare recipients will want to work, because they will be economically better off if they work. Most (not all) conservatives appear to believe that, once welfare recipients have a choice between welfare-based work requirements (such as workfare) and regular private-sector employment, they will respond to the new set of incentives by selecting to work in the private sector, because they will make more money there.

Unfortunately, it is not always the case that shifting from welfare to work means more disposable income. It depends on a number of interacting variables: (a) where the welfare recipient lives (states set greatly different benefit levels); (b) how big the family is (fewer children mean a smaller payment, more children mean a higher payment); (c) how many hours the recipient works and what the wage is (the minimum wage is greater than the federal minimum of $3.35 per hour in several states); (d) what arrangements are made to care for recipients' children while they are on the job (day care can cost over $2,000 per year per child); and (e) a variety of other work-related costs and taxes. While a two-person (one-child) family whose head switches from welfare to a full-time, year-round minimum-wage job will always realize an increase in gross income, in a few states a three-person (two-children) or larger family whose head makes the switch will end up with a very modest increase or (in one state) a decrease in gross income. The larger the family and thus the larger the welfare payment, the more likely it is that a minimum-wage job means only a modest increase or a decrease in gross income.

It is probably misleading, however, to make a comparison between the gross income provided by welfare with the gross income that work affords. In contemplating a switch from welfare to work, recipients (quite rationally) are more likely to compare the disposable income they get from welfare with the disposable income they get from a job. Welfare's gross and disposable income are the same, but work's disposable income is gross income minus (at least) day-care costs and Social Security taxes, plus (in many cases, but only if the worker takes advantage of it) the federal Earned Income Tax Credit. Day-care costs are not inevitable (many welfare recipients—like many other working parents—may be able to place young children with a parent or neighbor, and older children attend school), but if day care must be obtained, its cost can be substantial. Social Security taxes, 7.15 percent of income (raised to 7.51 percent on January 1, 1988), are unavoidable. When welfare is compared with disposable income (particularly where disposable income reflects day-care costs), the shift from welfare to a full-time, year-round job at the minimum wage becomes much less advantageous. While a two-person (one-child) family whose head switches from welfare to such a job will still generally realize an increase in disposable income, in a few states even such a small family will end up with only a modest increase or an actual loss of disposable income. A three-person (two-children) or larger family whose head makes the switch will typically end up with a loss of disposable income. The larger the family and thus the larger the welfare payment, the more likely a minimum-wage job is to mean a modest increase or a decrease in disposable income.

Because of all the variables mentioned, there is probably no way to show what will happen to all or most welfare recipients when they switch from welfare to work. It is possible, though, to take a few "typical" families and show, state by state, what moving from reliance on welfare to reliance on a minimum-wage job means to them in terms of an increase or decrease in disposable income. Table 6 provides such a state-by-state comparison for two different typical families in 1987. In both cases it is assumed that before the shift the family is receiving the maximum available AFDC benefit, but no other income; that after the shift the worker is working 40 hours per week, 52 weeks per year, at the applicable minimum wage, and is also taking full advantage of the federal Earned Income Tax Credit; and that the family's resulting gross income is diminished by day-care costs of $2,200 per child, plus the 7.15 percent Social Security Tax then applicable.[10]

The comparison in Table 6 between welfare and a minimum-wage job in certain instances overstates the economic advantage of taking the job. It assumes that the welfare recipient who takes the minimum-wage job will (a) work full-time and year-round for a total of 2,080 hours per year; (b) take full advantage of the federal Earned Income Tax Credit (EITC) in order to boost his or her income; (c) incur no significant transportation, clothing, tool, or other expenses (except for day care) in order to secure and hold the job; (d) pay no work-related taxes other than Social Security, such as state and federal income taxes; and (e) either need no health care or acquire a health-insurance plan

**Table 6**
**Maximum AFDC Payments for Two-Person and Three-Person Families versus Full-Time, Year-Round Minimum-Wage Job: State-by-State Comparison as of January 1987**

### Two-Person (One-Child) Family

(Annual Amounts)

| State | AFDC Payment | Income Afforded by Full-Time Minimum-Wage Job | | Gain/Loss of Income from Shifting from AFDC to Minimum-Wage Job | |
|-------|-------------|-------|------------|-------|------------|
| | | Gross | Disposable | Gross | Disposable |
| AL | $1,056 | $7,815 | $5,056 | +$6,759 | +$4,000 |
| AK | $7,980 | $8,750 | $5,924 | +$ 770 | -$2,056 |
| AZ | $2,796 | $7,815 | $5,056 | +$5,019 | +$2,260 |
| AR | $1,896 | $7,815 | $5,056 | +$5,919 | +$3,160 |
| CA | $5,976 | $7,815 | $5,056 | +$1,839 | -$ 920 |
| CO | $3,264 | $7,815 | $5,056 | +$4,551 | +$1,792 |
| CT | $5,712 | $7,852 | $5,091 | +$2,140 | -$ 622 |
| DE | $2,748 | $7,815 | $5,056 | +$5,067 | +$2,308 |
| DC | $3,432 | $8,938 | $6,099 | +$5,506 | +$2,667 |
| FL | $2,436 | $7,815 | $5,056 | +$5,379 | +$2,488 |
| GA | $2,568 | $7,815 | $5,056 | +$5,247 | +$2,488 |
| HI | $4,680 | $7,815 | $5,056 | +$3,135 | +$ 376 |
| ID | $2,940 | $7,815 | $5,056 | +$4,875 | +$2,116 |
| IL | $3,000 | $7,815 | $5,056 | +$4,815 | +$2,056 |
| IN | $2,352 | $7,815 | $5,056 | +$5,463 | +$2,704 |
| IA | $3,864 | $7,815 | $5,056 | +$3,951 | +$1,192 |
| KS | $4,008 | $7,815 | $5,056 | +$3,807 | +$1,048 |
| KY | $2,040 | $7,815 | $5,056 | +$5,775 | +$3,016 |
| LA | $1,656 | $7,815 | $5,056 | +$6,159 | +$3,400 |
| ME | $3,612 | $8,376 | $5,577 | +$4,764 | +$1,965 |
| MD | $3,228 | $7,815 | $5,056 | +$4,587 | +$1,828 |
| MA | $4,908 | $8,376 | $5,577 | +$3,468 | +$ 669 |
| MI | $4,644 | $7,815 | $5,056 | +$3,171 | +$ 412 |
| MN | $5,244 | $7,815 | $5,056 | +$2,571 | -$ 188 |
| MS | $1,152 | $7,815 | $5,056 | +$6,663 | +$3,904 |
| MO | $2,688 | $7,815 | $5,056 | +$5,127 | +$2,368 |
| MT | $3,384 | $7,815 | $5,056 | +$4,431 | +$1,672 |
| NE | $3,360 | $7,815 | $5,056 | +$4,455 | +$1,696 |
| NV | $2,748 | $7,815 | $5,056 | +$5,067 | +$2,308 |
| NH | $4,032 | $7,815 | $5,056 | +$3,783 | +$1,024 |
| NJ | $3,684 | $7,815 | $5,056 | +$4,131 | +$1,372 |
| NM | $2,520 | $7,815 | $5,056 | +$5,295 | +$2,536 |
| NY | $4,992 | $7,815 | $5,056 | +$2,823 | +$ 64 |
| NC | $2,700 | $7,815 | $5,056 | +$5,115 | +$2,356 |
| ND | $3,612 | $7,815 | $5,056 | +$4,203 | +$1,444 |
| OH | $2,976 | $7,815 | $5,056 | +$4,839 | +$2,080 |
| OK | $2,880 | $7,815 | $5,056 | +$4,935 | +$2,176 |

**Table 6** (continued)

| | | | | | |
|---|---|---|---|---|---|
| OR | $4,056 | $7,815 | $5,056 | +$3,759 | +$1,000 |
| PA | $3,588 | $7,815 | $5,056 | +$4,227 | +$1,468 |
| RI | $4,884 | $7,815 | $5,056 | +$2,931 | +$ 172 |
| SC | $1,896 | $7,815 | $5,056 | +$5,919 | +$3,160 |
| SD | $3,876 | $7,815 | $5,056 | +$3,939 | +$1,180 |
| TN | $1,428 | $7,815 | $5,056 | +$6,387 | +$3,628 |
| TX | $1,896 | $7,815 | $5,056 | +$5,919 | +$3,160 |
| UT | $3,612 | $7,815 | $5,056 | +$4,203 | +$1,444 |
| VT | $5,712 | $8,188 | $5,403 | +$2,476 | -$ 309 |
| VA | $3,528 | $7,815 | $5,056 | +$4,287 | +$1,528 |
| WA | $4,764 | $7,815 | $5,056 | +$3,051 | +$ 292 |
| WV | $2,412 | $7,815 | $5,056 | +$5,403 | +$2,644 |
| WI | $5,556 | $7,815 | $5,056 | +$2,257 | -$ 500 |
| WY | $3,840 | $7,815 | $5,056 | +$3,975 | +$1,216 |

that matches Medicaid in its scope and lack of cost sharing. In the real world, all minimum-wage workers are not so lucky. Many welfare recipients who shift to minimum-wage jobs will work fewer than 2,080 hours each year. Some will fail to use the EITC to full advantage. Many will have to incur substantial expenses to travel to work and meet other work-related needs in addition to day care. Some will be obliged to pay state, if not federal, income taxes. And many will have to pay significant sums out of pocket for medical care—especially if they have no health insurance, but also if they have a traditional health-insurance plan with deductibles and coinsurance that must be met before insurance coverage is triggered. In the real world, the move from welfare to a minimum-wage job may mean even lower levels of disposable income than Table 6 indicates, making work that much less attractive.

It is at times argued that, although AFDC recipients who do get jobs at the minimum wage will often initially end up with less disposable income, they will ultimately move up to higher-paying jobs within the firms that employ them and end up with more disposable income. Although the growth in the proportion of low-wage jobs may make this crossover increasingly less likely, in some cases it will certainly happen. To what extent welfare recipients' behavior will be influenced by this possibility is another matter. In deciding whether to remain on welfare or go to work, many—if not most—welfare recipients are likely to compare their current AFDC benefits with the actual amount (after day care and taxes) they can earn at a regular job and not with a future income that may or may not ever be attained.

The third faulty premise that underlies the liberal, conservative, and new-consensus approaches to welfare reform is that, once welfare recipients get good jobs at a substantial cost to society (in tax dollars

**Table 6** (continued)

## Three-Person (Two-Children) Family

### (Annual Amounts)

| State | AFDC Payment | Income Afforded by Full-Time Minimum-Wage Job | | Gain/Loss of Income from Shifting from AFDC to Minimum Wage-Job | |
|---|---|---|---|---|---|
| | | Gross | Disposable | Gross | Disposable |
| AL | $1,416 | $7,815 | $2,856 | +$6,399 | +$1,440 |
| AK | $8,988 | $8,750 | $3,724 | -$ 238 | -$5,264 |
| AZ | $3,516 | $7,815 | $2,856 | +$4,299 | -$ 660 |
| AR | $2,304 | $7,815 | $2,856 | +$5,511 | +$ 552 |
| CA | $7,404 | $7,815 | $2,856 | +$ 411 | -$4,548 |
| CO | $4,152 | $7,815 | $2,856 | +$3,663 | -$1,296 |
| CT | $7,080 | $7,852 | $2,891 | +$ 772 | -$4,190 |
| DE | $3,720 | $7,815 | $2,856 | +$4,095 | -$ 864 |
| DC | $4,368 | $8,938 | $3,899 | +$4,570 | -$ 469 |
| FL | $3,168 | $7,815 | $2,856 | +$4,647 | -$ 312 |
| GA | $3,072 | $7,815 | $2,856 | +$4,743 | -$ 216 |
| HI | $5,616 | $7,815 | $2,856 | +$2,199 | -$2,760 |
| ID | $3,648 | $7,815 | $2,856 | +$4,167 | -$ 792 |
| IL | $4,104 | $7,815 | $2,856 | +$3,711 | -$1,248 |
| IN | $3,072 | $7,815 | $2,856 | +$4,743 | -$ 216 |
| IA | $4,572 | $7,815 | $2,856 | +$3,243 | -$1,716 |
| KS | $4,836 | $7,815 | $2,856 | +$2,979 | -$1,980 |
| KY | $2,364 | $7,815 | $2,856 | +$5,451 | +$ 492 |
| LA | $2,280 | $7,815 | $2,856 | +$5,535 | +$ 576 |
| ME | $4,860 | $8,376 | $3,377 | +$3,516 | -$1,483 |
| MD | $4,140 | $7,815 | $2,856 | +$3,675 | -$1,284 |
| MA | $5,892 | $8,376 | $3,377 | +$2,484 | -$2,515 |
| MI | $5,676 | $7,815 | $2,856 | +$2,139 | -$2,820 |
| MN | $6,384 | $7,815 | $2,856 | +$1,431 | -$3,528 |
| MS | $1,440 | $7,815 | $2,856 | +$6,375 | +$1,416 |
| MO | $3,348 | $7,815 | $2,856 | +$4,467 | -$ 492 |
| MT | $4,248 | $7,815 | $2,856 | +$3,567 | -$1,392 |
| NE | $4,200 | $7,815 | $2,856 | +$3,615 | -$1,344 |
| NV | $3,420 | $7,815 | $2,856 | +$4,395 | -$ 564 |
| NH | $4,764 | $7,815 | $2,856 | +$3,051 | -$1,908 |
| NJ | $4,848 | $7,815 | $2,856 | +$2,967 | -$1,992 |
| NM | $3,096 | $7,815 | $2,856 | +$4,719 | -$ 240 |
| NY | $5,964 | $7,815 | $2,856 | +$1,851 | -$3,108 |
| NC | $3,108 | $7,815 | $2,856 | +$4,707 | -$ 252 |
| ND | $4,452 | $7,815 | $2,856 | +$3,363 | -$1,596 |
| OH | $3,624 | $7,815 | $2,856 | +$4,191 | -$ 768 |
| OK | $3,720 | $7,815 | $2,856 | +$4,095 | -$ 864 |

**Table 6** (continued)

| | | | | | |
|---|---|---|---|---|---|
| OR | $4,764 | $7,815 | $2,856 | +$3,051 | -$1,908 |
| PA | $4,584 | $7,815 | $2,856 | +$3,231 | -$1,728 |
| RI | $6,036 | $7,815 | $2,856 | +$1,779 | -$3,180 |
| SC | $2,388 | $7,815 | $2,856 | +$5,427 | +$  468 |
| SD | $4,392 | $7,815 | $2,856 | +$3,423 | -$1,536 |
| TN | $1,860 | $7,815 | $2,856 | +$5,955 | +$  996 |
| TX | $2,208 | $7,815 | $2,856 | +$5,607 | +$  648 |
| UT | $4,512 | $7,815 | $2,856 | +$3,303 | -$1,656 |
| VT | $6,864 | $8,188 | $3,203 | +$1,324 | -$3,661 |
| VA | $4,248 | $7,815 | $2,856 | +$3,567 | -$1,392 |
| WA | $5,904 | $7,815 | $2,856 | +$1,911 | -$3,048 |
| WV | $2,988 | $7,815 | $2,856 | +$4,827 | -$  132 |
| WI | $6,528 | $7,815 | $2,856 | +$1,287 | -$3,672 |
| WY | $4,320 | $7,815 | $2,856 | +$3,495 | -$1,464 |

spent for education, training, day care, health care, etc.), there will be no further costs to anyone. This is not true, because of the substantial zero-sum relationship between the long queue for jobs and the supply of jobs in our economy. Every job a welfare recipient gets, an unemployed nonwelfare recipient will not get (or a currently employed nonwelfare recipient will lose). Many of the displaced queue members will then end up joining the welfare rolls, which will cost us money.

In the final analysis, there is a kind of surrealistic quality to the welfare reform debate. Studies "cascade" out of government offices and private research centers; long-held ideological hatchets of the Left and Right are buried on the sacred ground of the new consensus; newspapers and magazines run lengthy features on the brave new world of welfare reform; Congress inches forward toward passage of yet another major "overhaul." Yet what emerges from all the sound and fury is an amalgamation of the two positions that have always been held, rather than a truly new approach. More bizarre still, the new glued-together doctrine is based on premises (reinforced by the gluing itself) that bear little relationship to the real world. It is assumed that the transformation of welfare recipients will shift large numbers of them into jobs, yet the only available evidence demonstrates that the number of current jobseekers far exceeds the number of available jobs. It is assumed that welfare recipients will gain economically by securing work, yet if they have two children or more, in most states they will be worse off if they get jobs paying the minimum wage (which are the jobs they are most likely, initially, to get), after paying for day care and Social Security. It is assumed that welfare recipients will hurt no one by getting jobs, but they will, in fact, displace others in the queue who would have gotten the jobs, but who now may end up on welfare.

Despite the hoopla, the welfare reform movement is no closer than it has ever been to creating a welfare system that will work (i.e., will, in fact, get most recipients into jobs, much less good jobs), that is fair, and that has an attractive ratio of benefits to costs.

## NOTES

1. The focus of this and the next two chapters is the "flagship" of the welfare system, Aid to Families with Dependent Children (AFDC), the program that is generally referred to when welfare is spoken of and the program whose reform lies at the center of the welfare reform debate. Although most AFDC recipients are children, while the adults (usually parents and typically women) who take care of them are usually referred to as caretakers, recipients and caretakers are here used interchangeably (unless the context clearly indicates otherwise) to mean adult caretakers.

2. Robert Pear, "Rewriting the Social Contract for America's Have Nots," *New York Times*, April 12, 1987, Sec. IV, p. 5.

3. Robert Pear, "Wide Backing Seen for Welfare Plan," *New York Times*, September 13, 1987, Sec. I, p. 27. Moynihan's cosponsors included a broad range of U.S. senators, ranging from liberal Democrats to conservative Republicans. Among the cosponsors were Majority Leader Robert Byrd (D-WV); presidential candidates (at the time) Joseph Biden (D-DE), Albert Gore, Jr. (D-TN), and Paul Simon (D-IL), and eight Republicans—Christopher Bond (R-MO), John Danforth (R-MO), John Chafee (R-RI), Thad Cochran (R-MS), David Durenberger (R-MN), Daniel Evans (R-WA), Mark Hatfield (R-OR), and Robert Stafford (R-VT).

4. Ibid.; and idem, "Why It's So Tough to Get Welfare Reform," *New York Times*, December 6, 1987, Sec. IV, p. 32.

5. U.S. Congress, House, Committee on Ways and Means, "Background Material and Data on Programs Within the Jurisdiction of the Committee on Ways and Means," March 6, 1987, pp. 428–29.

6. For most of the last decade, over 65 percent of AFDC caretakers have been continuously enrolled in the program for over 12 months; only 16–20 percent have been in the program for periods of six months or less. See Committee on Ways and Means, "Background Material," p. 434. Yet although most persons enrolled in the program at any point in time are in the midst of "spells" that last at least one year, that is, constitute a "permanent" welfare population, most spells of AFDC participation are relatively short. "While the large difference between the ever-began and point-in-time welfare groups may seem paradoxical, it is easily explained. . . . It occurs because the probability of being on welfare . . . at a given time is necessarily higher for longer-term recipients than for those who have shorter welfare . . . spells." (Ibid., pp. 439–40). It is, of course, the long-term welfare recipients, the permanent welfare population that relies on the program for support well beyond the initial 6-to-12 month emergency period following the birth of a child or the desertion or death of a spouse, who are the focus of both the welfare reform debate and this chapter. The short-termers, who use welfare for temporary assistance as it is intended, are generally not considered part of the welfare problem, are not the focus of

any of the solutions advanced by the parties to the welfare reform debate, and are not the subject of this chapter—although, as poor people who are generally not on welfare, they are very much the subject of this book. See particularly Chapter 7.

7. In March 1979, for instance, of AFDC mothers whose education level was known, 18 percent had an education of 8th grade or less; 40 percent had completed 1–3 years of high school; 36 percent had high-school diplomas; and only 6 percent had either some college education or were college graduates. Ways and Means Committee, "Background Material," p. 431.

8. For over a decade black AFDC caretakers have constituted over 40 percent of the total, and Spanish-origin caretakers have constituted over 12 percent of the total. Ways and Means Committee, "Background Material," p. 432.

9. The preceding draws heavily on Lester Thurow's discussion of zero-sum elements in the U.S. economic system. See Lester C. Thurow, *The Zero-Sum Society* (New York: Penguin, 1984), reprint of 1980 edition.

10. See Committee on Ways and Means, "Background Material," pp. 408–9, for a state-by-state summary of maximum AFDC benefits as of January 1987. The minimum wage assumed in Table 6 is $3.35 per hour, except for Alaska ($3.85 per hour), Connecticut ($3.37 per hour), the District of Columbia ($3.95 per hour), Maine, ($3.65 per hour), Massachusetts ($3.65 per hour), and Vermont ($3.65 per hour). The Earned Income Tax Credit payment assumed is $847, except for Alaska ($742), Connecticut ($842), the District of Columbia ($722), Maine ($784), Massachusetts ($784), and Vermont ($804).

# 7
# The Omitted Poor

Chapter 6 criticized both conventional and current welfare reform efforts on the grounds that their underlying assumption—changing long-term welfare recipients' motivation to work, job readiness, or both, will result in large numbers of recipients getting jobs, and good jobs at that—ignores reality. Specifically, such proposals ignore the enormous obstacle presented by the long queue of generally better-qualified unemployed jobseekers who are competing for a far smaller number of available jobs, plus generally better-qualified low-wage workers who are seeking to move up to a smaller number of good jobs. This chapter makes a different and more fundamental criticism of the welfare system and the attempt to reform it: Welfare—Aid to Families with Dependent Children (AFDC), in particular—does not even attempt to help most of the poor, and under most current reform proposals, welfare would continue to offer no help to the majority of those below the poverty line.[1]

By their very terms, the big federal welfare programs neglect most of the poor. AFDC, the flagship of the welfare system, is restricted by federal law to assisting only two categories of poor people: families with dependent children and pregnant women. States are not required to establish AFDC programs, but if they do (and all do), the programs must cover both of these categories. To be eligible for assistance a family must include a child who is deprived of parental support, due either to the death, continued absence from the home, or incapacity of a parent, or due to the unemployment of the principal wage earner. Families in which a parent is physically absent from the home or incapacitated are referred to as AFDC-Regular (AFDC-R). Federal law also permits states to provide eligibility to a narrow subcategory of families in which both parents live in the home, but the principal wage earner's lack of employment is the reason for lack of support. (The principal wage earner must have worked in 6 of the last 13 calendar quarters, have been unemployed for at least 30 days, have not refused a bona fide offer of employment or training for employment, and be doing no more than 100 hours per month of part-time work). The number of states that have taken advantage of this provision has ranged back and forth over the last decade from the low to mid–20s. As of 1986, 28 jurisdictions (states plus territories) participated in this AFDC-Unemployed Parent (AFDC-U or AFDC-UP) category. The states participating, however, accounted for over 70 percent of the total AFDC caseload and include most of the relatively high-benefit states. Finally, a single woman in the seventh month of a medically verified pregnancy is also eligible for assistance in the AFDC-R category.[2]

A family or single pregnant woman who meets these nonfinancial tests is not automatically eligible for AFDC. Both asset and income tests must also be met. Federal law provides that combined family assets may not exceed $1,000 or a lower amount determined by the state (excluding a home occupied by the family, $1,500 of equity in one automobile, and burial plots and funeral agreements). Federal law then directs each state to determine how much income a family or single pregnant woman may have in order to be even considered for benefits (gross income limit), establish how much a family must have to meet its essential needs (need standard), and then fix the percentage of need (100 percent or less) that constitutes the most it will actually pay in the form of cash grants (payment standard). Only if a family's gross income does not exceed the gross-income limit and the family's net or "counted" income is less than both the state's need standard and the (never higher and, in most states, lower) state's payment standard, will the family actually be eligible for a payment, which will not exceed the payment standard.[3] Table 7 compares, state by state, the payment standard—that is, the maximum net income an otherwise eligible family may have in order to qualify for AFDC benefits, as well as the maximum possible AFDC cash grant—with the poverty line:[4]

As may be surmised, the nonfinancial, asset, and income tests that must be met in order to obtain AFDC benefits prevent large numbers of the poor from getting any help from that welfare program. In 1985, of 3.3 million female-headed families with children, whose income fell below the poverty line, 2.1 million or 64.2 percent received AFDC or other forms of cash assistance—which means that 1.2 million or 35.8 percent did not. Of 2.5 million male-present families with children whose income fell below the poverty line, only 0.6 million or 25.9 percent received AFDC or other forms of cash assistance—leaving the

**Table 7**
**State Maximum AFDC Payment Standards for a Four-Person Family as a Percentage of the Poverty Line, January 1985**

| State | AFDC Payment Standard (per month) | Percent of Poverty Line |
|---|---|---|
| Alabama | $147 | 16 |
| Alaska | $800 | 87 |
| Arizona | $282 | 31 |
| Arkansas | $191 | 21 |
| California | $660 | 72 |
| Colorado | $420 | 46 |
| Connecticut | $636 | 69 |
| Delaware | $336 | 37 |
| District of Columbia | $399 | 44 |
| Florida | $284 | 31 |
| Georgia | $245 | 27 |
| Hawaii | $546 | 60 |
| Idaho | $344 | 38 |
| Illinois | $368 | 40 |
| Indiana | $316 | 34 |
| Iowa | $419 | 46 |
| Kansas | $422 | 46 |
| Kentucky | $246 | 27 |
| Louisiana | $234 | 26 |
| Maine | $465 | 51 |
| Maryland | $376 | 41 |
| Massachusetts | $463 | 51 |
| Michigan | $542 | 59 |
| Minnesota | $611 | 67 |
| Mississippi | $120 | 13 |
| Missouri | $308 | 34 |
| Montana | $425 | 46 |
| Nebraska | $420 | 46 |
| Nevada | $279 | 31 |
| New Hampshire | $429 | 47 |
| New Jersey | $443 | 48 |
| New Mexico | $313 | 34 |
| New York | $676 | 74 |
| North Carolina | $244 | 27 |
| North Dakota | $454 | 50 |
| Ohio | $360 | 39 |
| Oklahoma | $349 | 38 |
| Oregon | $468 | 51 |
| Pennsylvania | $444 | 48 |
| Rhode Island | $547 | 60 |
| South Carolina | $229 | 25 |
| South Dakota | $371 | 41 |
| Tennessee | $168 | 18 |
| Texas | $201 | 22 |

**Table 7** (continued)

| | | |
|---|---|---|
| Utah | $425 | 46 |
| Vermont | $622 | 68 |
| Virginia | $379 | 41 |
| Washington | $561 | 61 |
| West Virginia | $249 | 27 |
| Wisconsin | $636 | 69 |
| Wyoming | $390 | 43 |
| MEDIAN STATE | $379 | 41 |

great majority, 1.9 million or 74.1 percent, without any such assistance.[5] These data cover only families with children. When a broader net is cast, the number of poor Americans getting AFDC or similar assistance diminishes substantially. In 1984, of 7.3 million poor families, only 2.7 million or 37.4 percent received any public-assistance income. Of 6.6 unrelated individuals, only 0.5 million or 7.6 percent received public assistance. Since the term "public assistance" encompasses a number of programs, the number and percentage of poor actually getting AFDC payments would be somewhat smaller.[6]

AFDC is not alone in failing to help the majority of the poor. According to a Census Bureau report on the poor's use in 1985 of means-tested noncash benefits, 43.8 percent of all poor persons and 41.2 percent of poor households received Food Stamps; 38.3 percent of all poor persons were covered by Medicaid, and 39.9 percent of poor households had one or more member covered by Medicaid; and 16.7 percent of all poor persons and 27.6 percent of poor households resided in publicly owned or subsidized housing. A majority (67.2 percent) of poor households with children 5–18 years old received free or reduced-price school lunches, but this provided no help to poor families with younger children, poor childless families, or poor single persons.[7]

Ironically, as Table 7 makes clear, even if all poor persons in the United States qualified for AFDC—assuming that AFDC constituted their only source of income and that benefit levels have not changed appreciably—the poor would still almost all end up below the poverty line. For that is what AFDC, in particular, and the federal welfare system, in general, guarantees: poverty—sometimes a lesser degree of poverty, but continuing poverty. Even when Food Stamps are taken into account, as of January 1987 the median state combined benefit (i.e., the AFDC grant plus Food Stamp benefit) for a one-parent, three-person family had climbed to only 74 percent of the poverty line. In Alabama and Mississippi, the combined benefit was 46 percent of the poverty line; in all but ten states, the combined benefit remained below 90 percent of the poverty line; only in two states, Alaska and part of New York, did the combined benefit equal or exceed the poverty line.

Thus, even if all poor in the United States qualified for AFDC and Food Stamps at current benefit levels, the combination of AFDC cash and Food Stamps cash value would still leave virtually all of them poor—less poor, but still poor.[8]

When AFDC and most of the other programs that constitute the welfare maze are viewed from a distance, what is most striking is how many of the poor they omit. Equally striking are the incongruities in the system: state by state incongruities (a given poor person can get help in one state, not in another); need-versus-assistance incongruities (a poor person who qualifies for AFDC usually gets far less in cash and Food Stamps than is needed to get close to the poverty line and thus a minimally decent standard of living, but through Medicaid that person has one of the most generous health insurance plans in the country); and need-versus-need incongruities (a person on AFDC who needs no health care gets Medicaid, while a poor person whose work precludes eligibility for AFDC and who needs health care may be unable to qualify for Medicaid).

If welfare were reformed in the manner advocated by conventional liberals, conventional conservatives, or the new consensus, the situation would not get much better.[9] Welfare reform's chief objective, it must be remembered, is to transform welfare recipients into more highly motivated, more job-ready seekers after work. To the extent that some welfare recipients get work, however, some will end up worse off economically, and many will end up no better off economically (as discussed in the prior chapter). All those who end up worse off will, of course, still be poor, and a large portion of those who end up better off will also still be below the poverty line. Only some of the welfare recipients who end up better off economically will also escape from poverty. Meanwhile, welfare reform is likely to leave the nonwelfare poor—the omitted poor—somewhat worse off. Why? Because welfare recipients will have taken some of the jobs they would otherwise have filled. Whether welfare reform will improve the lot of the poor as a whole is a very open question.

Let us review these conclusions in detail, beginning with the poor on welfare. Let us assume that, thanks to welfare reform, the vast majority of long-term welfare recipients are transformed into such capable and motivated jobseekers that they distribute themselves evenly throughout the long queue of unemployed persons and get their proportionate share of the jobs that are available. This means, according to Katharine Abraham's research, that at any one time there will be at least two or three welfare recipients who do not get jobs for every one who does. The minority that does find work, meanwhile, will often get subminimum-wage, minimum-wage, or low-wage jobs—because such is the nature of a large number of the available jobs. As Table 8

**Table 8**
**Disposable Income of an AFDC Caretaker with Two Children and**
**Day Care Expenses, after Four Months on a Job: Pennsylvania,**
**January 1987**

| | | Food | | Social | Federal | State | Work | Disposable |
| | | | | --------Taxes-------- | | | | |
| Earnings | AFDC | Stamps | EITC | Security | Income | Income | Expenses | Income |
|---|---|---|---|---|---|---|---|---|
| 0 | $4,584 | $1,549 | 0 | 0 | 0 | 0 | 0 | $6,133 |
| $2,000 | $3,964 | $1,308 | $280 | $143 | 0 | 0 | $600 | $6,809 |
| $4,000 | $2,084 | $1,444 | $560 | $286 | 0 | 0 | $1,200 | $6,602 |
| $5,000 | $1,144 | $1,513 | $700 | $358 | 0 | $11 | $1,500 | $6,488 |
| $6,000 | 204 | $1,581 | $840 | $429 | 0 | $126 | $1,800 | $6,270 |
| $7,000 | 0 | $1,462 | $842 | $501 | 0 | $147 | $2,100 | $6,556 |
| $8,000 | 0 | $1,306 | $742 | $572 | 0 | $168 | $2,400 | $6,908 |
| $9,000 | 0 | $1,150 | $642 | $644 | 0 | $189 | $2,700 | $7,259 |
| $10,000 | 0 | 970 | $542 | $715 | 0 | $210 | $3,000 | $7,587 |
| $15,000 | 0 | 0 | 42 | $1,073 | $914 | $315 | $4,200 | $8,540 |
| $20,000 | 0 | 0 | 0 | $1,430 | $1,664 | $420 | $5,040 | $11,446 |

indicates, for a fairly typical poor person on welfare, shifting from welfare to a broad range of low-wage jobs can produce a reduction in disposable income and requires a fairly "high" low-wage job before most of the increase in earnings is translated into an increase in disposable income (at which point Medicaid eligibility is lost, leaving the family potentially uninsured).[10]

Even if welfare recipients who take low-wage jobs end up (depending in large measure on states' payment standards) with an increase in disposable income, many recipients—especially those with larger families—will still end up well below the poverty line. Table 9 compares, for a range of low-wage jobs, the preexpense, pretax gross income afforded by such jobs and the 1985 poverty line.

This comparison, it must be stressed, is between gross income and the poverty line. When gross-wage income is reduced by a number of unavoidable or difficult-to-avoid costs, the resulting net income will frequently fall below—or further below—the poverty level. Such expenses include Social Security taxes; potential federal income taxes and (where applicable) state income taxes; and the frequently unavoidable cost of day care, transportation to work (bus or subway fare or the cost of buying and maintaining a car), work clothes, and so forth. Even when gross income initially exceeds the poverty line, and despite the Earned Income Tax Credit or other wage-supplement or tax-reduction devices, the disposable income that remains to buy food, pay the rent, purchase clothing, and meet the other necessities of life may well be below the poverty line.

So far we have been examining the extent to which welfare reform's

**Table 9**
**Comparison of Low-Wage Jobs with 1985 Poverty Line**

Poverty Line (Annual Amount) =

| | | 1-Person $5,469 | 2-Persons $6,998 | 3-Persons $8,573 | 4-Persons $10,989 |
|---|---|---|---|---|---|
| Hourly Wage | Annual Income | ----------Wage | v. 2-Persons | Poverty Line-------- 3-Persons | 4-Persons |
| | | 1-Person | | | |
| $3.35 | $6,968 | +$1,499 | - $30 | -$1,605 | -$4,021 |
| $3.50 | $7,280 | +$1,811 | + $282 | -$1,293 | -$3,709 |
| $3.75 | $7,800 | +$2,331 | + $802 | - $773 | -$3,189 |
| $4.00 | $8,320 | +$2,851 | +$1,322 | - $253 | -$2,669 |
| $4.25 | $8,840 | +$3,371 | +$1,842 | + $267 | -$2,149 |
| $4.50 | $9,360 | +$3,891 | +$2,362 | + $787 | -$1,629 |
| $4.75 | $9,880 | +$4,411 | +$2,882 | +$1,307 | -$1,109 |
| $5.00 | $10,400 | +$4,931 | +$3,402 | +$1,827 | - $549 |
| $5.25 | $10,920 | +$5,451 | +$3,922 | +$2,347 | - $69 |
| $5.50 | $11,440 | +$5,971 | +$4,442 | +$2,867 | + $451 |

success (to the extent permitted by the shortage of jobs) in getting recipients off the rolls and into disproportionately low-wage jobs will actually increase their disposable income and lift them out of poverty. Until reform is attempted, of course, no one will know for sure. There is reason to believe, however, that in many cases recipients will be worse off or no better off; and even when they are better off, they will often fail to climb across the poverty line. We now turn to the impact of welfare reform on the majority of the poor: that is, the individuals and families who either qualify for welfare but choose not to take it or who are ineligible for welfare. What effect will the improvement of welfare recipients have on the omitted poor?

Let us assume that welfare reform succeeds in transforming long-term welfare recipients into such better-equipped and more-aggressive jobhunters that they are enabled to advance energetically through the long queue and obtain available jobs. It is reasonable to assume that the great majority of them (at least initially) will end up in low-wage jobs, since they will face considerable difficulty in competing effectively for any high-wage jobs that require advanced education and specialized training. The success of these welfare recipients in getting steady jobs of any kind is certainly good news for them, but it means that some of the other individuals in the queue, who would otherwise have secured those jobs, will not obtain employment—or will take longer to get it. In some cases these "losers" in the new game may actually enter the welfare system itself. Precisely because of welfare reform, the choice would not be entirely irrational, since a brief stint on welfare may be the most effective and least costly way for them to get further education, training, and help with day care and health insurance, all of which may increase their odds of getting a job, once they again return to the long queue. Most of those in the queue whom the improved welfare recipients displace would, of course, be ineligible for welfare: single women who are not pregnant or pregnant less than seven months; single men; childless couples; couples with children, where the primary earner has over 100 hours of work; couples with children who have met the 100-hour test but not any one of the asset or income tests. All these would be shut out of the welfare system; the queue is their only recourse. The successful march of welfare recipients into the queue spells for many of them simply a lengthier time of unemployment. In many cases, it also means a prolongation of poverty.

Perhaps the assumption made above, however, is too pessimistic. The assumption—to repeat—is that if long-term welfare recipients are transformed into job-ready and motivated members of the long queue for work, most will end up in low-wage jobs, and to the extent they do so, they will prevent nonwelfare poor from obtaining those jobs. Let us assume, then, the other possible outcome and consider its consequences for the nonwelfare poor. Suppose that every new wave of welfare recipients, advancing with great speed through the queue, succeeds not only in getting jobs but in getting high-wage jobs that permit a departure from poverty. Well and good, but have they not largely just preempted other poor members of the queue of unemployed persons and low-wage workers from getting those jobs? Will not most welfare recipients who get out of poverty do so at the expense of the nonwelfare poor?

The competition within the queue for good jobs is perhaps not so bleak in its consequences—not so much a beggar-thy-neighbor matter—as these questions suggest. While welfare recipients compete with the unemployed poor and the working poor, the competition also takes place with the unemployed nonpoor and the working nonpoor (e.g., children and spouses of well-paid workers, well-paid workers looking for a second job, persons with substantial unearned income). To the extent that welfare recipients preempt the latter's pursuit of good jobs, the persons preempted may complain, and their families' incomes may remain static, but society gains a net reduction in the number of poor people at no cost to the taxpayers.[11]

It is highly improbable, however, that most or even a large percentage of the long-term welfare recipients, whose transformation (if it happens) results in their advancing through the queue so as to get otherwise unattainable employment (if that, too, happens), will both secure good jobs and displace only the nonpoor unemployed and nonpoor workers, thus producing a net reduction in the number of poor people. While such a happy result is surely to be hoped for (except, of course, by the displaced persons), it can hardly be expected. Even to the limited extent that a portion—one might imagine them as wavelets—of transformed welfare recipients year after year get good jobs that pull them out of poverty at the "mere" expense of disappointed but nonpoor unemployed and working persons, significant moral and policy questions surely arise. Is it fair for government to help welfare recipients at the expense of nonpoor persons who are competing for the same jobs? Is it just to tax the nonpoor to help welfare recipients to take away good jobs from them? The fact that the jobs that welfare recipients would get are jobs that other people (poor and nonpoor) might have taken cannot be ignored, even if the answer to the question posed here is that such a preemption—and the imposition of part of the cost of the preemption on those who are preempted—is on balance a morally and socially desirable objective.

It is important, of course, not to drift too far from probability in these matters. The discussion of the impact of welfare reform (liberal, conservative, and new-consensus) on long-term welfare recipients and those they compete with in the queue for scarce jobs (and even scarcer good jobs) should focus primarily on where most recipients will end up and whom most of them will displace. Given (1) the job-related characteristics of the welfare population (lower education, lower skills, less work experience, less motivation) compared to those of the nonwelfare unemployed and working poor (who score better in each category); (2) the racial and sexual makeup of the welfare population (disproportionate number of blacks, Hispanics, and women) and the *de facto* discrimination that still pervades our society; and (3) a variety of other disadvantages that disproportionately burden the welfare population (physical distance from available jobs, limited understanding of what employers want and how they behave, the stigma attached to welfare recipients by some employers, and so forth)—it seems unavoidable that most long-term welfare recipients, even if truly transformed into more job-ready and motivated jobseekers, will have great difficulty competing effectively with non-welfare recipients within the long queue for jobs and particularly good jobs. Most are not likely to get jobs rapidly, unless extraordinary job-placement measures are taken, in any regional market where the queue is very long. New waves of improved welfare recipients will be joining the queue, as the prior waves partially and slowly seep into jobs. Most who get jobs will end up in low-wage jobs, which means many will end up still poor. Finally, many who get jobs will end up preempting the nonwelfare poor (both unemployed and working) who would otherwise have gotten the jobs; some of the displacees will then go onto welfare themselves and others will remain poor for longer periods of time. Welfare reform, as conventionally conceived, as well as according to the new consensus, is less likely to result in a reduction of poverty than in a recycling and recomposition of America' poor.

## NOTES

1. While welfare in this chapter still refers primarily to Aid to Families with Dependent Children (AFDC), the focus is widened somewhat to include a number of other welfare programs, including Food Stamps and Medicaid.

2. U.S. Congress, House, Committee on Ways and Means, "Background Material and Data on Programs Within the Jurisdiction of the Committee on Ways and Means," March 6, 1987, pp. 388–90, 401–2; and Susan Robillard, Legislative Fiscal Bureau, State of Wisconsin, "Aid to Families with Dependent Children," January 1987.

3. Committee on Ways and Means, "Background Material," pp. 405–18; and Susan Robillard, "Aid to Families." Federal law fixes the gross income limit at 185 percent of the state's need standard. Each state uses a different formula for determining its need standard and payment standard.

4. Committee on Ways and Means, "Background Material," pp. 413–14. The median state payment standard is for 50 states plus the District of Columbia. The poverty line for a four-person family was $10,989 per year—or $916 per month—in 1985.

5. Ibid., pp. 631, 634.

6. Bureau of the Census, "Characteristics of the Population Below the Poverty Level: 1984," Series P–60, No. 152, June 1986, pp. 93–98, 120. Unrelated individuals receiving AFDC payments would, presumably, consist entirely of pregnant women.

7. Bureau of the Census, "Receipt of Selected Noncash Benefits: 1985," Series P–60, No. 155, January 1987, pp. 2, 23, 36, 42.

8. Committee on Ways and Means, "Background Material," pp. 406–7.

9. The ultraliberal position that all poor persons, regardless of family status or employment, should be entitled to welfare benefits substantially higher than the poverty line, would, of course, result in eliminating poverty. This position, however, has two enormous drawbacks. First, it rests on a basic premise that all poor people who can work should be given a choice between a nonpoverty income and going to work (at jobs many of which provide a substantially lower income). Second, it would generate an enormous public cost because of the simultaneous increase in payments to poor persons not working previously and a shift to welfare of low-wage workers. These two problems have discredited the ultraliberal position with most analysts and kept it from receiving serious consideration by policymakers at any level of government.

10. Committee on Ways and Means, "Background Material," p. 404. Pennsylvania's AFDC benefit levels are fairly typical: In January 1985, for example, the median state maximum benefit for a four-person family was $379, compared to Pennsylvania's $444; by January 1987, the median state maximum benefit had risen to $415, while Pennsylvania's had risen to $466.

11. There may actually be some cost to the taxpayers. A former welfare

recipient is likely to end up paying lower taxes than a nonpoor person would pay on the same income. There will be some cases where the opposite is true, but probably fewer. The aggregate loss of tax revenue to the government, all other things being equal, must be made up by raising taxes somewhere. Since the welfare caseload will have marginally declined, however, all other things will not be equal, and there may be no necessity to make up the revenue shortfall.

# 8
## The Prisoners of Welfare

The greatest failure of the U.S. welfare system is the narrowness of the frame of reference it imposes on our thinking about the poor. Welfare in this country serves only a fraction of the poor. It helps this fraction of the poor in very limited and rigid ways: giving them cash or cash substitutes, paying their medical bills, and taking care of them (since they are presumed to be incapable of taking care of themselves) in various ways. Welfare's cash, cash surrogates, and caretaking lift virtually none out of poverty: To the extent that recipients do get out, it is largely by finding work and forming (or re-forming) families. By design and in practice, welfare offers no help at all to the majority of the poor. Precisely because it serves such a truncated segment of the poor, gives that segment the fruits of work without offering work itself, and neglects both the majority of the poor and their participation in the working world, the welfare system encourages us to think of welfare and the poor—of welfare and the job market—as things apart.

Tragically, the parties in the welfare-reform debate and the major efforts to remake welfare (liberal, conservative, new-consensus) have so far accepted this same narrow frame of reference. The issues the parties debate are, How might the fraction of the poor who now get welfare be helped in a better, ultimately less costly manner? How should the basic methods we use to take care of this fraction be improved?

The limited frame of reference that shapes the welfare system and constrains the terms of the welfare reform debate is not without its virtues. It helps keep the problem simple. It helps make the options for change more manageable and cheaper. By concentrating on only a fraction of the poor, and by then concentrating on making better a defined cluster of existing entitlement programs, it is possible to avoid a large number of disquieting facts, troubling questions, and radically different options. In narrowness there is comfort.

In the end, though, this approach ensures failure. The poor who get welfare, and the poor who do not, cannot be neatly segmented and handled. They are in large measure the same people, living together in the same communities, shifting from on welfare to not on welfare, creating each other's problems, and (literally) creating each other. The poor woman on welfare was probably once a poor woman not on welfare. If her child was born out of wedlock, that child may well have been fathered by a poor man not on welfare. Her daughter may well become a poor woman on welfare; her son may well become a poor man not on welfare.

The interrelationship between the poor who get welfare and the poor who do not is not merely a matter of random biological connections. It is a matter of multiple and powerful dependencies—of choices that influence decisions, of decisions that influence further decisions. The availability of welfare to women influences the decision to have children, raise children, live independently, get married, and work. Women's access to welfare influences the decisions of men to father children, live independently, get married, and work. Precisely because welfare's influence reaches far beyond the families and single pregnant women who legally qualify for it to the broad community of the poor as a whole, it is essential when analyzing welfare and its reform to focus on the poor as a whole.

Just as welfare and welfare reform cannot be divorced from the broad community of poor people that they directly or indirectly influence, they cannot be considered apart from the job market. Getting welfare benefits—or indirectly receiving them as some poor men do—is a real-world alternative to pursuing work or taking a job where one is available. The effort to move large numbers of long-term welfare recipients into jobs is severely restricted by the long queue—a labor market queue—of non-welfare recipients competing for the limited number of jobs (and the even more limited number of good jobs) available. To attempt to reform welfare as if it were a handful of programs that functioned in isolation from the job market—to seek to redo the welfare system without dealing effectively with its relationship with the long queue composed of unemployed workers pursuing a far smaller number of jobs, plus low-wage workers seeking higher-paying jobs—makes no sense at all.

If the underlying purposes of the welfare system are ever to be achieved; if true welfare reform is ever to occur; if the poor on (and off) welfare are ever to be freed from the nightmare prison of insufficient income, induced irresponsibility, perverse incentives, self-loathing, paternalistic caretaking, and red tape that welfare has created; then those of us who designed the system and control its future must free ourselves from the narrow framework that governs our thinking. Rather than ask, How might the same fraction of the poor be helped in a different, less costly manner?, we need to begin asking, How might all the poor be helped to get out of poverty? Rather than ask, How might we establish a better system of being the poor's caretakers?, we need to begin asking, How can we provide impoverished American adults the jobs and income they need to take care of themselves?

The poor, it is often said, are trapped by welfare. Yet we—the non-poor, primarily white majority who do most of the worrying about welfare, write most of the books and articles, and write most of the regulations and statutes—are equally the prisoners of welfare. For decades we have permitted a narrow frame of reference about welfare, grounded in a kind of studied ignorance about the poor people of this country and their participation in the long queue of unemployed and low-wage workers competing for a far smaller number of available jobs, to obscure our understanding of why the poor are poor, to exaggerate the importance of welfare as an instrument for helping the poor get out of poverty, and to delay our examination of job creation and wage supplementation as the most practical means of eliminating poverty in this country. For the poor to get out of poverty, they must escape from their welfare prison. For the poor to escape from their welfare prison, we must escape from our own.

# PART THREE
## ENDING POVERTY

# 9

# The Right Not to Be Poor

Poverty in the United States will be eliminated only when the poor secure the right not to be poor. However much we might wish poverty to be eliminated without creating such a right, the supply of jobs and the structure of wages in the U.S. economy present such an enormous barrier to the elimination of poverty that the only practical way to end poverty in this country is to create a right not to be poor, to implement that right through acts of government, and to finance the implementation by expending public funds. What form such a right ought to take and how such a right ought to be implemented and financed will be discussed in subsequent chapters. The establishment of the legal right not to be poor, however, must be considered first.

Do poor Americans today have a basis for claiming under the U.S. Constitution that they have a right not to be poor? If so, what might be the specific constitutional foundation for such an assertion? If no credible constitutional basis now exists for a right not to be poor, do state constitutions or the common law provide any basis for a right not to be poor? Finally, if existing law provides no foundation for a legal right not to be poor, what would be the pros and cons of enacting a federal statute that creates a legal right not to be poor?

The U.S. Constitution, primarily through the interpretation by the U.S. Supreme Court of the Bill of Rights and the Fourteenth Amendment, confers on the poor and on groups (e.g., blacks) that are disproportionately poor a broad array of narrow rights—that is, rights that apply to very specific situations in which the poor face demonstrable economic disadvantage as they come up against the policies or operation of government. Some of these rights make poverty irrelevant to participation in the political process. Others explicitly aim to put the poor in the same position that nonpoor persons would occupy with respect to the purchase of necessary goods or services—particularly the purchase of legal representation. Still other rights do not explicitly seek to equalize the status of the poor and nonpoor, but their effect is to treat groups that are disproportionately poor in a manner similar to the treatment of groups that are disproportionately nonpoor. No constitutional provision or interpretation exists, however, that vests either the poor as a whole or any group that is disproportionately poor with a general right not to be poor.

The body of law that makes poverty irrelevant to taking part in the political process focuses on the right of the poor to vote or stand for elective office without having to pay poll taxes or filing fees. In 1964, the ratification of the Twenty-fourth Amendment to the U.S. Constitution prohibited the imposition of poll taxes in federal elections.[1] Two years later, the U.S. Supreme Court held that under the Equal Protection Clause of the Fourteenth Amendment, state and local voting fees were similarly proscribed.[2] These constitutional actions invalidated poll taxes altogether; they do not merely exempt the poor from paying poll taxes that the nonpoor might be asked to pay. With respect to the right to stand for elective office, however, the U.S. Supreme Court has taken the exemption route. Applying the Fourteenth Amendment's Equal Protection Clause, the Court held that candidates without the funds to pay filing fees cannot be required to pay them, but states may impose filing fees on candidates who have the ability to pay.[3]

In addition to eliminating financial impediments to poor people's participation in the political process, the Court has also struck down fees that obstruct the poor's access to the judicial system. For instance, the Court has held that indigent defendants may not be required to pay filing fees in order to have access to appellate courts or to initiate other kinds of postconviction proceedings, nor may the poor be compelled to pay a fee to file for divorce in a state civil proceeding.[4]

Perhaps the largest body of law conferring rights on the poor aims to place the poor in the same economic position as the nonpoor with respect to the purchase of a short list of fundamental goods and services. As with the rights of the poor to vote or stand for office, most of these rights have to do with the poor's relationship with government, particularly the judicial branch. The most famous such right, and no doubt the most important, is the right to legal counsel, regardless of ability of pay. (From an economic perspective, it would technically be more accurate to describe this as the right of poor people to have someone else pay the cost of their legal representation. Such representation is not free. Rather, either the lawyer providing it pays for it in the form of foregone income that might otherwise have been earned, or, more typically, the lawyer's fees are paid by the taxpayers through the government.)

In the leading case, *Gideon v. Wainwright,* the U.S. Supreme Court declared in 1963 that the Sixth Amendment's guarantee of the right "to have the assistance of counsel" in all criminal prosecutions required states to provide indigent defendants with legal representation at every "critical stage" of the proceedings.[5] The *Gideon* case marked neither the beginning nor the end of the evolving doctrine that the poor enjoy the same economic status of the nonpoor vis-à-vis the judicial system. Several years before, the Supreme Court had declared that indigent defendants were entitled to transcripts of their criminal trial proceedings, where that was necessary to the conduct of their appeals.[6] In the same year in which the Court handed down *Gideon,* it held that a state must furnish an indigent criminal defendant with counsel when the defendant is making an appeal guaranteed by law.[7] Over 20 years after *Gideon,* a very different Supreme Court has continued to give poor people rights to the same benefits that the nonpoor would be economically able to enjoy in judicial proceedings. In a 1985 case, for instance, the Court held under the Fourteenth Amendment's Due Process Clause that, at least where a capital crime is alleged, an indigent defendant who makes a preliminary showing that his sanity at the time of the alleged offense is likely to be a significant factor at his trial is entitled to access to a state-provided psychiatrist.[8]

While the U.S. Supreme Court has handed down dozens of cases that either eliminate financial burdens on the poor (e.g., filing fees) or compel the state to provide the poor with benefits (e.g., legal counsel) that the nonpoor can usually afford, it is important to understand the narrow scope of these opinions. First, they apply only to situations where a poor person enjoys an underlying constitutional right that all U.S. citizens, regardless of income, also enjoy (e.g., the right to run for elective office or the right to employ a lawyer in a criminal case). The underlying right is never specific to poor people. It confers benefits on the U.S. citizenry in general. Second, the Court's opinions confer specific rights on the poor only where the poor's attempts or ability to exercise their underlying constitutional rights are thwarted by their lack of money. Third, the Court requires that the inability of the poor to exercise an underlying constitutional right, due to lack of money, must either be the consequence of the imposition of a specific burden by government (e.g., the imposition of filing fees) or arise within the context of governmental action (e.g., the prosecution of a poor person for a criminal offense). There must be a positive act of thwarting, and the thwarting agency must be government. No right exists where government simply takes no action or where the thwarting agency is a grocery store, a landlord, a hospital, or some other facet of the private marketplace.

Adhering to this distinction, the Court held in 1980 that though a poor woman may have a constitutional right to an abortion during the first two trimesters of pregancy, if she is unable to pay for one, the state need not provide a subsidy.[9] Here, the poor woman's exercise of her underlying constitutional right to an abortion, which she could not exercise due to lack of funds, was not thwarted by a specific act of government. Rather, it was thwarted (depending on one's viewpoint) by either governmental inaction (i.e., the failure to provide an abortion-specific or a general subsidy) or the cost of the abortion in the marketplace. The result: no constitutional right to an abortion subsidy at public expense.

The decisions of the U.S. Supreme Court discussed above explicitly intended to confer rights on poor people, although, as mentioned, such rights fall within a narrow range that meets the threefold test just outlined. There is another important body of Court decisions that has benefited the poor as well—but coincidentally, as a by-product of other purposes (at least from the Court's official point of view). The intent of these decisions was generally to treat certain groups that happened to be disproportionately poor in the same manner as certain groups that happened to be disproportionately nonpoor. Most of these decisions are based on the Fourteenth Amendment's Equal Protection Clause. Most struck down state or local laws or ordinances that treated blacks and whites differently.

The most famous case was the 1954 ruling in *Brown* v. *Board of Education,* in which the Court invalidated "separate but equal" public schools for black and white children.[10] Prior to *Brown,* a trickle of cases had struck down what the Court considered to be some of the most egregious examples of official racial discrimination. In 1879 the Court invalidated a state statute that excluded blacks from juries.[11] In 1915 the Court struck down the use of a literacy test as a condition for voting, because it contained a grandfather clause that had the effect of imposing the test upon all blacks but only on a small fraction of whites.[12] Following the *Brown* decision, the floodgates of justice opened. Federal courts at all levels agreed to review, and consistently struck down, a broad range of racially discriminatory laws and ordinances, as well as discriminatory practices promoted or tolerated by government, in areas ranging from municipal boundaries to election districts.[13]

Taking their cues from these cases, advocates for other racial or ethnic minorities, the handicapped, and women have sought to use the Fourteenth Amendment's Equal Protection Clause—as well as its Due Process Clause—as a means for redressing their grievances. This is not the place to recount in detail the extent to which the U.S. Supreme Court and lower federal courts have ruled in favor of or against such plaintiffs, or to analyze the soundness of the complex legal doctrines that evolved. The point being made here is that groups that were usually poor to a disproportionate extent (i.e., compared to the incidence of poverty in the population as a whole) often gained additional constitutional rights as a result of the federal judiciary's decisions. The disproportionate poverty of blacks, Hispanics, Native Americans, persons with handicaps, and women was no doubt a factor in motivating their advocates to take their grievances to court. Such disproportionate poverty was also undoubtedly noted by the federal courts as they considered their decisions. But poverty *per se* was not an official factor in the courts' decision making. To the extent that poor people benefited when blacks were allowed to serve on juries, or attend once all-white schools, and so forth, such benefits were coincidental to other constitutional rights that the federal courts intended to vindicate.

Like the Supreme Court interpretations of the U.S. Constitution that either eliminate financial burdens of the poor (e.g., filing fees) or compel the state to provide the poor with benefits that the nonpoor can usually afford (e.g., legal counsel), federal constitutional decisions that coincidentally benefit segments of the poor population by striking down discriminatory laws and practices are narrower in their legal scope than their historical impact might suggest. The Fourteenth Amendment's Equal Protection Clause and all the other constitutional grounds for judicial intervention apply to the affirmative conduct of government. While the courts have gone a long way, precisely because of the vulnerability of the groups seeking protection and the importance of the rights being vindicated, to expand (some would say unduly) the meaning of "conduct" and the meaning of "government," the reach of the Constitution ends, and the federal judiciary's capacity to extend its power ends, where conduct by government ceases. The federal courts have never held that the Constitution itself (as opposed to constitutionally valid statutes enacted by Congress or state governments) forbids discrimination that results from either true governmental passivity or the conduct of private persons or organizations. Constitutional rights may arise where government affirmatively misbehaves. No constitutional rights (as distinguished from constitutionally valid statutory rights) arise where government truly takes no action or where the misbehaving entity is a soda-fountain operator, a realtor, or a private employer.

In short, the U.S. Constitution provides no satisfactory foundation for a right not to be poor. Because of the Constitution's inherent limits and the ways it has been construed by the federal judiciary, neither the extensive body of constitutional law conferring specific rights on the poor, nor the even greater body of constitutional law that benefits disproportionately poor groups as a coincidental by-product of establishing rights for those groups, offers much hope that either the poor as a whole or groups that are disproportionately poor will ever secure a broad constitutional right not to be poor. Perhaps the best case that could be made for such a right has already been attempted, and it failed miserably. During the late 1960s and early 1970s, lawyers working for the Legal Services Program of the federal Office of Economic Opportunity (OEO) sought to establish that the Fourteenth Amendment's Equal Protection Clause guarantees every U.S. citizen a "right to life" that includes the right to receive a minimum welfare payment at public expense. Their effort, which eventually culminated in a welfare recipients' challenge of Maryland's maximum payment, was decisively rebuffed by the Supreme Court in 1970 in the case of *Dandridge* v. *Williams*.[14] Given the conservative direction the Supreme Court has taken during the Reagan administration, it would be unreasonable to hope that a renewal of this or any other attempt to establish a constitutional right not to be poor would be favorably received by the federal judiciary.

The way the Constitution reads and has historically been interpreted—not the judicial philosophy of the current Supreme Court—is the primary reason why such a hope is unreasonable. With respect to the effort to establish a general constitutional right of the poor not to be poor, two constitutional obstacles present themselves. First, no provision of the U.S. Constitution states or implies an underlying right of access to a minimal or decent or adequate standard of living. Second, even if such an underlying right could be found, a poor person's inability—because of lack of income—to enjoy such a right is generally not thwarted by action on the part of government, but is, at worst, the result of governmental inaction (i.e., a failure to provide high enough social-insurance payments, create enough jobs, and sufficiently augment wages) and would most likely be found to be the result of activity within the private economy.

With respect to any effort to get disproportionately poor groups (e.g., blacks, women) out of poverty by attacking discrimination of some kind, the most one could theoretically hope for would be to achieve a more even-handed distribution of unemployment and low-wage jobs among the races and between the sexes by securing a judicial holding that the current distribution is the result of impermissible discrimination. Poverty would not be ended for any group or for the population as a whole. It would just be more fairly spread around. To achieve even this much, however, would require overcoming the second legal hurdle mentioned above: demonstrating that the uneven allocation of unemployment and low-wage jobs is the result of constitutionally impermissible action on the part of government—not the result of governmental inaction or activity within the private economy. It is an enormous legal obstacle, and not simply because of all the data that would have to be gathered, analyzed, and presented. The fact is that, however unfair the uneven distribution of unemployment and low-wage jobs may be, there is little reason to believe that much of it results from direct governmental action and a great deal of reason to believe that virtually all of it results (depending on one's viewpoint) from either governmental passivity or a combination of private prejudice and private habit.

It is no accident that the U.S. Constitution confers rights on the poor only insofar as they interact with government. The authors of the Constitution feared government as much as they believed in its necessity. They believed that there was an inherent conflict between citizen and government, and that unless restrained by specific prohibitions, government would overreach its powers. While the main purpose of the Constitution was to create a powerful new central government, its secondary purpose was to control the federal government's overreaching by splitting up its power and giving individuals specific rights against the federal government itself. This secondary objective of safeguarding individuals against the federal government, left incomplete in the Constitution's original seven Articles, permeates the Bill of Rights that the first Congress quickly adopted. That objective was expanded in the wake of the Civil War to protect individuals—particularly blacks—against abuse by state and local government with the adoption of the Fourteenth and Fifteenth Amendments.

During the last several decades, in particular, legal scholars and federal judges have debated vociferously about exactly which citizens have which rights against which kind of governmental action. The debate betweeen those who advocate a so-called strict construction of the Constitution and those who urge a more flexible approach, designed to adapt underlying constitutional purposes to the changing conditions and values of U.S. society, is precisely a debate about the ways in which the Constitution should be applied to conflicts between citizens and governmental action. The terms of the debate do not apply to problems caused by governmental inaction or private activity.

In sum, neither the purpose of the Constitution, nor the language of the Constitution itself, nor 200 years of judicial interpretation, nor either of the competing schools of thought about how to go about applying the Constitution, lends support to the view that the Constitution can be fairly construed to vest America's poor with a legal right to reverse the inaction of government that permits poverty to continue or to alter the operations of the private economy (i.e., the creation of an insufficient number of jobs and the payment of low wages), which are proverty's primary cause. There is no constitutional right not to be poor, and there will probably never be one.

The U.S. Constitution is, of course, not the only potential basis for establishing the right of the poor not to be poor. State constitutions and the common law should also be examined. A detailed survey is not possible here, but it should suffice to say that neither state constitutions nor the common law provide any legal basis for a right not to be poor. State constitutions generally mirror the structure of the U.S. Constitution. They establish governments, they allocate power, and they vest individuals with rights vis-à-vis government action. Many entitle children to receive an education at public expense, but beyond that they generally do not go. None gives poor people the right not to be poor. Common law entitles the destitute poor—once they've died, and if there's no other person "bound to perform such function"— to have their bodies decently covered and carried to the graveyard at the expense "of him under whose roof the body lies."[15] The poor who remain alive, however, enjoy no benefits under common law.

If the poor in the United States are ever to secure the right not to be poor, therefore, the right must come through the enactment of statutes. The U.S. Constitution has been consistently interpreted over the last 50 years to permit Congress to enact, implement, and finance such a statutory right. (State constitutions would also permit state legislatures to do likewise.) We must turn, therefore, from the realm of constitutional interpretation to the realm of public policy. Should laws be enacted to grant the poor the right not to be poor? If the poor were granted specifically enforceable rights to obtain concretely defined benefits (more cash, a job, a wage supplement), which, if taken advantage of, would result in their income rising above the poverty line—and if those rights were translated into reality through the enactment of national programs and full-scale financing—would the public benefits outweigh the public costs? The question should be considered from at least three perspectives: that of the poor, that of the rest of us (the nonpoor), and that of American society as a whole.

From the perspective of the poor, it seems obvious that the benefits would outweigh the costs. The benefits to poor people of no longer being poor would be enormous. Their intake of protein and other nutrition would increase. Their choice of housing and the quality of the housing they select would improve. Crimes related to poverty (that the poor generally commit against each other)—murder, rape, robbery, burglary, child abuse, spouse abuse, and drug-related crimes—would probably decrease.[16] Apart from these specific improvements, the poor would benefit by an increase in the control over their own lives. Increased purchasing power represents a part of this. More money to spend not only permits the purchase of additional goods and services but greatly widens the choice of goods and services that potentially could be purchased. The poor, if no longer poor, would also gain greater control of various nonfiscal aspects of their lives. As their economic stake in society increases, their political stake is likely to increase as well. They will vote more, and thus exercise a greater influence in municipal, local, state, and federal elections. As a result, elected officials will respond to them more effectively. Agencies of government—police, fire, sanitation, streets, parks, and so forth—will also respond more promptly and effectively. Public school systems in particular will be more responsive. The former poor who dislike the education their children are getting in public schools will have an increased ability to "vote with the dollars" by enrolling their children in previously unaffordable private schools or moving to living quarters in previously unaffordable communities. Responding to the former poor will become a matter of survival for the teachers and administrators who depend for their livelihood on the public schools.

While the benefits to the poor of enjoying a right not to be poor may for the most part be obvious, some potential disadvantages—to them—should also be considered. First, will not the creation of a right not to be poor reduce the motivation of the poor to exert themselves to get out of poverty? It is arguable that to the extent that self-help is rendered unnecessary to achieving a minimum living standard, many of the poor will refrain from enrolling in the schools, undertaking the enterprises, and in general taking the risks that today elevate many of them not only above the poverty line but into the middle class and beyond. The establishment of a right not to be poor could result, arguably, in the poor as a whole—or at least a substantial percentage of them—ending up economically worse off in the long run. Second, to the extent that a guarantee of nonpoverty reduces the poor's incentive to exert themselves, will there not be a parallel reduction in their innovative contributions to the economic well-being of our entire society—including the well-being of the former poor along with the well-being of the rest of us? In other words, a guarantee of nonpoverty may arguably induce the poor child—whose deprivation would otherwise have spurred the child to graduate from high school, finish college, get a Ph.D. in physics, and win the Nobel Prize for devising a way to produce cheaper energy—to refrain, because of the security offered by the guarantee, from embarking on a course that would greatly benefit all former poor people as well as society as a whole.

In individual cases, it may indeed be true that a guarantee of nonpoverty will reduce the incentive to achieve. In other individual cases, however, the opposite may hold true. The establishment of a right not to be poor may eliminate the listlessness and aimlessness that often accompany deprivation. Formerly poor people, no longer paralyzed by want, may be more highly motivated to attend school, achieve great things, and improve not only their own lot but society's overall condition.

Regrettably, there is simply no way to determine whether the incentive to achieve that results from the continuation of poverty or the incentive to achieve that results from the elimination of poverty produces the greater level of achievement. Controlled scientific studies are not practical, because the achievements in question are too complex, too numerous, and extend too far into the future to define or measure. Subjective analysis provides the only help, and it leads to no definitive conclusion. One must call it a wash.

Even if the incentive question yielded a conclusive negative answer, it would still have to be balanced against the enormous, positive, and tangible benefits accruing to the poor as a result of creating a right not to be poor. Those benefits include, at a minimum, improved nutrition, better housing, increased purchasing power, and greater influence over elected officials and public services. In the final analysis, there can hardly be doubt that on balance the poor would be much better off if they could exercise a right not to be poor.

Would the poor's possession of a right not to be poor help or hurt the rest of us, that is, the nonpoor?

There are many reasons why the elimination of poverty is in the self-interest of the rest of us. Poor people commit more crimes than other people. Sometimes we are the immediate victims. More often we suffer indirectly: spending money on burglar alarms and other security systems; choosing not to live in "bad neighborhoods" whose architecture, liveliness, and proximity to work we may actually prefer; haunted subtly but powerfully by the fear of violence or violation. Ending poverty would presumably reduce the level of crime we endure, reduce our expenditures for home security systems, expand our choices of where to live, and remove some of the fear we endure whenever we walk in the dark or return home alone or hear strange noises in the night.

Poor people often do not have health insurance.[17] When they get sick and receive care, the hospitals and doctors who treat them shift the costs to the insurance companies or self-insured employers that insure most of the rest of us. Our wages, salaries, and dividends are reduced acordingly. Ending poverty would presumably result in a more even distribution of health insurance. Low-income people already buy health insurance with their own out-of-pocket funds to a suprising extent.[18] Lifted out of poverty, the former poor would probably increase their purchase of health insurance to the extent that current national health-insurance policies remain static, and their ability to contribute to the cost of premiums would increase to the extent that current arrangements are replaced by policies that either offer individuals and firms incentives to provide health-care coverage or mandate such coverage. Under any scenario, lifting the poor above the poverty line would thus reduce the necessity for cost shifting, which in turn would make it possible for insurance companies to reduce the premiums (or at least the premium increases) they charge the rest of us, and for self-insured employers to curb the growth of their per-employee health expenses. This in turn would permit employers to pay the never-poor majority higher wages, salaries, or dividends.

Poor people, indeed, impose a host of other costs on the rest of us. Committing more crimes, they make police protection more expensive. Setting more fires, they make fire protection more expensive. Raising more handicapped, violent, and other "problem" children, they make public education more expensive. Committing more child abuse and spouse abuse, they make publicly funded social services more expensive. Unable to care as well for themselves, their children, or their parents when mental illness or other disabilities strike, they make not only public programs but private charities more costly than would otherwise be true. Ending poverty would greatly reduce—though hardly eliminate—all these fiscal burdens on the rest of us.

Widespread poverty also results in the imposition of a disproportionate burden of taxation on the nonpoor. Because poor people maintain their homes less well than other people, the valuation of the property owned by the rest of us accounts for a disproportionately higher share of property taxes. If poverty were ended, the formerly poor would take better care of their homes, their property would increase in value, and the burden of property taxation would be redistributed. Similarly, because poor people earn less, they pay lower income taxes, thus shifting the burden of income taxation to the rest of us. If poverty were ended, the formerly poor would pay higher taxes, and the rates the rest of us pay (all other things being equal) could decline.

These self-interested reasons for establishing the right not to be poor must be offset, of course, against compelling self-interested reasons for not creating such a guarantee. Implementing the guarantee means spending money, which could mean the elimination of government programs or subsidies for the middle class and wealthy, higher taxation for the rest of us, or both. Another effect of the guarantee would be a greater demand by the once-poor for the goods and services the rest of us also buy, which may mean an inflation of the cost of those goods and services. A guarantee of the right not to be poor may mean less pressure on workers to accept wage cuts and benefit reductions, which may mean more aggressive unions, which may mean more and longer strikes—an outcome some of the nonpoor may applaud, but some of the nonpoor are likely to bemoan.

Is the creation of a right not to be poor a good thing or a bad thing for the rest of us? No definitive answer can be given. It depends in part on how much we value the advantages and disadvantages that will result. It also depends on how the right is implemented. There are more costly and less costly ways of eliminating poverty. Such a right could also be implemented rapidly or slowly, which would influence its impact on inflation. It is a premise of this book that the creation of a right not to be poor, if implemented in certain ways, would serve not only the self-interest of the poor but the self-interest of the rest of us. That is, however, a proposition about which reasonable people can certainly differ.

It is also a premise of this book that the establishment of a right not to be poor would benefit American society as a whole. We are more than a nation of self-interested persons, each seeking to maximize our personal advantage. We are also a culture. Admittedly, we constitute a mixture of many separate subcultures with divergent and even conflicting histories and aims. Yet all (or at least the great majority of us) also belong to and consciously adhere to a common set of values, a common vision of our past, a common purpose for our future.

At the heart of our culture are the twin concepts of freedom and equality. Every observer of U.S. society, from Alexis de Tocqueville on down, has noted this. Freedom and equality pervade our rhetoric, define our social and political debates, permeate our institutions. Reconciling the drive for liberty and equality with each other, with the other values of the U.S. system (powerful local government, the rule of the majority), and with the imperatives of government itself (the need for law, the need for stability) has been the ongoing challenge of U.S. history. Though liberty and equality have suffered as many defeats as victories, in the end they have consistently triumphed in American history (though the cost, as in the Civil War, has included the slaying of hundreds of thousands of men and the laying waste of half the nation).

The advancement of liberty and equality—the liberation of the colonies from British rule, the emancipation of the slaves, the movements for equal rights for racial minorities and women, the elevation of the status of the worker during the New Deal—defines not only the U.S. view of itself but its image of its role in the world. Since our creation as a self-made nation, we have offered ourselves as a model for the world. Today most of us still view the United States as a model. While we recognize that our appeal to other countries has diminished during the last several decades, we sense that some nations (or, at least, large numbers of people in other nations) still share our view of ourselves. The model we offer is a model of liberty and equality.

Poverty is the blemish on the American model. Nothing undermines our self-image more—nothing undermines the model we offer the world more—than the 33 million, the 14 percent of our population, who cannot maintain an adequate standard of living in this land of plenty. The poor are not merely an embarrassment to us as we look at ourselves and face other nations. The wretched slums in which the poor live (within sight of the U.S. Capitol itself, within minutes of the United Nations)—teeming with criminals, drug pushers, violent parents, malnourished children—do not merely diminish the admiration we have for our own society, give pain to our foreign friends, and invite sneers from our foreign adversaries. The harm done goes much further. Poverty in the United States deeply wounds the cause the United States has always sought to advance in the world (despite great backsliding and hundreds of errors): the advancement of human rights. The presence of millions of poor in this rich nation discredits our assertion that we stand for human rights. The prevalence of poverty in the United States lends strength to the argument that human rights are a charade—an argument that dictators of both the Right and the Left are more than inclined to use to justify the brave new worlds they build on the graves of their enemies.

In the end, however, the question of whether the poor should have a right not to be poor ought not to be made too complex or transported too far from U.S. shores. It is useful to investigate the constitutional issue. It can hardly be surprising, though, that the Constitution does not seem to offer much room for the creation of a general right not to be poor. It is useful as well to examine the self-interest of both the poor and the rest of us. That the poor would generally be better off not being so, and that the elimination of poverty would probably benefit the nonpoor far more than it would harm the nonpoor (though some may disagree with this contention), can hardly be surprising conclusions. The impact of eliminating poverty on America's achievement of its core purposes of liberty and equality here at home, and its effectiveness in promoting liberty and equality throughout the world, also represents an intriguing inquiry. There, too, the result of the inquiry is hardly surprising: If poverty were eliminated, we would be much closer to fulfilling our fundamental purpose of achieving liberty and equality within our borders, and our historical task of promoting liberty and equality across the globe would be both easier and more successful.

None of these inquiries, unfortunately, disposes of the question, Should the poor have a right not to be poor? None of these inquiries can settle the question. In the final analysis, it is neither a legal nor a utilitarian issue. It is a moral issue. Legal and utilitarian considerations inform the answer, but they alone cannot provide an answer. Moral judgments must be made to come to a final resolution.

The dominant moral question is, Is poverty just or unjust? More particularly, do we as a society believe that poverty is just or unjust?

More than a third of the poor are children. Do we as a society believe it just that children, poor through no fault of their own, should remain poor? Or do we believe that impoverished children should be lifted out of poverty as a matter of justice?

A tenth of the poor are over 65. Do we as a society believe it just that old people, regardless of the cause of their poverty, should remain poor? Or do we believe that impoverished elders should be raised out of poverty as a matter of justice?

Most of the poor adults under 65 either want to work or are working, many full-time and year-round. Do we as a society believe it just that people who want to work, or who are doing work, should remain poor? Or do we believe that the working poor should—if they work full-time and year-round—not be poor, as a matter of justice?

If we conclude that whether the poor remain impoverished or get out of poverty is not a matter of justice—the attitude toward the poor that prevailed in the United States and most societies until the twentieth century—the matter comes to an end. The poor can be left to their fate. If they remain poor, justice has not been offended. If they climb out of poverty, that is wonderful, but justice has in no way been enhanced.

If we believe, however, that because poverty (or at least most poverty: the poverty of children, the handicapped, the elderly, those who seek but cannot find work, and those who are already working) is unjust, we can proceed to the next step. Should the injustice be ended? And, if so, how?

This book rests on the belief that poverty is unjust and that affording every poor American a means by which that person can easily escape from poverty is required as matter of decency, fairness, and equity in a wealthy society such as ours. Some reasonable people will no doubt disagree. Most will agree. There is no way to prove the proposition in an objective manner. It is a matter of values and belief.

To conclude that poverty is unjust is not necessarily to conclude that it should be ended. The mechanism chosen for eliminating an injustice could theoretically produce an even greater injustice. The constitutional and utilitarian analyses presented earlier relate to this matter of the greater injustice. There is no reason to believe, however, that all or even most of the mechanisms that might be chosen to eliminate the injustice of poverty would produce a greater injustice.

Assuming, therefore, that poverty is unjust and that it can be eliminated without producing a greater injustice, what specific mechanisms for eliminating poverty should be chosen?

This question will be taken up in great detail in subsequent chapters. Here, a more general discussion is in order. Like any "good," the elimination of poverty can at times come into conflict with other goods. The specific mechanisms for eliminating poverty that ought to be implemented should therefore be those that most promote and least impair the other relevant goods.

It is not too difficult to define those other goods. They include:

1. The promotion of work.
2. The preservation of the family.
3. The imposition of the lowest level of cost and taxation.
4. The establishment of the least degree of government.

Each will be briefly discussed in turn.

## PROMOTING WORK

The poor generally want to get out of poverty by working. Work is as fundamental to poor people as it is to the rest of us. It is as much a safeguard of their sanity as it is a safeguard of our own. Work is as much an act of creativity for poor people as it is a creative endeavor for the rest of us. It is as much the key to their social standing as it is the key to ours. While there may be some poor people on welfare, and some not on welfare, who would prefer to remain in poverty and have middle-class people take care of them until they die, the vast majority of the poor would rather free themselves from their middle-class caretakers and obtain jobs that allow them to take care of themselves. All the surveys of the poor ever conducted point to this conclusion.[19] The poor's own behavior—that is, the fact that most poor adults who can work are either seeking employment or holding jobs—makes the point even more clearly.

Yet eliminating poverty creates the possibility of discouraging work. If every poor person were simply given $15,000 cash, for example, people working at jobs that paid less than $15,000—as well as many people employed at jobs that paid more than $15,000, but who valued the loss of income less than the gain of leisure—might stop working. This book assumes that any effort to eliminate poverty should both encourage and expect work. To that end, a number of potentially controversial assumptions are made, which should be candidly set forth:

First, everyone—including those intially classified as unable to work—should be encouraged to work. The classification of individuals as unable or able to work will always involve some degree of arbitrariness. In some cases, fraud, due process, and simply the complexity of government will result in some individuals receiving classification as unable to work, despite the fact that they really can work. In other cases, persons legitimately classified as unable to work will improve (either physically or mentally) and become able to work. To encourage work, not only should periodic reevaluations of classifications take place, but those who are classified as unable to work should always know that they will always make more money if they work.

Second, everyone (other than children and the elderly) who is classified as able to work should be expected to work in return for receiving money. The debate as to whether there should be a work requirement has gone on now for several decades in this country. The arguments on both sides are complex and fascinating. It serves little purpose here to recapitulate the debate, but it is worthwhile to note that in recent years the entire debate has begun to take on a surrealistic tone in the wake of the massive entry of women into the labor force. The principal argument of the opponents of a work requirement is that women with young children should be permitted to choose freely between staying at home and working. Yet millions of women with children in this country, who either do not wish to participate in the welfare system or who do not qualify for welfare benefits, feel that they have no choice—and in some cases truly have no choice—but to find jobs. The opponents of a work requirement have yet to formulate a coherent principle that justifies giving one group of mothers with children a free choice between welfare and work, when another group of mothers with children (which is paying for a portion of the first group's benefits) feels compelled to work and in many cases has no legal means of obtaining an adequate income other than by working. In any event, the assumption is made here that in a just system of eliminating poverty, every poor person aged 15–64 who can work should be expected to work in return for receiving money. Few will dispute that this assumption is widely shared by the U.S. public.

Third, working more hours should always result in more income, and working at a higher-wage job should always result in more income. These propositions will not generally be disputed.

## PRESERVING THE FAMILY

The largest program in this country that provides cash to the poor—AFDC—discourages family formation. Again, this issue is surrounded by debate, but several things seem to be fairly clear. Because a woman can often gain AFDC (and other) benefits if she has an "unformed" or "broken" family (i.e., one or more children, and no spouse), and often loses benefits if she marries the children's father or another man, AFDC discourages family formation and encourages family break-ups relative to what would occur if AFDC did not exist. The program certainly does nothing to encourage family formation. This is foolish and destructive. The elimination of poverty should at the very least be neutral with respect to family formation, and preferably should promote it.

## HOLDING DOWN COSTS AND TAXES

Because poverty is so widespread in this country, its elimination will be costly. How costly, and who bears the cost, is the question. It seems indisputable, however, that the cost of eliminating poverty should be held to the least amount necessary to accomplish the objective and that devices that thus keep the basic cost down should be adopted. A collateral objective is that the cost should if possible be met by eliminating other government programs that either the elimination of poverty renders unnecessary or policymakers determine to be of lesser value. Another collateral objective is that, if the cost of eliminating poverty cannot be met by reprogramming existing spending, the resulting burden of new taxes should fall least on those with lower incomes and most on those with higher incomes, that is, should be based on ability to pay.

## CURBING THE ROLE OF GOVERNMENT

Finally, the elimination of poverty should be accomplished to the greatest extent feasible without expanding the size or role of government. Ideally, the size and role of government should be reduced. How this might be achieved will be discussed later.

The remainder of this book will deal largely with the mechanics of eliminating poverty. It is important to understand that such an emphasis on mechanics is entirely proper. Once the fundamental decision is made to give poor people the right not to be poor as a matter of justice, the rest of the solution *is* mostly a matter of mechanics. The poor are a huge but measurable number of individuals and units (i.e., single individuals and families). The number of poor who cannot work is definable; the number who seek work but cannot find jobs is definable; the number who are already working is definable. The amount of money that must be gotten to them to raise them above the poverty line is definable. The problem resembles lots of other mechanical problems, such as making spaghetti, building a bridge, or purchasing a radio. The task is clear; the ingredients are identifiable; the constraints are known. The challenge is how to accomplish the task efficiently, quickly, cheaply.

A correct assessment of the problem must, of course, underlie any sound mechanical solution. Neglect of this principle—or, simply, an incorrect assessment of the problem—largely explains why past efforts to deal with poverty in the United States failed.

Past efforts either assumed without analysis, or asserted on the basis of inadequate analysis, that correcting deficiencies in the poor population themselves or the network of caretaking services surrounding them would lead to the elimination of poverty. It was postulated that the poor needed to be motivated to overcome their antipathy to work; needed remedial education, training, and other support services to make them more job-ready; or needed day care, health insurance, housing assistance, legal services, and other services designed to help them deal with the symptoms of poverty until they got good jobs. The shortage of jobs was ignored. The fact that so many available jobs pay very low wages was ignored. Because they were based on the incorrect assessment that the problem was generally the poor themselves, rather than the limitations of the job market, past efforts failed. They did not fail, however, because they were mechanical. They failed because, based on false premises, the wrong mechanics were applied.

To transform the right not to be poor into a reality, we must build upon an accurate assessment of the major causes of poverty—that is, the shortage of jobs and the great number of low-paying jobs in this country—a series of mechanical solutions that correct for those labor-market shortcomings as efficiently and as inexpensively as possible. The task is doable. It is a question of tackling it the right way.

## NOTES

1. The Twenty-fourth Amendment (Section 1) states: "The right of citizens of the United States to vote in any primary or other election for President or Vice President, for electors for President or Vice President, or for Senator or Representative in Congress, shall not be denied or abridged by the United States or any State by reason of failure to pay any poll tax or other tax." The amendment was adopted by Congress in 1962 and ratified by the requisite number of states in 1964. It essentially codified a decision of the U.S. Supreme Court, *Breedlove* v. *Suttles,* 302 U.S. 277, 58 S.Ct. 205, 82 L.Ed. 252 (1937) that, under the Equal Protection Clause of the Fourteenth Amendment, poll taxes could not be imposed in federal elections.

2. *Harper* v. *Virginia Bd. of Elections,* 383 U.S. 663, 86 S.Ct. 1079, 16 L.Ed.2d 169 (1969).

3. *Lubin* v. *Panish,* 415 U.S. 709, 94 S.Ct. 1315, 39 L.Ed.2d 702 (1974) (absent reasonable alternative means of ballot access, a state may not require from an indigent candidate filing fees he cannot pay, denying a person the

right to file as a candidate solely because of inability to pay a fixed fee); *Bullock* v. *Carter,* 405 U.S. 134, 92 S.Ct. 849, 31 L.Ed.2d 92 (1972) (filing-fee system held to violate equal protection laws, because system used criterion of ability to pay as condition of being on ballot, thus excluding some candidates otherwise qualified, denying undetermined number of voters opportunity to vote for candidates of their choice). See, also, *Turner* v. *Fouche,* 396 U.S. 346, 90 S.Ct. 532, 24 L.Ed.2d 567 (1970), applying the Equal Protection Clause to strike down a provision that limited membership on a school board to those with interest in real property.

4. *Burns* v. *Ohio,* 360 U.S. 252, 79 S.Ct. 1164, 3 L.Ed. 2nd 1209 (1959) (indigent defendants in criminal cases may not be required to pay filing fees in order to have access to appellate courts, as this would deny them equal protection of the laws); *Smith* v. *Bennett,* 365 U.S. 708, 81 S.Ct. 895, 6 L.Ed. 2nd 39 (1961) (state's refusal to docket indigent prisoner's petition for a writ of habeas corpus without the payment of a statutory filing fee denies the prisoner the equal protection of the laws guaranteed by the Fourteenth Amendment); *Boddie* v. *Connecticut,* 401 U.S. 371, 91 S.Ct. 780, 28 L.Ed 2nd 113 (1971) (requiring a poor person to pay $60 filing fee to commence suit for divorce in state court violates Due Process Clause of the Fourteenth Amendment). But see *Ortwein* v. *Schwab,* 410 U.S. 656, 93 S.Ct. 1172, 35 L.Ed. 2nd 572 (1973), holding that the Equal Protection Clause of the Fourteenth Amendment does not prohibit a state from requiring an indigent person, whose public-assistance payment has been reduced after an evidentiary hearing that meets minimal due-process requirements, to pay a $25 appellate court filing fee to secure judicial review of the agency decision.

5. *Gideon* v. *Wainwright,* 372 U.S. 335, 83 S.Ct. 792, 9 L.Ed. 2nd 799 (1963).

6. *Griffin* v. *Illinois,* 351 U.S. 12, 76 S.Ct. 585, 100 L.Ed. 891 (1956).

7. *Douglas* v. *California,* 372 U.S. 353, 83 S.Ct.814, 9 L.Ed. 2nd 811 (1963). But see *Ross* v. *Moffitt,* 417 U.S. 600, 94 S. Ct. 2437, 41 L.Ed.2nd 341 (1974), where the court held that, under the Fourteenth Amendment's Due Process Clause and Equal Protection Clause, an indigent defendant convicted of a crime, who had received free counsel for his first appeal "of right" from his conviction to an intermediate state appellate court, was not entitled to counsel when taking a subsequent discretionary appeal to the highest state court.

8. *Ake* v. *Oklahoma,* 470 U.S. 68, 105 S.Ct. 1087, 84 L.Ed.2nd 53 (1985). In the decades between *Gideon* and *Ake,* the Supreme Court extended the right to free counsel to indigent juveniles accused of acts of juvenile delinquency. See *In Re Gault,* 387 U.S. 1, 87 S.Ct. 1428, 18 L.Ed.2d 527 (1967). Federal courts have also extended the right to free counsel to persons detained on grounds of mental illness. See, for example, *Heryford* v. *Parker,* 396 F.2d 393 (10th Cir. 1968) ("It is the likelihood of involuntary incarceration—whether for punishment as an adult for a crime, rehabilitation as a juvenile for delinquency, or treatment and training as a feeble-minded or mental incompetent— which commands observance of the constitutional safeguards of due process.")

9. *Harris* v. *McRae,* 448 U.S. 297, 100 S.Ct. 2701, 65 L.Ed.2d 784 (1980) and *Williams* v. *Zbaraz,* 448 U.S. 358, 100 S.Ct. 2694, 65 L.Ed.2d 831 (1980).

10. *Brown* v. *Board of Education,* 347 U.S. 483, 74 S.Ct. 686, 98 L.Ed. 873 (1954). On the same day, the Court, acknowledging that the Fourteenth

Amendment did not apply to the District of Columbia, because it was a branch of the federal government, invoked the Fifth Amendment's Due Process Clause, which does apply to the federal government, to disallow the District's legally segregated school system.

11. *Strauder* v. *West Virginia,* 100 U.S. 303 (1879).

12. *Guinn* v. *United States,* 238 U.S. 347, 35 S.Ct. 926, 59 L.Ed.1340 (1915).

13. See, for example, *Gomillion* v. *Lightfoot,* 364 U.S. 339, 81 S.Ct. 125, 5 L.Ed.2d 110 (1960) (Alabama statute redefining the boundaries of a city so as to deprive blacks of their preexisting municipal vote invalidated under the Fifteenth Amendment), and *Gaffney* v. *Cummings,* 412 U.S. 735, 93 S.Ct. 2321, 37 L.Ed.2d 298 (1973) (equal population districts that fence out a racial group so as to deprive the group members of their vote may be unconstitutional).

14. 397 U.S. 471, 90 S.Ct. 1153, 25 L.Ed.2d 491 (1970). See Samuel Krislov, "The OEO Lawyers Fail to Constitutionalize a Right to Welfare: A Study in the Uses and Limits of the Judicial Process," 58 Minn.L.Rev. 211 (1973).

15. 22 Am Jr 2d, Dead Bodies § 8.

16. M. Harvey Brenner has estimated that the 1.4 percent rise in unemployment during 1970 was "directly responsible" for 1,740 additional homicides and 7,660 state prison admissions, as well as 1,540 additional suicides, 26,440 additional deaths from cardiovascular-renal disease, 879 additional deaths from cirrhosis of the liver, and 5,520 additional state mental hospitalizations during the period 1970–75. Brenner further estimated that this increase in unemployment cost the U.S. society $6.6 billion in lost income and added outlays for incarceration and hospitalization, in addition to $2.8 billion annually for welfare and unemployment payments, over the same period. M. Harvey Brenner, "Personal Stability and Economic Security," *Social Policy,* Vol. 8, No. 1 (May–June 1977): 2–4. For evidence of the same relationships from the early 1900s through the mid–1970s, see M. Harvey Brenner, "Influence of the Social Environment on Psychopathology: The Historic Perspective," in *Stress and Mental Disorder,* edited by James E. Barrett et al. (New York: Raven Press, 1979). Brenner's research focuses primarily on unemployment as opposed to poverty; and it does not "prove" that more unemployment directly causes more homicides, state prison admissions, and so on (or that less unemployment would directly cause fewer homicides, state prison admissions, and the like); such research is certainly sufficient, however, to lead a reasonable person to conclude that relatively greater poverty is related to a relatively greater incidence of crime and that a reduction in poverty would contribute to a gradual reduction in the crime rate.

17. In 1985, 11.2 million persons below the poverty line and under age 65 had no health insurance. They constituted 32.3 percent of all nonelderly uninsured persons. Deborah J. Chollet, Employee Benefit Research Institute, "The Erosion of Health Insurance Coverage Among the Nonelderly Population: Public Policy Issues and Options." Statement before the U.S. Congress, House, Committee on Small Business, May 6, 1987. See Chapter 11 for a more detailed discussion of the uninsured.

18. In 1985, of 18.3 million persons aged 18–64 whose hourly wage was less than the federal minimum wage, 2.8 million had private insurance not provided by their employers. Of 8.8 million whose hourly wage was between 100 and

124 percent of the minimum wage, 0.8 million had private, nonemployer insurance. See Deborah J. Chollet, "Erosion of Health Insurance Coverage."

19. See, for example, Leonard Goodwin, *Do the Poor Want to Work: A Social-Psychological Study of Work Orientations* (Washington, DC: Brookings Institution, 1972).

# 10
# The Mechanics of Justice

The reasons that the poor are poor in the United States must govern the mechanics of ending poverty.

The poor in this country are not poor primarily because of their own deficiencies. Rather, poverty in this country results primarily from an imbalance between the jobs the poor seek or hold and the jobs made available by the U.S. economy. The number of poor who are unemployed (including welfare recipients and so-called discouraged workers, as well as the officially unemployed), when added to the nonpoor who are unemployed, far exceeds the total number of jobs available at any time. The number of poor persons holding low-wage jobs, together with the number of nonpoor persons holding low-wage jobs, vastly exceeds the total number of unfilled good jobs (i.e., full-time, year-round jobs, paying substantially above the minimum wage and offering health insurance and other fringe benefits) offered by the U.S. economy at any time. As poor individuals, pursuing their own self-interest, seek to advance their relative position vis-à-vis one another, as well as vis-à-vis nonpoor individuals, within the queue for jobs so as to maximize their employment, income, and benefits, both losers and winners emerge. No one poor individual is inevitably a loser or winner, but because of the aggregate imbalance there will inevitably be millions of unemployed poor people who do not get jobs at any given time, and inevitably millions of the poor who do get jobs will not get the good jobs available—just as there will inevitably be millions of poor people who win in the struggle for employment, high wages, and decent fringe benefits.

The poor who lose out in the scramble for jobs and the competition for good compensation, and who thus remain below the poverty line, include:

- Unrelated individuals who get no job, or who work part-time or part-year for low wages;
- Single parents who get no job, or who work part-time or part-year—or even full-time and year-round—at low-wage jobs;
- Married childless couples, neither of whom gets a job, or only one of whom works full-time and year-round but at a low-wage job, or both of whom work part-time or part-year for low wages;
- Married couples with children, neither adult with a job, or only one adult working full-time and year-round but at a low-wage job, or both adults working part-time or part-year for low wages.

Each case is unique. A single person who is unemployed and would normally be poor, or a family supported solely by part-time low-wage work that would normally be poor, may have sufficient unearned income, or live with well-to-do relatives or friends, such that the person or family would be classified as above the poverty line. The vast majority of low-income and moderate-income persons under 65, however, obtain the bulk of their income from their own or their spouses' work. They depend solely or almost entirely on their position in the queue for jobs to get out of poverty. The inability of persons in the queue to climb high enough within the queue to obtain steady jobs with good wages (thus failing to preempt or displace others in the queue who succeed in getting those jobs and wages) means for most of them a period—and sometimes a life—of poverty.

## THE POOR WHO CANNOT WORK OR WHOM WE DO NOT EXPECT TO WORK

While poverty arises primarily from the imbalance between the aggregate number of persons seeking employment and pursuing good jobs (on the one hand) and the number of unfilled jobs and vacant good jobs available (on the other hand), there is an important secondary cause. Some of the poor cannot work. Some of the poor we do not expect to work. In 1984, 5.2 million people in the United States were poor (15.4 percent of the poor population) because disability or illness prevented them from holding jobs or because old age exempted them from employment (or compelled them to retire).[1] Most qualified for one or more of this country's social insurance programs, such as Social Security or Supplemental Security Income (SSI).

The failure of the U.S. social insurance system to lift those who cannot work or whom we do not expect to work above the official poverty line surely ranks as one of this nation's greatest embarrassments. How can U.S. policymakers—to be specific, how can the U.S. Congress—justify treating handicapped citizens and elderly citizens so shabbily? All the stock answers fail. Congress cannot claim ignorance, since both popular press accounts and official reports (including some of Congress's own) have chronicled the fact that millions of the handicapped and elderly remain poor. Nor can the poverty of the handicapped and elderly possibly be justified on the grounds that such persons ought to be working instead of receiving handouts, or that their incentive to seek work will be impaired by affording them a higher income, or other arguments drawn from the welfare debate. It is conceded from the start that handicapped and elderly persons should not be expected to work. It is a given that encouraging them to work is a secondary priority (and some would argue, at least in the case of the elderly, no priority at all). Their entitlement to a decent standard of living through social insurance is government policy. Indeed, politicians go to great lengths to mask the welfare components of Social Security and to obscure the fact that it is at best at intergenerational insurance scheme. Instead, they characterize Social Security as a true insurance system, under which workers contribute premiums while they are young into their own generation's account and then draw annuity-like benefits from that account, once they reach 62 or 65.

The only rationale that policymakers can offer for failing to end the poverty of handicapped and elderly citizens is their desire to save money. Even that rationale is a weak one. In 1984, it would probably have cost somewhere between $7.5 and $12.0 billion to bring all the handicapped and elderly up to the poverty line.[2] This is hardly an outlandish amount in the context of a federal budget that in 1984 neared (and now exceeds) $1,000 billion.[3] The mechanics of identifying the handicapped and elderly who are poor and transferring additional dollars to them pose no significant obstacle. If a general increase in the minimum Social Security benefit level is deemed too expensive, Social Security could be modified to provide certain categories of beneficiaries with additional cash. If tinkering with Social Security is deemed dangerous, then the SSI program could be amended specifically to guarantee that all handicapped and elderly persons—whether currently eligible for SSI benefits or not—be thenceforward entitled to SSI payments sufficient to raise their income to the poverty line. There are, no doubt, technical problems and administrative costs with either a Social Security or an SSI approach, but such difficulties surely do not pose barriers large enough to thwart what is fundamentally a very simple task: giving handicapped and elderly people whose incomes fall below the poverty line monthly checks sufficient to raise their incomes to that line. The mechanics are straightforward. It is a matter of spending the cash.

## THE POOR WHO ARE UNEMPLOYED

Eliminating the poverty of the poor who lack work also boils down to a willingness to spend the cash, but the details are far more complex.[4] This is so because the most equitable and efficient way to spend the cash is to hire the unemployed poor to perform community-service jobs—jobs that afford them (assuming they work full-time and year-round, and together with the wage supplements discussed in the next section) an income above the poverty line, but jobs that also always make it economically advantageous for them to accept any regular private-sector or government employment. Although hiring the poor who are unemployed to perform community-service jobs is both equitable (in the sense that it does not give the unemployed poor a benefit that is unfair to the rest of the U.S. population) and efficient (in the sense that it costs less than any other approach), the solution is not a simple one because of the many administrative arrangements that must be put in place to allow the endeavor to succeed.

Conventional solutions for getting the unemployed poor out of poverty, because they ignore the fundamental fact of the job shortage, will simply fail. They have failed in the past; they are failing today; they will fail in the future. No other device or gimmick, neither new nomenclature nor computerization, can squeeze millions of unemployed poor people into jobs that don't exist.

The nonsolutions fall generally into three categories: cutting welfare benefits; education and training; and providing day care and health insurance. Each is a nonsolution precisely because it is premised on a false assumption: the availability of jobs.

The strategy of eliminating or slashing welfare benefits rests on the belief that women receiving welfare—or the men who depend on their welfare payments for survival—will, if denied free money, conclude that the best way to get money is to seek, secure, and hold jobs that afford them money. The availability of enough jobs is assumed without inquiry. It is undoubtedly true that, if denied free money, former welfare recipients and their dependents will seek other means of obtaining money—and that one (but by no means the only) way of obtaining money that will be pursued is paid work. It is also true that some of them will secure and hold paying jobs. All or even most of them cannot secure and hold paying jobs, however, because, when added to the nonwelfare unemployed with whom they are competing for work, their number greatly exceeds (in the nation as a whole, and in most regions of the nation) the number of available jobs.

The cut-welfare strategy, because of its focus on welfare recipients and their dependents, also largely ignores the unemployed poor who are not on welfare. Cut-welfare strategies, in order to justify cutting benefits for welfare recipients, will often note the inequity of giving free money to one group of unemployed poor people, while another group of unemployed poor gets nothing; but from then on, the other group of unemployed poor fades from the scene. It is important to note, however, that eliminating or slashing welfare benefits in order to induce recipients and their dependents to seek jobs contributes nothing to the motivation of the unemployed poor who are not on the dole to pursue work. If anything, cutting welfare worsens the plight of the unemployed poor not on welfare by greatly increasing the competition for a scarce supply of available jobs.

The education-and-training strategy founders on exactly the same false assumption. The theory is that, if the unemployed poor were only properly educated and trained for employment, they would go out and seek, secure, and hold jobs. Insufficient education and outdated training block their access to jobs. Proper remedial education and up-to-date training will clear the path, permitting both welfare recipients and other unemployed poor people to flow like a mighty river into readily available jobs. The availability of jobs is assumed without question, without examination, without analysis. The premise of the education-and-training solution, alas, has no basis in fact. Education and training are valuable in and of themselves. In the long run, education and training are the key to the successful evolution of the entire U.S. economy (and any other nation's economy). In the short run, education and training will also undoubtedly help some unemployed poor people get jobs that unemployed nonpoor individuals will otherwise fill. Yet, in the short run, education and training are inherently incapable of getting a relatively large number of unemployed poor persons, who are competing both with each other and with a large number of unemployed nonpoor persons, into a comparatively smaller number of available jobs. As educators and trainers surely ought to understand, a larger number cannot fit into a smaller one.

The most recent strategy (part of the new consensus) for getting the unemployed poor into jobs is to provide them with day care and health insurance. As with education and training, day care and health insurance are valuable in and of themselves and will undoubtedly help some welfare recipients, as well as nonwelfare-recipients, compete more effectively for available jobs. Neither day care nor health insurance, however, can alter the laws of basic mathematics. They cannot shoehorn a relatively larger number of unemployed poor, who are competing with one another and with a large pool of unemployed nonpoor, into a comparatively smaller number of jobs. Like the education-and-training strategy, the day-care-and-health-insurance strategy rests on a fundamentally false assumption, and it will fail to make a significant dent in the problem of the unemployed poor because it does nothing about the shortage of jobs.

In short, the only way to get all (or even most) of the unemployed poor out of poverty is to put enough money in their hands—and the most equitable and efficient way to do that is to hire them for newly created community-service jobs that encourage them to move on to any private or regular government jobs that come open.

A simple cash-transfer program (whether accomplished by expanding the welfare system's list of eligibles and increasing their benefits or creating a negative income tax that affords the poor a large refundable tax credit equal to the difference between their income and the poverty line) would get the unemployed poor out of poverty, but it would be neither equitable nor efficient. It would be inequitable to give unemployed poor persons sufficient public funds to get them out of poverty, while employed poor persons must work (often at difficult or unpleasant jobs) to earn the same (or smaller) amounts of money. It would be inefficient just to give unemployed poor persons enough money to get them out of poverty, because that would encourage millions of poor persons who are unemployed and seeking work to halt their pursuit of employment and would encourage millions of both poor and nonpoor persons who are already working to give up their jobs. That a guaranteed annual income at or above the poverty line would encourage some of the poor who are unemployed or working to cease either the search for work or work itself is obvious: If you can get X thousands of dollars for free, and X thousands of dollars is more than you now have, why not take it? A guaranteed annual income at or above the poverty line would also encourage some of the nonpoor who are working to cease working. If you can get X thousands of dollars for free, and if X thousands of dollars is less than the Y thousands you now have—but X thousands is enough for you to live on, and you greatly desire leisure, while to get Y thousands you must work—then why not accept X thousands and get your life of leisure at the price of an income loss equal to the difference between Y and X? Exactly how inefficient a guaranteed income would be is unknown. It is impossible to predict the full extent to which assurance of a free income at or above the poverty line would induce unemployed poor people to abandon the search for work or would encourage employed poor and nonpoor persons to give up low-wage (and, conceivably, high-wage) jobs. It is inevitable, however, that a guaranteed annual income would substantially increase the cost of eliminating poverty, thus imposing a higher-than-necessary tax burden on the nonpoor majority of the population.

There are other objections to a simple cash-transfer program. The unemployed poor say they want to work, and most of them undoubtedly do. A cash-transfer program fails to give them the jobs they want. It also fails to produce anything—other than the elimination of the unemployed poor's poverty—in return for the taxpayers' expenditure. Finally, a cash-transfer program invites cheating. People who have jobs and income will have an incentive to hide their employment and income in order to get free (i.e., at no cost to them) money from the government. The cost of policing a cash-transfer program could be substantial.

The most equitable and efficient way of providing the unemployed poor a means of getting out of poverty is, therefore, to offer them paid work to the extent that they cannot find better-paid work in the private economy or in regular government positions. Affording the unemployed poor the opportunity to work does not inequitably benefit them vis-à-vis other poor persons who are already working. Both must work for their daily bread. Providing the unemployed poor with jobs that actually paid enough to lift them out of poverty would inequitably benefit them vis-à-vis poor persons already working the same number of hours at existing jobs, if those existing jobs did not provide an income higher than the poverty line. This potential inequity can be corrected, as the next section will discuss, by providing to all low-income workers a carefully constructed wage supplement that elevates them all above the poverty line.

Providing the unemployed poor with jobs that get them above the poverty line is also a moderately efficient means of ending their poverty. Unlike cash that can be obtained without working, jobs that require work offer no inducement to low-wage workers, whose earnings put them above the poverty line, to quit their current, regular, unsubsidized jobs. Why work for less when you're already working for more?

It is true that providing the unemployed poor with jobs that get them slightly above the poverty line may induce workers whose earnings do not get them above the poverty line to quit their regular jobs, so that they can transfer to community-service jobs that provide them a higher income. Therefore, to make the jobs the unemployed poor get a more fully efficient means of ending poverty, it is necessary (as noted above) that currently employed low-wage workers receive a wage supplement that raises their income above the poverty line as well. Offering to the unemployed poor jobs that get them out of poverty—combined with offering low-wage workers a wage supplement that raises them above the poverty line—is almost fully efficient in that there would be no incentive for already employed poor persons to give up their existing jobs and impose on the taxpayers the cost of rehiring them for community-service jobs.

To achieve maximum efficiency, the total income an unemployed person gets by working full-time and year-round at a community-service job should actually be somewhat less than the total income an already-working poor person can obtain by working the same number of hours at an existing job. Both should end up above the poverty line, but the person who already has a regular private-sector or government job should always end up a little bit further above. This will ensure that persons will have an incentive to transfer from community-service jobs to regular jobs whenever the latter become available (and not *vice versa*), which achieves the efficiency objective of holding down public spending to the lowest level necessary to achieve the goal of eliminating poverty. The wage supplement provided to poor persons who work, to be discussed in the next section, should be carefully crafted to achieve this result.[5]

Offering the poor, unemployed population jobs that get them out of poverty has other virtues. Since poor, unemployed persons say they want to work and there is abundant evidence that this is largely true, affording them jobs provides them the means of getting out of poverty that *they* prefer. Offering poor, unemployed persons jobs also gives society, which pays the tab, a direct return on its expenditure: useful work performed for the public good. Finally, offering this population jobs would greatly reduce cheating. Many individuals (poor and otherwise) will cheat to get something for free; few individuals (poor and otherwise) will lie about their income so that they can qualify for a program that requires them to perform work to get money—especially when, working the same number of hours, they can achieve a higher income at a private-sector or regular government job. The cost of policing a community-service-jobs program can thus be kept to a minimum.

Community-service (or public-service or public-works) jobs have a mixed reputation in the United States. Although the community-service projects sponsored by the Civilian Conservation Corps, Works Progress Administration and Public Works Administration of the New Deal stirred up great controversy in their day, they have come down to us as generally popular programs that greatly improved U.S. national parks, courthouses, schools, roads, and other public facilities; that for the most part kept corruption and inefficiency in check; and that did not cost too much. The CETA (Comprehensive Employment and Training Act) projects of the 1970s bear an entirely different image: make-work, corrupt, expensive. Whether the difference between CCC and CETA merely reflects a difference in appearance or in reality, the last major attempt to carry out community-service projects on a national scale left a bitter taste that must be acknowledged—and washed away—if another, necessarily much greater and necessarily permanent program of hiring the unemployed poor is to be carried out successfully.[6]

There is no inherently correct way to establish and administer a massive community-service-jobs program in the United States. Any number of approaches could succeed. Any successful approach, however, will have to meet the following criteria.

First, every unemployed person between the ages of 15 and 65 whose own income is less than the poverty line should be eligible.[7] Whether eligibility should be based on the relationship between total household income and the poverty line, or the unemployed person's individual income and the poverty line, is a tricky question. Each answer results in mirror-image negative and positive outcomes.

An example will help explain why a dilemma exists. Imagine a woman with one child, who holds a job paying $11,000 per year (or any other amount somewhat over the poverty line), and who is engaged to marry an unemployed man. Let us initially assume that total household income is used to determine the man's eligibility for a community-service job. His household income, if he gets married and joins the family, automatically becomes $11,000, which exceeds the poverty line for a three-person family and causes him to lose eligibility for a community-service job. His household income, if he remains single, is zero, which is below the poverty line for one person and allows him to obtain a community-service job. The household-income approach, therefore, discourages family formation. It penalizes the man in question, if he gets married and joins the family, by taking away his eligibility for a job, while it rewards the man, if he remains unmarried and does not join the family, by extending eligibility to him. There is, however, a benefit to the household-income test: It ensures that low-income individuals who belong to nonpoor families and who, therefore, arguably do not warrant eligibility for a job paid for by the taxpayers, will not impose an unnecessary burden on taxpayers.

The alternative, of course, is to determine eligibility solely on the basis of the relationship between the individual's own income and the poverty line for a single person. Were this approach taken, the man in our example would face no disincentive to marry and join the family. Whether he did so or not, he would be counted as poor and would be eligible for a community-service job. The woman and child and he would all benefit economically by his joining the family: The expenses of two separate households could be pared down to one, while real family income would grow by the extra wages he earns. The individual-income test, therefore, promotes family formation, but it imposes a price. As in our example, though a family is already above the poverty line in the absence of one of the family member's bringing home a paycheck from a community-service job, one or more unemployed family members would still be entitled to obtain community-service jobs—jobs the family does not need to get out of poverty and that therefore impose an unnecessary expense on the taxpayers.

There appears to be no way out of the dilemma. A choice between two not-so-goods must be made. The individual-income test, on balance, seems to do the most good and least harm. Promoting family formation is an objective that permeates our legal system, including our tax laws. Only the welfare system encourages family dissolution, and that effect has justly earned it much opprobrium. The individual-income test will no doubt result in some nonpoor units receiving money they do not need, but it is to be doubted that many unemployed persons who form part of middle-income and high-income families will actually take the low-paying jobs offered by community-service programs just because they happen to be eligible. The kind of work these community-service jobs will require, and the fact that (as part of the family's total income) the income generated by the community-service job will be taxed at a relatively high rate by the federal government, will further deter middle- and high-income unemployed persons from seeking such jobs. The actual cost of offering the "undeserving rich" community-service jobs will probably be far less in fact than it is in theory.

Second, poor individuals eligible for community-service jobs should be entitled—and, if they sign up, should perhaps be required—to work for exactly 35 hours per week at the minimum wage. (Poor individuals who hold part-time jobs in the private sector or government would be entitled—and, if they signed up, required—to work for a smaller, but nonetheless specific number of hours per week at the minimum wage. The exact number of hours would be fixed by formula.)[8] Permitting the unemployed poor to work at least 35 hours per week, and paying them at least the minimum wage, are necessary in order to permit them to earn a minimal income: Thirty-five hours at the federal minimum wage equals $117.25 per week or $6,027 per year, just above the 1987 poverty line of $5,500 for a single person, but below the 1987 poverty line of $7,400 for a two-person family.[9]

It may also make sense, should an unemployed (or partially employed) poor person choose to work, to require that individual to work 35 hours per week (or, in the case of a partially employed person, the lesser amount determined by formula) in order to retain the community-service job. A minimum-hour requirement may be necessary in order to plan and implement community-service-jobs projects efficiently. Such a requirement also imposes on the unemployed poor the same responsibility that others who earn money must assume: the obligation to work a minimum number of hours or lose the job. The requirement thus serves to familiarize them with the demands that will be placed on them by regular private-sector or government employers, an education that can be expected to help provide a bridge to those other jobs as they come open.

Whether a 35-hour minimum requirement is imposed or not, 35 hours should function as the maximum level of weekly employment. Persons holding community-service jobs should be encouraged, not just occasionally but every week, to attempt to find better private-sector or regular government employment. They will need time, however, to search for other work. Giving them 5 hours "off" every week provides them with that time. An additional, critical function of the 35-hour maximum is the economic incentive it provides to try to find a regular job that, by typically providing more hours of work, affords a higher income.

Third, community-service jobs should all be useful jobs that serve true community needs. Avoiding make-work should be a high priority, both to return real value to the taxpayers footing the bill and to preserve political support for the program. There is surely enough work to do. Any person who has driven through the inner core of a U.S. city or who has taken back country roads through depressed rural areas, and who has not been struck by the enormity of the legitimate work that needs to be done in our country, has surely been driving blind. There are sidewalks, alleys, streets, and freeways littered with broken glass and garbage; parks overgrown with weeds, benches and shelters in disrepair, basketball courts and tennis courts in ruins; empty lots, filled with debris, which could grow vegetables and fruit for undernourished children; grafitti-marked, shabby, public buildings; boarded-up homes. Beyond the regions that a passer-by can see from the window of a car lie even larger realms of unmet needs: homes seeping hot air in winter through holes inches wide; infirm, unattended old people, unable to shovel the walk, mow the lawn, rake the leaves, buy groceries, or visit friends; schools; day-care centers; senior-citizen centers; libraries, museums; community organizations. This list barely scratches the surface.

Fourth, community-service jobs should not displace existing private-sector or regular government jobs. Both the purpose of community-service jobs and the politics of preserving a strong community-service-jobs program require a clear and strong prohibition against displacement. From the perspective of society as a whole, it serves no purpose to hire one unemployed person at the price of laying off another. The inefficiency is compounded by the unfairness of paying for the wages of the unemployed person with the taxes of the person who is displaced. Apart from the merits of prohibiting displacement, such a prohibition is needed for political purposes. Without a strong antidisplacement provision, a community-service program will face the fierce opposition of public-employee unions in particular and organized labor in general. Distinguishing community-service jobs that do not cause displacement from those that might is, of course, not an easy task. Cities, counties, and states differ widely in what they are willing to hire regular public employees to perform. Each region has established its own pattern, however, of what does—and what does not—fall within the reach of regular public employment. The key to consensus as to what types of community-service jobs might be created is to identify and follow these regional patterns, regardless of whether some other region's pattern is different.

Fifth, a national community-service-jobs program must reflect several characteristics of the unemployed poor and the communities they inhabit, if it is to be effective. Many of the unemployed poor can contribute very little besides their labor to the work they are hired to do. They have time; they have energy; they have willingness. They often do not have cars, tools, and materials. If the unemployed are to be expected to seek, secure, and hold the jobs created by a community-service-jobs program, the jobs created must be labor-intensive, and should depend to the least possible extent on vehicles, machinery, and other capital.

The many and diverse private, nonprofit organizations (often entirely secular, but frequently connected to churches), which play a critical role in the life of poor communities, must also be taken into account. Without the support of such organizations, community-service-jobs programs are likely to founder: They will be resisted, undermined, and boycotted. On the other hand, there arises the opposite danger of allowing a politically powerful community organization to gain control of the local community-service-jobs program and use it for the organization's own ends, rather than the program's purposes. Striking the proper balance between cooperation and independence—between responsiveness to local constituencies and accountability to the nonlocal taxpayers who foot the bill—presents a difficult challenge, but unless that challenge is acknowledged forthrightly from the beginning, it cannot be met.

Local bureaucrats and politicians present much the same test of skill. Their expertise, influence, and power cannot—should not—be ignored. At the same time, their fiscal appetites and political instincts will encourage them to seek to capture and absorb a local community-service-jobs program and use it for their own purposes, rather than the purposes of the program. The temptation—so much new money, so many jobs to be given out—will be difficult to resist. Achieving the greatest degree of local cooperation, without capitulating to local pressures to divert a community-service-jobs program from its intended purposes, may constitute the program's severest challenge.

Sixth and finally, the public's ambivalent attitude toward programs that provide money or benefits to poor people must be frankly acknowledged. On the one hand, most voters and taxpayers believe in helping poor people get jobs. On the other hand, many of the same voters and taxpayers have the nagging feeling they are being swindled by government programs meant to serve the poor, a feeling sustained by widespread abuse in welfare programs and reinforced by the press's proclivity to ferret out such abuse. In and of itself, the public's visceral resentment of abuse is not a political problem, but when whipped up and brought into focus by interest groups and elected officials who oppose community-service jobs for their own reasons, public resentment can provide momentum sufficient to topple such a program. Designing a program so as to minimize the possibility of abuse, frequent monitoring in order to detect abuse, and immediately and forcefully correcting abuse when it occurs, are key elements in winning the public's long-term support for and defusing opposition to a community-service-jobs program.

Important as fighting abuse itself is the need to counter the possible image of abuse with evidence of success. To survive, a national community-service-jobs program must produce visible evidence that it is accomplishing worthwhile tasks. The general public, the press, and key interest groups must see what is being achieved. Citizens must experience, from day to day, the fact that their own lives and communities have improved because of what the community-service-jobs program has done. Experts' reports and government audits, however favorable, will not suffice. Ordinary voters and taxpayers, local reporters and editors, union officials and business executives must be able to observe with their own eyes that, notwithstanding occasional abuses, their streets, their parks, their neighborhoods, their schools have become demonstrably more attractive. The most effective response to the public's profound fear of getting ripped off (again!) by another do-good program is to create a program that leaves visible signs of its success in every city and county in the United States.

These considerations suggest that a community-service-jobs program will be most successful in getting off the ground and maintaining public and political support in the face of predictable opposition, if its administrative structure meets the following criteria:

1. Jobs should require unemployed poor persons to furnish their time and energy, but should not require the use of cars, tools, or other materials.[10]
2. Community organizations and local governments should not be excluded from the process of deciding what jobs to create, but neither should they be

permitted to dictate what is done with money raised by the federal government. A balance between local involvement and central responsibility must be struck. One approach would be to invite community organizations and local governments to submit competitive bids proposing which specific local jobs projects should get carried out. The bids would then be ranked on the basis of preannounced criteria and the best proposals chosen for funding. The administrators of the community-service-jobs program would confine themselves to (a) identifying the broad categories of work to be performed, (b) determining the criteria to be used in deciding which proposals to fund, (c) ranking and selecting proposals based on these criteria, and (d) monitoring performance. For each proposal selected, a contract should be signed, specifying the number of persons to be hired, the manner of their hiring, the jobs to be created, the outcome of the project and its cost. Consistent with striking a balance between local involvement and central responsibility, it may make sense to give community groups and local government broad discretion in implementing their contracts and to try to hold them accountable through at-risk arrangements and incentives, rather than detailed regulations and sanctions. If community groups and local governments fail to achieve their specific contractual goals with the money they receive, they would be required to achieve them anyway with money they themselves raise; if, on the other hand, they achieve their goals prior to spending all the money they receive, they should be able to keep the difference.

3. Of all the criteria used in approving projects, two should be fundamental. First, the projects that create the greatest number of jobs at the lowest total cost should receive priority. Second, projects should be approved only if they result in jobs that produce visible improvements quickly and continuously, both within the neighborhoods and valleys of the poor and throughout the affected cities and counties.

As noted before, there is no magic formula for establishing a successful national community-service-jobs program. The suggestions outlined above, if followed, will help, but the ingredients most critical to success are commitment and leadership.

Like it or not, millions of unemployed poor Americans will remain unemployed and poor for years to come, unless we make a commitment to offer them publicly funded community-service jobs that let them get out of poverty. These community-service jobs can and should be offered in a manner that ensures that, insofar as possible, all available private-sector and regular government jobs are filled. Even when community-service jobs are clearly made the jobs of last resort, however, hundreds of thousands of such jobs will have to be created. There will be a large, inescapable, public cost. Paying that cost requires a major long-term commitment by the American people and their Congress.

As important as commitment is leadership. The endeavor has been undertaken before—the CCC, CETA, and so forth—but the community-

service-jobs program we now need to create stands on a different footing. The others were designed and perceived to be temporary. They
were meant to last until the crisis passed; then they would be repealed
(whether the crisis passed or not, they indeed were repealed). Whether
or not the assumption of temporariness was justified in the past, it
cannot be justified today. The community-service-jobs program we need
to establish in the United States today must be a regular program for
the foreseeable short-term future, that is, at least the next 10–30 years.
The problem of millions of unemployed poor may get better or worse
from year to year, but it will be a massive problem for years and
decades. We had better get used to the idea. Having gotten used to the
idea, we had better get down to the practical, no-nonsense, trial-and-
error, let's-roll-up-our-sleeves-and-make-the-thing-work, somewhat
boring business of making such a large regular program run properly.
In pursuing the mechanics of justice, what we require most, after commitment, is leadership wise enough to understand this challenge and
capable enough to meet it.

## THE POOR WHO ALREADY WORK

Eliminating the poverty of the poor who have jobs is also largely a
matter of cash.[11] Their wages bring them within various degrees of
proximity to the poverty line. Yet for many of the poor who are employed less than full-time and year-round and for all those already
employed full-time and year-round, working 40 hours per week for 52
weeks per year is insufficient to get them to or above the poverty line.
Their wages must be supplemented in order to convert full-time, year-
round employment (2,080 hours of work) into employment that gets
their familes out of poverty.

Wage supplementation is neither a novel nor a difficult concept. The
federal Earned Income Tax Credit (EITC) already offers certain low-
wage workers the opportunity to receive periodic wage supplements.
Introduced as a temporary provision by the Revenue Adjustment Act
of 1975, the EITC was made permanent in 1978. The credit is available
only to low-income workers who have dependent children. It was intended to offset the burden imposed on those workers by Social Security
payroll taxes. Workers claim the EITC, however, as a credit against
their federal income-tax liability. To achieve the original objective of
offsetting Social Security taxes, which often exceed federal income-tax
obligations, Congress made the EITC refundable. Workers can claim
the credit in full, even if it exceeds the amount of their federal income-
tax liability, which means the federal government may pay them
money (a refund) rather than their paying any taxes to the government.

Eligibility for the EITC is based on the entire taxpaying unit's gross income. In 1987, eligibility was limited to families with gross incomes under $15,432. Once eligibility is established, the family's earned income determines the amount of the credit. In 1987, as earned income rose from $0 to $6,922, the amount of the credit rose from $0 to $851; as earned income continued to rise to $15,432, the amount of the credit then proceeded to decline steadily to $0. Under the Tax Reform Act of 1986, these figures will be adjusted for inflation in subsequent years. Workers, by filing Form W–5 with their employers, may claim advance payment of their EITC. In other words, at the option of each worker, the credit may be obtained at the same time the employer pays wages (Circular E includes several pages of tables telling employers how much of the EITC to add on to worker's paychecks, depending on whether the employer uses a weekly, biweekly, semimonthly, monthly, or other payroll period). Alternatively, the EITC may be claimed retroactively when a family files its federal income-tax return.[12]

From the perspective of both the worker and the employer, the EITC—particularly if the worker files Form W–5 with the employer—operates as a wage supplement, notwithstanding Congress's purpose of merely offsetting Social Security taxes. The EITC has been expanded in the past, most recently in 1986 for tax year 1987. Further enlarging the amount of this wage supplement represents neither a conceptual nor a practical challenge. It requires merely a willingness on the part of Congress and the president to incur a higher tax expenditure, that is, to forego a larger loss of revenues to the U.S. Treasury. The question is, Is the EITC the most desirable form of wage supplement, or would another kind of wage supplement be preferable?

To answer this, we need to determine exactly what we are looking for in a wage supplement. Several criteria—criteria that the EITC has met—are obvious. It should not be available to single persons for whom a full-time year-round job at the minimum wage is already adequate to get them above the poverty line. Conversely, it should help persons with families for whom such a job is insufficient to lift them above the poverty line.[13]

A wage supplement should also be neutral with respect to marriage and arguably should promote marriage. The EITC partially achieves this objective by offering extra income to both unmarried and married workers. Any other wage-supplement scheme should do the same. The EITC rules governing the definition of earned income, however, partially undermine the objective of marriage neutrality and offer a "perverse" incentive for marriages not to form (or to dissolve). This marriage disincentive, and the cost of correcting it, will be discussed later.

A wage supplement should also not discourage childbearing by reducing income in inverse proportion to the number of children, nor should it encourage childbearing by providing so much extra money if a first child is present—or an extra child is born—that childbearing decisions are influenced by the availability of the extra dollars. The EITC, of course, does not impose a penalty for children, and it is unlikely that any other wage-supplement scheme would be constructed to do so. The EITC does reward the bearing of a first child in that it requires the presence of a dependent child in order for the worker to qualify for the credit. It is highly unlikely, however, that a low-wage worker without a child would be induced to bear a child in order to take advantage of the EITC. Not just a child but work is required to get any portion of the credit. More or less full-time year-round work is necessary to secure the maximum credit (in 1987, $851 per year). Yet the maximum credit is hardly a magnificent sum. It is extremely unlikely that any woman would be influenced to bear a first child in order to obtain the added cash afforded by the EITC, given her or her spouse's obligation to work to obtain the EITC and the modest amount of extra cash the EITC provides. The EITC thus scores well against the childbearing criterion. Any other wage-supplement scheme should do likewise. With respect to any additional children, the EITC clearly offers no incentive, since regardless of the number of children, the EITC credit amount is flat. Whether a wage supplement can be constructed that remains neutral with respect to childbearing, while also providing large families proportional amounts sufficient to get them above the poverty line, will be discussed shortly.

Another set of key wage-supplement criteria involves the incentive to work. Workers should always gain—when wages and the wage supplement are added together—if they work more hours (at least up to 40 hours per week) and if they work at higher-wage jobs. These work incentives are important, not only because they promote work *per se* but because they promote the efficiency of a wage-supplement program. The more low-wage workers engage in work, and the higher their wages, the smaller the gap between their income and the poverty line, and thus the fewer tax dollars need to be devoted to the wage-supplement program. The incentive to work at higher wages also functions to deter employers from lowering their wages—an incentive employers always have as they pursue maximum profits, but which a wage supplement strengthens by cushioning the economic harm to workers of a wage reduction. The more a wage supplement is structured so as to encourage workers to pursue higher-wage jobs, the more employers will hesitate to lower their wages (fearing both employee resistance, resulting in work-site unrest and loss of productivity, and the loss of valued employees to competing firms). Like the incentive to work at higher wages itself, deterring employers from lowering their wages also promotes the efficiency of a wage-supplement program. The more employers continue paying workers out of their companies' pockets, the smaller the gap between workers' income and the poverty line, and thus the fewer the tax dollars that need to be devoted to the wage-supplement program.

The federal EITC generally operates in a manner consistent with these work-incentive criteria. By working more hours, or by working at higher wages, or both, the low-wage worker always gains in total income (wages and wage supplement combined). Once (as the formula stood in 1987) the worker's income reaches $6,922 and the worker attains the maximum $851 credit, the relative incentive to work (i.e., compared to the incentive before the maximum credit was attained) does diminish, in that additional dollars of earned income generate a decreasingly smaller EITC, such that the sum of wages and credit rises at a slower pace. Specifically, for each dollar of wages in excess of $6,922, ten cents are subtracted from the credit. Nonetheless, it always pays to work more hours, and it always pays to work at a higher-wage job, because the result is always a total higher income. While the specific features of the EITC work incentive should perhaps be altered in introducing a different kind of wage supplement, the basic structure of the EITC should serve as the model for any wage-supplement effort.

Yet the EITC is not the optimal wage supplement. It fails to meet several critical criteria.

First, because of its historical linkage with offsetting Social Security taxes, it does not directly relate to the goal of eliminating poverty. In 1987 a worker with one child, who held a full-time, year-round, min-imum-wage, regular private-sector or government job ($6,968/year) and who took advantage of the maximum EITC available ($851), ended up with an income ($7,819) that somewhat exceeded the poverty line ($7,400) for that family size.[14] A worker with two children (or one unemployed spouse and one child), who held such a job ($6,968/year) and who took advantage of the maximum EITC available ($851), ended up with precisely the same income ($7,819), which was significantly below the 1987 poverty line ($9,300) for that family size.[15] The larger the family size, the less the EITC serves as a vehicle for getting out of poverty. The one modification of the EITC that is most needed in order to make it a better wage supplement is to allow workers who have the same family income below the poverty line and who work the same number of hours, but who have different numbers of dependents, to obtain different wage supplements—different enough to let each family get above its respective poverty line.

Second, although the EITC is partially neutral toward marriage, in that it permits both unmarried and married persons to claim (all other factors being equal) the same amount of credit, the EITC rules govering the definition of earned income will in certain cases discourage the formation (and, possibly, the survival) of marriage. An example provides the best explanation. Ozzie and Harriet, an unmarried couple living together, have a child. Their entire income comes from their employment, and both work nearly full-time, year-round, at minimum-wage jobs ($6,700/year). If they remain unmarried (or, had they been married to begin with, if they should get divorced) and should Harriet retain custody of their child, Ozzie's income would remain the same, but Harriet's earnings of $6,700 would let her claim the maximum EITC of $851. Total income: $6,700 + $6,700 + $851 = $14,251. If Ozzie and Harriet get married (or, had they been married to begin with, they stay married), their combined earnings of $13,400 let either one of them claim a smaller EITC of $203. Total income: $6,700 + $6,700 + $203 = $13,603. Unmarried, Ozzie and Harriet have a combined income (all wages plus EITC) which is $648 greater than if they were married.

To what extent such a marriage penalty would actually deter our Ozzie and Harriet—plus the tens of thousands of low-income single men and women, with or without children, who have no moral objection to living together outside of wedlock—from considering marriage or getting married cannot, of course, be quantified. It is also necessary to point out that the EITC's disincentive to marriage may be partially or entirely neutralized (if not reversed) by the marriage incentives built into the rest of the tax system, that is, the tax rates applied to single persons versus the rates applied to married persons filing jointly. The point here is simply that the EITC, when considered by itself, does offer a partial disincentive to low-income persons to form marriages, and that it would be desirable if the EITC or any other wage-supplement scheme had the opposite result.

Creating an incentive to marry, regrettably, comes at a price. The price? A much less efficient—that is, more costly—wage-supplement program. The EITC or any other wage-supplement scheme could be designed to make not family income but individual income the basis for determining the amount of the credit. Regardless of the income of the "other adult," either low-income parent—presumably the one with the lower income—would be entitled by virtue of a dependent child to claim a wage supplement. (Only one of the parents, not both, could "use" each dependent child by claiming a credit.) The parent's individual income would determine the amount of the supplement. The number of dependents either would not (as in the case of the current EITC) or would (assuming EITC is amended) vary the amount of the wage supplement. The relationship between the parent claiming the supplement and the other adult—that is, whether they are unmarried or married—would then be irrelevant. From an economic perspective, this arrangement would never discourage marriage. To the extent that two can live more cheaply than one, it would encourage the adults in question to live together, whether married or not. Arguably, it would encourage marriage in that its neutrality toward marriage would not undermine other features of the tax system (i.e., lower rates for married couples filing jointly) that generally make marriage a more economically advantageous arrangement.

Regrettably, eliminating the EITC's marriage penalty bears a price. Let us return to our example. Under the old (i.e., current) EITC formula, the marriage of Ozzie and Harriet cost the federal government an EITC payment of only $203, while had they lived together (or separately) without being married, the federal EITC cost would have been $851. Marriage penalized our couple to the tune of the $648 difference, and thus the price of eliminating the marriage penalty—that is, the price of rewarding marriage as highly as nonmarriage—is an extra $648 in federal tax dollars (foregone federal revenue) that the taxpayers must ultimately bear (all else being equal) in the form of reduced government spending, higher taxes, or both. Multiply the example by millions of real cases, and the dollars add up. There would also be an important nonpolitical cost. In a few cases, though Harriet may be working a minimum-wage job, Ozzie may be pulling down $50,000 a year. Under the current EITC formula that uses total family income, Harriet's minimum-wage job would not entitle her to claim any credit. Eliminating the current EITC's marriage penalty in the manner just outlined would let Harriet claim the full credit, regardless of Ozzie's princely income. The inequity of this outcome would surely find little political favor. It would not be unreasonable to conclude that, however regrettable may be the partial marriage penalty built into the current structure of the EITC, the fiscal and political cost of correcting that penalty under an alternative wage-supplement program would do far greater harm.

In the end, what this discussion should make clear is that the criteria that a wage-supplement program ought to meet do not all run in the same direction. Some incentives go one way, some incentives work the other way. Encouraging low-wage workers to work more hours and pursue higher-wage jobs suggest a larger per-hour supplement. But the incentive to work is then dampened by the relatively high tax on the supplement necessary to phase it out by a reasonably low income cut-off level. If, to strengthen the work incentive as the supplement is phased out, the tax rate is lowered, the income cut-off level must be raised, which diminishes the efficiency of the program by increasing the total cost to the taxpayers. Which choice? Marriage is somewhat penalized by using family income as the basis for calculating a wage supplement, but correcting that penalty by using individual income to determine the amount of the supplement again undermines the efficiency of the program by augmenting its cost. Which choice?

Recognizing the large number of difficult choices and the pros and cons of the alternatives should improve, rather than paralyze, the decision-making process. To get the single largest segment of America's poor—the working poor—over the poverty line, their wages will have to be supplemented. The federal Earned Income Tax Credit is not merely a great step forward; it is an exciting precedent for further action. Unlike most of what the federal government has done to eliminate poverty, the EITC directly attacks the problem, meets many of the criteria for a sound wage-supplement program, and provides a commitment of substantial federal resources (in the form of tax expenditures or foregone revenue). The task that lies ahead is either to modify the EITC or replace it with another wage-supplement program, in a manner that preserves EITC's strengths, but corrects its weaknesses—particularly its failure to provide low-wage workers a wage supplement that varies with the number of dependent children and thus, in all cases, afford low-wage workers a total income that lifts them out of poverty.

## THE CHALLENGE OF SIMPLICITY

Just as the explanation of poverty advanced throughout this book is a simple one, the recommendations for eliminating poverty advocated in this chapter are simple. The government of the United States should:

- Eliminate the current welfare system;
- Give enough money to the handicapped poor who cannot work and the elderly poor whom we do not expect to work to raise their incomes to the poverty line;
- Offer community-service jobs to the poor who are fully or partially unemployed;
- Provide wage supplements to poor families headed by workers that are sufficient, should they work full-time and year-round, to raise such families' income over the poverty line;
- Design the cash transfers, community-service jobs, and wage supplements in such a way that work is always encouraged; more work is always encouraged; work at regular private-sector or government jobs is always encouraged; work at higher-paying jobs is always encouraged; and marriage is encouraged to the greatest extent possible;
- Afford all low-income persons, on the basis of their ability to pay, access to day care and health insurance (discussed further in the next chapter).

Such simplicity naturally invites criticism: If the causes of poverty are indeed so simple, why doesn't everyone agree on them? If the solutions are truly so simple, why weren't they adopted long ago? Are you saying that the experts and Congress are stupid—so stupid that poverty's simple causes and solutions escape their comprehension? Or are you saying that the experts and policymakers are malevolent—that they understand poverty's simple causes and solutions perfectly well, but intentionally refuse to enact the necessary laws? These questions deserve answers. The answers must come at several levels.

The first answer is that the existence of the job shortage and the existence of such a large supply of low-wage jobs have historically been ignored and continue to go unnoticed by large segments of the U.S. public and by a large percentage of the country's policymakers. There are some good reasons for this lack of recognition. Accurately counting both unemployed jobseekers and available jobs on a local, state, and national basis and at regular intervals, and then comparing the two, is a time-consuming and costly enterprise. No private or public organization carries out such a count or makes such a comparison today. Every month the Bureau of Labor Statistics tells us what the official unemployment rate stands at, but neither the BLS, nor the Census Bureau, nor anybody else tells us what the official jobseeker-to-jobs ratio or job-shortage rate happens to be. The Census Bureau does periodically publish tables showing that millions of Americans subsist below the poverty line, though they work full-time and year-round. The federal government also counts and publicizes what workers earn. Such data strongly suggest the presence of a large and possibly growing number of low-wage jobs in the U.S. economy. Although the raw data may permit such a tabulation, however, no private or public organization periodically and systematically measures the wage structure of the U.S. economy; that is, how many workers (by age, sex, race, region, family size, etc.) hold jobs paying $3.35 per hour, $3.35–3.40 per hour, $3.40–$3.45 per hour, and further appropriate increments in a given week (and the monthly and annual equivalents of these data). In short, because data directly demonstrating the existence and perpetuation of a job shortage and the prevalence of low-wage jobs are either not collected or not tabulated, the fact of the job shortage and the fact that so many jobs are low-wage jobs have been ignored or downplayed.

Katharine Abraham's pioneering work on the ratio of jobseekers to jobs, demonstrating empirically that the number of unemployed jobseekers far exceeds the number of available jobs, ought to have sparked a recognition of the importance of collecting such data and the value of publicizing the information. Her research, regrettably, has been almost entirely ignored by the academic community. It has hardly begun to penetrate the world of policymakers. As a result, the school of thought that holds—on the basis of the large number of jobs advertised in newspapers and other anecdotal information—that the number of unemployed jobseekers approximately equals or is less than the number of available jobs continues to command the faith of a large segment of the population and a substantial number of policymakers. Just as proof of the earth's roundness required years of repetition and publicity before it replaced the belief in a flat earth, Abraham's demonstration of a job shortage will no doubt require a fair amount of independent corroboration and widespread dissemination in the academic and popular media before the false notion of a job sufficiency (or job surplus) finally losses its grip.

A second reason why the simple nature of poverty's causes and solutions has gone unacknowledged in this country has to do with the fiscal and policy implications of making such an acknowledgement. Admitting the simple causes and implementing the simple solutions advanced here will require a major expenditure of public funds and a major realignment of public priorities. Income transfers for those unable to work or whom we do not expect to work, community-service jobs for the unemployed, and wage supplements for workers will all cost a great deal of money. Such expenditures also imply a reduction in the importance (if not the outright repeal) of a whole host of other antipoverty programs that seek to educate and train the poor, take care of the poor, or otherwise address the symptoms of poverty, each of which is backed by powerful constituencies, both outside and inside government. On the other hand, not admitting poverty's simple causes and not pursuing the kind of simple solutions advanced here does not require wrenching decisions to expend more public dollars or rearrange public priorities. The status quo can continue. Entrenched constituencies need not be threatened. When the exploration and pursuit of a new and simple approach promises to impose such fiscal and other pain, can it be wondered that policymakers shrink from the exploration and pursuit?

The third answer is perhaps the most important. It helps to explain why basic raw data about the job shortage and prevalence of low-wage jobs have not been properly collected and widely disseminated. It also helps to explain why painful fiscal and policy choices have been avoided. Yet it has its own, independent, rationale.

The third answer is that it is difficult for nations to admit simple unpleasant truths about themselves. It is difficult for nations to admit big shortcomings. Examples abound. Turkey's massacre of Armenians, Russia's decimation of the *kulaks*, Germany's slaughter of the Jews, South Africa's vicious policy of *apartheid*. These simple brutal facts of history rise up, quietly but persistently, to confront the people and leaders of Turkey, the U.S.S.R., Germany, and South Africa. Their instinctive response has been to deny, ignore, downplay, expurgate, blame the victims, excuse the criminals in their midst.

Avoidance in all its forms is no stranger to our own history. The destruction of Native American populations and culture, the enslavement and segregation of blacks, the imprisonment without cause of Japanese-Americans—these are just some of the blots on our history we would prefer to forget. So we pretend nothing ever happened; we

hide the facts; we deny their validity; we challenge their obvious meaning; we clean up the history books; we point fingers elsewhere; we
excuse our fellow-citizens as "well intentioned."

Compared to the massacre, enslavement, and imprisonment of whole
populations by nations (including our own), which then try to deny or
ignore horrors they have carried out in order to preserve their self-
esteem, the general failure of the United States' public and policymakers to acknowledge the simple causes of the poverty in our midst
and to enact the simple (if costly) programs that could quickly eliminate
poverty constitutes a far, far milder form of denying truth in order to
protect an important symbol of our national dignity and greatness. The
symbol is the genius of the U.S. economy. We generally take pride in
our economic system. It has provided most Americans—the clear majority—with an extremely comfortable standard of living, by world
standards. The opportunities it has provided and continues to provide
for millions of people—many of whom are the grandchildren of slaves,
sharecroppers, peasants, wage slaves, and refugees—to climb up the
ladder of economic opportunity is profoundly linked with this society's
most fundamental social and political values: equality, liberty, and the
pursuit of happiness. An assault on the U.S. economic system is felt
by many as an assault on the nation itself.

Accepting the simple explanation of poverty and the simple mechanics of eliminating poverty advanced here will require, however,
embracing the conclusion that the U.S. economy today has fundamental deficiencies and must be corrected in major ways. By contrast, not
inquiring about, not accepting, and not directly correcting for the job
shortage and low-wage jobs—that is, denying the simple explanation
and simple solutions advanced here—seems to permit us to reaffirm
our faith in the basic goodness of the U.S. economy and by extension
the virtue of the United States itself. This, at least, is how the choice
must subconsciously present itself to millions of people and thousands
of key policymakers. Can there be any wonder that, given such a choice,
they consciously or unconsciously deny the simple unpleasant truth
about the American economy and reaffirm their faith in the American
system?

The choice is, of course, a false choice. Just as it is possible for a job
shortage to exist at the same time that thousands of jobs go begging,
it is possible to acknowledge that poverty is deeply rooted in the shortcomings of the U.S. economy and can be eliminated only if major new
initiatives are undertaken and simultaneously assert that the U.S.
economy is indeed a good one, providing the vast majority of jobseekers
with jobs, providing most of them with good jobs, and sustaining our
society's most basic values of liberty, equality, and the pursuit of happiness. The flaw in the gem and the beauty of the gem need not be

mutually exclusive. Acknowledging the truth of both the flaw and the beauty represents, rather, the first step toward correcting the flaw, while preserving the beauty for its real—not imagined—virtue.

## NOTES

1. In 1984, 1.9 million poor persons aged 15–64 did not work because of disability or illness, and 3.3 million poor persons were 65 and over as of March of the following year. Bureau of Census, "Characteristics of the Population Below the Poverty Level: 1984," Series P–60, No. 152, June 1986, pp. 5, 37.

2. The lower estimate assumes that, since the handicapped and elderly represent 15.4 percent of the poor population, they would account for an equal percentage of the total income deficit (i.e., the total amount it would take to raise all poor persons to the poverty line), which stood at $46.3 billion in 1984. The higher estimate assumes that most of the handicapped and elderly live alone and that their mean income deficit would therefore be the same as the mean deficit for unrelated individuals, which came to $2,274 in 1984. See ibid., p. 22. The income deficit will be discussed further in Chapter 12.

3. For the first time in U.S. history, federal outlays were projected to exceed $1,000 billion—$1 trillion—in Fiscal Year 1987. Office of Management and Budget, "Special Analysis: Budget of the United States Government," Fiscal Year 1988, p. A–5.

4. In this section "the unemployed poor" refers both to those who cannot find any work and those who work less than 35 hours per week.

5. As will be discussed in the next chapter, maximum efficiency requires not only that the unemployed poor and the regularly employed poor end up with roughly the same cash income (with the latter coming out a bit ahead), but that they end up with roughly the same total benefit package—that is, wages plus wage supplement plus day-care subsidies plus health insurance.

6. The community-services job program should, of course, be abolished if the ratio between unemployed jobseekers and available regular jobs were ever to get close to 1:1. Since it is improbable that this will happen at any time in the foreseeable future, however, such a program is considered here to be a permanent addition to the public-policy landscape. The ratio between unemployed jobseekers and available regular jobs is far more likely to be relevant to the scope of the program, that is, the number of community jobs that should be made available. As the economy worsens, that number is likely to rise; as the economy improves, the number is likely to decline; other demographic factors may also influence the number of community jobs needed at any one time.

7. The choice of age 15 as the lower eligibility limit is arbitrary. The Census Bureau frequently uses age 15 when counting the number of poor householders and workers, and thus it is used here. See, for example, Bureau of the Census, "Characteristics of the Population," pp. 13–21 and 36–49. Ages 16, 17, or 18 might be chosen—with equal arbitrariness. The critical policy question is, At what age should a teenage parent be entitled to a community-service job? Teenage parents who were eligible for such a job but who preferred not to work

(whether their intention was simply to stay at home or, it would be hoped, to attend school) could, of course, decline to accept community-service employment, but under the arrangement proposed here they would not be entitled to any other independent source of publicly subsidized income. If they did not wish to work, they would have to remain at home with their own parents (who, if unemployed and poor, would be entitled to community-service jobs and who, if employed but poor, would be entitled to a wage supplement) or secure child-support payments from their children's absent parents (who, if between 15 and 65, unemployed, and poor, would be entitled to a community-service job and who, if employed but poor, would be entitled to a wage supplement). Age 65 is chosen as the upper eligibility limit because at that age virtually every American is eligible for Social Security retirement benefits. Eligibility could be extended beyond 65 for those ineligible for Social Security.

8. In the case of partially unemployed persons, they should be required to work the difference between 35 hours per week and a number equal to their weekly earned income divided by the minimum wage. This formula will ensure that they work a total number of hours (i.e., community-service-job hours plus regular-job hours) that provides them all the work they need to equal the income of completely unemployed poor persons, but gives them no more work (at public expense, it must be remembered) than is necessary to achieve that goal.

9. "1987 Poverty Income Guidelines for All States (Except Alaska and Hawaii) and the District of Columbia," *Federal Register,* 52, No. 34 (February 20, 1987): 5341.

10. In many cities and most rural areas, unemployed poor persons will typically have to use cars—their own or friends'—to get to work, but use of cars on the job should not be required.

11. In this section, the poor who have jobs means those family heads working (a) entirely in community-service-jobs programs, (b) partially in community-service-jobs programs and partially in regular private-sector or government jobs, and (c) entirely in regular private-sector or government jobs, whose annual family income is reasonably projected to be less than the applicable poverty line and whose annual family income would continue to remain below the applicable poverty line if the family head worked full-time and year-round.

Because, in the case of a single person, a full-time, year-round job at the minimum wage exceeds the poverty line for one person, there is no need to provide single people with wage supplements. A single person who works solely full-time and year-round at a community-service job, and who thus is employed for only 35 hours per week and 52 weeks per year at $3.35 per hour, would have an income of $6,097. A single person who works solely full-time and year-round at a regular private-sector or government job, and who thus is employed 40 hours per week and 52 weeks per year at $3.35 per hour or more, would have a minimal income of $6,968. A single person working full-time and year-round at a combination of the two kinds of jobs—community-service and regular—would have, based on the formula assumed here, an income between the two figures (see n. 8, above). For a single person, therefore, any full-time year-round combination of jobs would produce an income that exceeds the poverty line, which was $5,500 in 1987 (see "1987 Poverty Income Guidelines," n. 9, above).

Thus, wage supplementation here refers to augmenting the earned income of poor families (i.e., multiperson family units) by increasing the take-home pay of the family's first 2,080 hours of work per year (whether performed by one full-time, year-round worker, two part-time, year-round workers, etc.), such that, if the family's workers do perform 2,080 hours of work in a year, the family will have an annual income above the poverty line.

12. The description here of the federal Earned Income Tax Credit is drawn from the following sources: Congressional Budget Office, "Reducing Poverty Among Children," May 1985, pp. 56 et seq.; U.S. Congress, House, Committee on Ways and Means, "Background Material and Data on Programs Within the Jurisdiction of the Committee on Ways and Means," June 6, 1987, pp. 607 et seq.; and Internal Revenue Code, Circular E, January, 1987, p. 12.

13. The most a full-time year-round worker can earn at the federal minimum wage (40 hours per week × 52 weeks per year × $3.35 per hour) is $6,698, which is less than the 1987 poverty line of $7,400 for a two-person family and even further below the 1987 poverty lines for larger families. See "1987 Poverty Income Guidelines," n. 9 above. Unless the federal minimum wage is raised in 1988 or later, the gap between a minimum-wage job and the poverty line for two-person and larger families will continue to increase annually, as the poverty line is adjusted annually for inflation and as inflation (while slower now than in earlier periods) continues to occur.

14. "Poverty Income Guidelines," n. 9, above.

15. Ibid.

# 11
# Day Care and Health Insurance

The elimination of poverty in the United States through the "mechanics" described in the preceding chapter will permit the once-poor to meet most of their basic needs, such as food, shelter, clothing, and so forth, without further help from government.[1] Most of the once-poor's basic needs will be fairly consistent from month to month, regardless of external factors. Certain costs that cannot be avoided may fluctuate somewhat with the weather (e.g., in northern climates utility costs will peak in the winter),[2] but generally, individual preferences of a discretionary nature (e.g., taking a vacation) will most influence the need for major infusions of additional cash in any given month.

Two needs depart from the pattern. First, once-poor people who hold jobs, and who have children too young to attend school or whose hours of work make it impossible for them to be at home when their children have returned from school, will often face the extraordinary cost of paying for day care. A single parent who must place one child in day care for eight hours each working day, for 52 weeks each year, could easily run up a bill, at the very modest rate of $1.00 per hour, of $2,080 annually. Some parents may be obliged to pay more. A 1984 congressional report noted:

> Full-day care is expensive, often prohibitively so for the care of more than one child. A sampling of fees in several states shows child care costs for preschool children range from $45 per week on the low end [$2,340 for 52 weeks] to more than $75 per week on the high end [$3,900 for 52 weeks]. According to testimony from the Children's Defense Fund, the

cost of caring for preschoolers in group or center care ranges from $2,200–
$3,200 per year, and in family day care from $1,200–$2,200 per year.[3]

The Census Bureau reported that during the winter of 1984–85, of 5.3
million women who were employed, had at least one child under 15,
and paid cash for day care, the median weekly child-care cost was
$37.50, which equals $1,950 for 52 weeks. If the child was less than
one year old, the median cost was higher: $41.60 per week or $2,163
for 52 weeks. If the woman worked full-time, the median cost was also
higher: $40.50 per week or $2,100 for 52 weeks.[4] It takes no great
mathematical talent to recognize that many once-poor workers will,
because of the cost of child care, end up with dramatically lower disposable incomes, which for all practical purposes pushes them back
into poverty again.

Second, once-poor people who suffer a major accident or illness, and
who are not covered by health insurance, face the extraordinary cost
of paying doctors' and hospital bills. Yet health insurance, which shifts
most of the burden of those bills to an insurance company, is itself an
extraordinary cost. This is especially so for family coverage. Like day
care, family health-insurance premiums can easily amount to $1,500–
$2,000 per year. Again, it requires no special mathematical talent to
conclude that many once-poor individuals and families will, because
of the cost of health insurance, end up with substantially smaller disposable incomes that for all practical purposes leave them poor once
more.

Although we have so far been discussing the once-poor as if they
were distinguishable from never-poor low-income persons, the distinction serves no useful purpose when it comes to day care or health
insurance. If there is a basis for helping the once-poor meet the extraordinary costs of day care and health insurance, then the never-
poor should be helped in exactly the same manner. Why should the
two groups be treated differently? Their income is the same. Their
needs are the same. For the balance of this chapter, therefore, the focus
will be on all low-income persons (defined roughly, and arbitrarily, as
all single individuals and families below 175 percent of their respective
poverty lines), the costs all of them face in obtaining adequate day care
and health insurance, and the mechanisms available for providing all
of them with subsidized day care and health insurance.

Day care is the easier of the two extraordinary costs to discuss. The
broad policy issues are fairly clear: Should low-income persons be subsidized in their efforts to purchase day care? How great should the
subsidy be? How should it be administered? The major choices are also
fairly straightforward. The low-income population can be left to fend
for themselves, or they can be subsidized. A subsidy can be flat or

progressive. A subsidy can be provided in the form of vouchers, a tax credit or deduction, direct reimbursement of private day-care centers, or the direct establishment and operation of day-care centers.

Whichever choice is made (other than a decision to provide no subsidy at all), there will be a certain degree of inefficiency; that is, low-income persons who would otherwise have taken care of their children's day-care needs by placing their children with parents, relatives, or friends who were glad (or at least willing) to provide the care at no or minimal cost, will take advantage of the subsidy and impose arguably unnecessary costs on the taxpayers. Whether such cost shifting is nonetheless justified, and how extensive it will be, can be debated. It will certainly take place.

The central principle that underlies this book—that all poor people who can work and whom we expect to work should be entitled through work to get out of poverty, maintain a decent living standard, and meet their own needs in the marketplace—suggests that a day-care-voucher approach makes the most sense. Under this approach, low-income persons who are responsible for the care of children between birth and some appropriate cut-off age (perhaps 12 or 13), who work a minimal number of hours, and who certify that free or minimal-cost day care is not available to them, would be entitled to receive a voucher entitling them to buy day-care services from specified categories of providers. To deter use by those who truly need no help in obtaining day care, the program should require every eligible person to pay something for the voucher. The value of the voucher would be based on the person's income and the number of children for whom day care is sought. The lower the income and the larger the number of children, the greater the face amount of the voucher; the higher the income and the smaller the number of children, the smaller the face amount of the voucher. Voucher holders would then shop around for the day-care arrangements that best suit their pocketbooks and meet their needs, and upon finding a suitable home or center, they would sign over the voucher to the provider. The provider would usually receive some cash directly from the person placing the child and would redeem the voucher for cash with an agency of government. Providers receiving and redeeming vouchers would be regulated by the state, but to keep costs down, regulations should be kept minimal.

Needless to say, any number of other arrangements might—and perhaps should—be tried. The details are less important than the objective: (1) providing assistance to low-income persons in proportion to their income; (2) permitting parents the greatest possible freedom of choice in deciding where their children shall be physically located and which individuals shall take care of their children; (3) promoting day care that meets minimal standards of quality; and (4) constraining the total cost of the day-care subsidy. The latter concern cannot be over-emphasized. Helping low-income persons buy adequate day-care services will be an expensive proposition. The cost will have to be constrained to maintain popular and political support.

It should be noted that some of the dilemmas that confront the proper design of a wage supplement also confront the design of a good day-care subsidy. Dilemma #1: Using differences in family income to calculate different day-care subsidies so that lower-income individuals get a larger subsidy, while higher-income individuals receive a lower subsidy, seems only fair; yet it somewhat discourages work and higher wages by imposing (on top of a wage-supplement "tax" and other government taxes) a day-care tax; that is, each extra dollar of income earned will be reduced by the amount of day-care subsidy lost. Dilemma #2: Unmarried adults will arguably face a disincentive to marry, if their combined family income is used to calculate eligibility for and the amount of a day-care subsidy; yet using solely the individual income of the parent of the child to determine eligibility for and the amount of a child-care subsidy could result in families with large combined incomes getting unjustified subsidies. As with wage supplements, there is no way to avoid these dilemmas completely. They are inherent in any scheme that seeks to provide help based on need, but that also seeks to eliminate help that is unneeded. The best that can be done is first, to recognize that a difficulty exists, and, second, attempt to fashion subsidy formulas that do not offer too many and too great perverse incentives.

The second extraordinary expense that low-income persons will face, health care or health insurance, is far more complex. During the last several years the number of uninsured Americans has been rising dramatically. In 1977 approximately 26 million, over 13 percent of the population under 65, lacked health insurance at any point in time. By 1980 the number had risen to roughly 28 million, or nearly 14.5 percent of the under–65 population. By 1983 the number had climbed to about 35 million, just over 17 percent of the under–65 population.[5] As of 1985, it had risen further to 37 million, well over 17 percent of the under–65 population.[6] Simultaneously, for a portion of the period in question, the percentage of nonelderly persons with private health insurance actually dropped—from 75.8 percent in 1982 to 73.9 percent in 1985—notwithstanding the general growth in U.S. population as a whole.[7] Contrary to conventional wisdom, the number and percentage of uninsured have grown and the percentage of insured has declined in the face of the U.S. economic recovery.

The main focus here is on the economic impact of both the lack of insurance and the cost of insurance. A low-income (as well as, in some cases, a moderate-income or even high-income) family that is hit by a serious accident or illness can run up thousands of dollars in health-care costs, wiping out its savings, forcing it into debt, and possibly pushing it into backruptcy, unless the health-care providers agree to forgive the amounts due them. A low-income family that seeks to forestall these risks by buying insurance is still likely to incur significant medical costs (for over-the-counter drugs, for dental care and vision care, and for the deductible and coinsurance not covered by its policy), but its biggest economic loss is the cost of insurance itself. As already mentioned, a family's premium can easily run from $1,500 to $2,000 per year. Yet because "going bare" can lead to thousands of dollars in medical bills, huge debt, and bankruptcy, many low-income families are willing to suffer a substantial reduction in their standard of living in order to secure health insurance.

While protection against the economic cost of accident or illness is the primary reason that motivates individuals to obtain health insurance, health-insurance coverage also appears to serve a nonfinancial purpose. There is some evidence that people with health insurance get more health care, and there is at least reason to believe that (all else being equal) people who get more health care enjoy better health. A 1986 survey sponsored by the Robert Wood Johnson Foundation, for instance, reported that 31 percent of the uninsured said they had no regular source of health care, compared to about 16 percent of the insured. The uninsured visited doctors and other ambulatory providers of care an average of 3.2 times per year, compared to 4.4 times for the insured. Over 41 percent of the uninsured had made no ambulatory visits in the preceding 12 months, compared to somewhat over 32 percent of the insured. Ironically—or, perhaps, predictably—the uninsured used emergency rooms more than the insured.[8]

The relationship between insurance coverage and utilization of health-care services is fairly straightforward. It is hardly a surprise that the Robert Wood Johnson survey found that, compared to those who lack insurance coverage, those who have coverage are more likely to go to a regular doctor. The relationship between utilization of health-care services and actual health status, on the other hand, is a complex one. A day in the hospital or a visit to the doctor is not necessarily good for your health, and avoidance is not necessarily bad for your health. Utilization of health services is likely to improve health status only if a real need for care exists and the care provided is medically appropriate.

What, then, do the studies conclude about the relationship between utilization of health services and health status? Unfortunately, the evidence is limited. The Robert Wood Johnson survey provides some evidence that the health of the uninsured is worse than the health of the insured. According to the survey, slightly more of the uninsured

(12.2 percent) reported their health to be poor or fair compared to the insured (11.7 percent), even though far fewer of the uninsured (12.4 percent) reported that they had chronic or serious illnesses, compared to the insured (20.9 percent).[9] While self-reporting can be inaccurate, there is no reason to believe that it would be more inaccurate for the uninsured than for the insured. The problem with using this particular survey is that the numbers are just too raw and too close to permit much confidence that it demonstrates a positive relationship (all other factors being equal) between insurance coverage and health status. Other studies are no more definitive. So we are left with the opinions of the experts, who seem to have concluded that (all other factors being equal) health insurance on the whole does improve health status.

While there thus remains an open question about whether the lack of health insurance presents a real health risk, and while there has also been some uncertainty about the actual number of the uninsured because of the different surveying methodologies used by different organizations, all the surveys of the uninsured population seem to be in agreement as to the uninsureds' characteristics.[10] The uninsured are disproportionately young, disproportionately low-income, and strongly connected to the labor force. Roughly one-third are children (0–17 years of age); another one-third are young adults (18–35 years of age); the remainder are scattered from age 35 to age 64; virtually none are 65 or older, thanks to Medicare. Roughly one-third have incomes below the poverty line; another one-third have incomes between approximately 100 percent and 200 percent of the poverty line; the remainder are scattered across higher income brackets. The uninsured population's largest occupational category is full-time worker, followed by part-time worker. The remainder consist largely of unemployed persons, housekeepers, handicapped persons, retired persons, students, and preschoolers. In short, young low-wage workers, their spouses, and their children constitute the bulk of the uninsured.[11]

Most uninsured workers are either self-employed or hold jobs in small firms. In 1982, for instance, 27 percent of uninsured workers were self-employed, and 40 percent worked in firms with fewer than 25 employees.[12] This information raises what may be the trickiest issue with regard to providing the uninsured with insurance: Should the solution ignore employers even though the workplace is where most people get their health-insurance coverage, and even though a nonemployer solution could induce those employers who now provide coverage to cancel it? Or should all employers be required to provide health insurance, even though many of the small employers who now fail to do so are so marginal that a mandate that may average $1,500 or more per employee for family coverage could push them into bankruptcy, cause layoffs, or result in wage reductions? Does a solution exist somewhere between these alternatives which guarantees that the uninsured will get insurance, but avoids both alternatives' unattractive side-effects?

If poverty were eliminated as proposed in this book—by providing poor people who cannot work or whom we do not expect to work with additional cash; by offering the unemployed poor community-service jobs; and by offering the employed poor wage supplements—the number of low-income Americans who lack health insurance is likely to rise, if nothing else is done. Virtually the entire AFDC population that has enjoyed Medicaid coverage will lose it (assuming Medicaid, as it now exists, remains in existence), because their incomes will be too high. Most of the nonAFDC population (both those once below and those always above the poverty line) who previously lacked health insurance are likely to remain uninsured. It is true that a small percentage of the once-poor who previously lacked health insurance will use some or all of their additional income to buy individual health insurance or to join employer-sponsored plans they feel they now can afford. On balance, though, the total number and percentage of uninsured will probably rise substantially, unless a new affordable health-insurance program is put in place.

It can be argued that, once poverty has been eliminated, the once-poor who are uninsured—together with everyone else who is uninsured—should be left to decide for themselves whether to spend their money to buy individual health insurance or join whatever employer-provided coverage may be available. Government, it can be argued, should keep hands off. Most advocates of nonintervention will probably agree that, in order to achieve equity, any premiums that the uninsured choose to pay for individual insurance should be deductible from their gross income, to simulate the exclusion from income of employer-paid premiums now enjoyed by insured persons covered by employer-sponsored plans. (Some advocates of nonintervention will argue that the path to equity should be to eliminate the existing exclusion from income of employer-paid premiums and thus rid the marketplace of even that degree of government interference.) Beyond achieving tax equity, the proponents of a market solution will maintain, government should not get involved. With poverty eliminated, every single person or family has enough to maintain a decent living standard; they should then be free to choose how to spend their money, specifically whether to buy health insurance or not. If raising the poor above the poverty line does not realistically give them enough disposable income to afford health insurance, the solution is to increase the incomes of persons just above the poverty line to a somewhat higher level. At that higher income level, then, they should be free to decide whether to buy insurance or not. Government should not interfere.

Under such a scenario, a percentage of the low-income uninsured will indeed buy health insurance, as they do today. Those who are sick or averse to risk will disproportionately seek to buy insurance. The sick will naturally have trouble obtaining private coverage at any price, because of insurers' underwriting standards. The healthy who are simply averse to risk, and who are willing to accept a reduced level of consumption of food, housing, clothing, transportation, entertainment, and so forth, should have no problems securing an individual policy for a premium of $500–1,000 per year or a family policy for a premium of $1,500–2,000 per year.[13]

Under a strictly voluntary scenario, however, the great majority of the low-income uninsured are likely to remain uninsured. Their disinclination to buy coverage will arise, not from a dislike of the insurance product itself, but from a judgment that they cannot afford its price—that is, a determination that they will unacceptably reduce their consumption of food, housing, clothing, and other necessities or valued goods and services by spending scarce dollars on health insurance.

The policy question we must decide, therefore, is whether low-income persons who are uninsured should be encouraged with public dollars or required to obtain subsidized health insurance? If so, who should bear the cost?

The consequences of the three major choices—(1) no subsidy and no mandate, (2) a subsidy but no mandate, and (3) a subsidy and a mandate—are fairly clear.[14] If the answer is neither to subsidize nor require health insurance, roughly 10–15 percent of the U.S. population will continue to have none. They will continue to be exposed to the financial disaster that typically follows a medical disaster. They will continue to forego receiving care, which presumably means they will fail to obtain some necessary care. They will continue to have accidents and get sick at the same rate, will continue to go to hospitals and doctors at the same rate, and will continue to generate the same charity-care and bad-debt costs at the same rate, which means that "uncompensated care" costs will continue to be shifted to those who do buy or provide insurance. It was estimated that in 1982 uncompensated hospital charges alone, which were largely shifted from the uninsured to the insured, amounted to $6.2 billion.[15]

If the uninsured were offered the chance to obtain subsidized health insurance, but were not required to buy it, it is probable that the percentage of uninsured would decline from 10–15 percent to perhaps 5–10 percent. Some would take advantage of the subsidy; some would not; until experiments are conducted on the effect of a voluntary subsidy plan, the impact of a voluntary subsidy approach cannot be precisely determined.[16] To the extent that such an approach does reduce the percentage of the uninsured, it will presumably reduce the problems associated with lack of insurance: exposure to economic disaster, failure to utilize health-care services, and cost shifting to those who do buy insurance.

Yet a voluntary subsidy approach has significant fiscal problems and other disadvantages. Sick and risk-averse potential uninsureds, who previously elected to use their own scarce resources to cover the entire cost of insurance, are likely to take advantage of a subsidized program in order to reduce their out-of-pocket costs, while maintaining substantially the same coverage. To the extent that these individuals simply transfer from unsubsidized to subsidized insurance, there will be no net increase in the percentage of insureds, but the program will generate a major cost.[17] The uninsureds who never bought insurance but who now join the program will also generate a major cost. Finally, unless a means is adopted for deterring employers who currently provide health-insurance coverage from terminating it, some employers may cancel or fail to renew their health-insurance plans, let their low-income employees use the subsidized government program, and take care of their high-income employees simply by raising salaries.[18]

The combined effect of these actions by uninsured persons and employers means that a voluntary subsidy program will be more expensive to the taxpayers than anticipated and will result in a major displacement of private spending with taxpayer dollars. Those individuals and companies that now already pay twice for health care (once for the uninsured whose costs are shifted to them, and once for their own health insurance) are likely under a voluntary subsidy scheme to end up paying four times for health care: first, for the uninsured who choose not to participate in the program and whose medical costs are shifted to them; second, for the uninsured who join the program and whose subsidy is borne in part by them; third, for the previously insured who cancel their own or whose bosses cancel their coverage, who then join the program, and whose subsidy is borne in part by them; and, finally, for their own health insurance.

A mandatory subsidy program, that is, one that requires all low-income persons to obtain insurance coverage and then provides them with income-adjusted subsidies, solves most of the problems discussed above. The number of uninsured persons would decline from 10–15 percent to 0–5 percent.[19] Utilization of health-care services would increase substantially. Cost shifting would largely come to an end. The great obstacle would be cost. According to a recent study by Patricia Danzon and Frank Sloan, covering the uninsured could increase public costs by as much as $8.0–14.4 billion.[20] An equally great obstacle is the issue of whether all or most of the cost of insuring employees should be imposed on their employers. Either way, a major problem arises.

If no responsibility is imposed on employers, the consequence discussed earlier will surely arise: Employers with large numbers of low-wage workers will cancel their health-insurance plans, let their low-wage employees obtain subsidized coverage from the government, and provide their high-income employees enough money to buy individual health insurance. In many cases, employers could in this manner substantially reduce their total spending associated with health care. If, on the other hand, employers' incentive to cancel health insurance is itself eliminated by imposing a mandate to pay for coverage, a different set of adverse effects occurs because of the added costs imposed on employers. As noted earlier, individual premiums can easily amount to $300–500 per year while family premiums can easily be $1,500–2,000 per year. If compelled to absorb these costs (or most of these costs), some employers will go out of business. How many? There is no way to predict. Others will lay off workers. How many lay-offs? It is impossible to tell. Other employers will simply reduce wages in order to pay for the added premium cost. How many employees will have their incomes lowered and by how much? Again, there is no way to be precise. Just as some of the proponents of an employer mandate probably underestimate its adverse effect on jobs and wages, its opponents probably exaggerate the harm. The truth is probably somewhere in between, but it is unknown.

Which choice, then, will it be—a voluntary system without subsidies, a voluntary system with subsidies, or a mandatory system with subsidies? If the latter, should employers be required to pick up the cost of their employees' coverage? As with so many of the choices confronted in this book, the answer depends ultimately on what objectives we most value. How important is it that everyone be protected against the high cost of health care? How important is it that those with low incomes not be deterred by their empty pocketbooks from obtaining the care they need? How important is it that a woman's limited economic resources not prevent her from obtaining good prenatal care? How important is it that parents' depleted bank accounts not keep them from providing their children with basic well-baby care? How important is it that people who utilize health services pay for what they use, to the extent they can afford to pay, rather than take a free ride on the insurance of others? On the other hand, how important is it that people be free to make their own decisions about how they live their lives? How important is it that they be free to decide how to dispose of their own income, rather than have government dispose of it for them? How important is it to avoid burdens on small (and some large) employers who now do not provide health-insurance coverage? How important are the businesses, jobs, and wages that would be eliminated as the price for mandated employer coverage?

In considering what choice to make, it is worthwhile taking into account some of the related choices we have already made. On our behalf, state and federal governments have already decided to require insurance in several critical areas. We require that employees be insured against the risk of work-site accidents: workers' compensation. We require that employees be insured against the risk of unemployment: unemployment compensation. We require that workers be insured so that they will have a minimal pension in old age: Social Security. We require that workers obtain old-age health insurance: Medicare. In many states, anyone who gets a driver's license must buy automobile accident insurance. A mandatory health-insurance scheme backed up by subsidies—either one in which employers were mandated to provide their employees with insurance coverage or one in which employees were required to purchase insurance, based on their ability to pay—would be in step with these other social insurance mechanisms. Why not mandate health insurance for the nonelderly, if we already mandate that workers have workplace accident insurance, unemployment insurance, old-age pensions, and old-age health insurance?

On balance, the arguments favoring a mandatory subsidy scheme appear to outweigh the arguments against it. Health insurance is essential: essential to protecting people against the catastrophic cost of major health problems, essential to encouraging the utilization of necessary care, essential to avoiding cost shifting. Yet most low-income uninsureds are unlikely to buy health insurance unless required to do so. Requiring them to forego a portion of their income in order to obtain health insurance, either through the imposition of a mandate on their employers or the imposition of a direct tax, does not seem like a harsh or unreasonable requirement in a society in which they are already required (in effect) to spend a portion of their income to buy other needed forms of insurance, such as workers' compensation, unemployment compensation, Social Security, and Medicare.

How a mandatory subsidy scheme should be implemented is an enormous question—the proper subject of a separate book. Several key points, however, should be made here.

First, the decision to require all low-income persons—or, for that matter, all Americans—to obtain health-insurance coverage does not require that a government program like Medicaid or Medicare must be established. Individuals and employers could, and arguably should, be directed to shop around for the private individual or group coverage that best suits their needs. Government could, and arguably should, be limited to (1) requiring that citizens be enrolled in the private-sector individual or group plan of their or their employers' choice, (2) ensuring that the plan meets minimal standards of adequacy, and (3) paying any subsidy deemed to be appropriate.

Second, a substantial minority of uninsured persons will not be covered by an employer mandate. Therefore the only way to obtain universal coverage is to impose a personal duty on these individuals to obtain insurance. If no employer mandate is imposed, then securing universal coverage would require that all the uninsured be subject to such a personal duty to obtain insurance. The uniqueness of a federal law that imposes an affirmative personal duty on citizens to buy insurance should be recognized forthrightly. Only two other kinds of federal legislation require Americans to act in such an affirmative way: the draft laws and the tax laws. While workers are required, from an economic perspective and to some extent from a legal perspective, to participate in government programs providing them with workplace accident insurance, unemployment compensation insurance, old-age pensions (Social Security), and old-age health insurance (Medicare), the duty is not a personal one. Technically, they can always decide not to work, thus exempting themselves from any federal mandates under these programs.

Third, because of the major disadvantages, that is, the business failures, lay-offs, and wage reductions that would result from mandating employer coverage, policymakers should seriously consider the radical approach of separating the financing—but not the purchase—of health insurance from the workplace. Specifically, the following alternatives should be explored:

- Impose a health-insurance tax on all U.S. citizens, based on their ability to pay, and deposit the tax in a national health fund;
- Give each citizen a voucher (perhaps a credit card), good for 12 months of health insurance, whose value varies with the citizen's age, sex, and (perhaps) region;
- Require unemployed citizens to purchase individual insurance that meets minimal standards;
- Require employed citizens to turn over their vouchers (as well as their unemployed spouses' vouchers and their children's vouchers) to their employers, and require the employers to purchase group insurance that meets minimal standards;
- Permit individuals and employers who can obtain plans meeting the minimal standards that cost less than the value of their vouchers to accept cash rebates equal to the difference from their insurers (whether traditional indemnity carriers, PPOs, or HMOs) as a means of inducing competition and thus holding down the aggregate cost of health care;
- Establish local "risk-sharing plans" for individuals or groups whose high risk precludes them from obtaining health-insurance coverage in the private market, require the uninsurable to join these plans, and subsidize the difference between the vouchers that the uninsurable would "pay" to these plans and the actual cost of administering the plans;

• Finally, permit insurers (whether traditional plans, PPOs, or HMOs) and the risk-sharing plans to redeem the vouchers they acquire for cash from the national health fund.

This approach would entirely replace the current system of financing health insurance primarily with employers' dollars. Employers could always choose to supplement their employees' vouchers, if they wanted to buy more generous insurance packages, but presumably most employers would elect not to do so. Yet it is not clear that employers would be hurt by this radical change. For many small employers, it would be a lesser disruption than a mandate requiring them to pay for their employees' insurance. Nor would large employers clearly suffer any economic harm (unless the cost of financing the arrangement resulted in a more than countervailing tax increase.) From the country's point of view, this approach would solve several problems at once: It would guarantee nearly universal coverage; it would require citizens to pay a fair share for their health insurance, thus eliminating cost shifting; it would preserve the private insurance marketplace; and it would promote cost constraint, as individuals and employers (who would still be involved in the actual purchasing of insurance) seek to buy the best coverage at the lowest cost. Yet it is a radical approach, which would disrupt long-established relationships and require the creation of a major new federal bureaucracy. It is only because of the serious flaws that plague the current employer-based system of financing health insurance, and the problems inherent in attempting to reform the current system, that justify taking a careful look at alternatives (there may be others) that shift the burden of financing health care to another base.

Finally, it must be understood that not all uninsureds will get covered under even a mandatory plan. People will fall through the cracks, either by accident or design. Street people, for instance, will often simply fail to show up and obtain the voucher or card or other evidence they need to buy insurance or show they have it. Criminals, drug dealers, and other individuals who do not wish their names and addresses to come to the attention of the government will intentionally steer clear. Others will refuse to participate on principle. Yet some of these people will get sick, be hospitalized, get care, and generate costs. Developing an effective method for including them in the program—and making them pay their fair share (which may be nothing, but may be a substantial sum)—is critical to the success of a mandatory program.

Of all the components of a sound system for eliminating poverty, with the possible exception of the one that offers the unemployed poor community-service jobs, the most complex component is probably that which would require low-income uninsureds (or all uninsureds) to obtain health-insurance coverage. On top of the "generic" complexities that arise from identifying eligible persons, enrolling them in the program, requiring them to pay their fair share of the program's cost, there come into play the special complexities that stem from the underlying intricacies of the health-insurance sytem, such as insurers' underwriting and rating practices. On top of all this, there is the truly knotty problem of whether to mandate employer coverage.

Yet, as with the other components of a sound system for eliminating poverty, these technical difficulties can either be overcome or mitigated. They should not be permitted to mask the fundamental issue: our willingness—or unwillingness—to ensure that all our fellow citizens obtain health insurance and to pay the accompanying price.

## NOTES

1. If this society decides, now or in the future, that increasing the incomes of the poor to the poverty line will still not provide them with enough income to meet most of their basic needs, then the major policy response should be to use the methods described here (i.e., direct cash transfers for those who cannot work or whom we do not expect to work, community-service jobs for those who can work but are unemployed, and wage supplements for those already working) to increase the poor's disposable income to whatever alternative income level is deemed sufficient to allow them to meet their basic needs.

2. Even such utility costs can often be leveled off by enrolling in expense-averaging plans offered by the utility companies.

3. U.S. Congress, House, Select Committee on Children, Youth, and Families, "Families and Child Care: Improving the Options," December 28, 1984, pp. 17–18.

4. U.S. Bureau of the Census, "Who's Minding the Kids? Child Care Arrangements: Winter 1984–85," Series P–70, No. 9, pp. 10, 26.

5. Margaret B. Sulvetta and Katherine Swartz, National Health Policy Forum, "The Uninsured and Uncompensated Care: A Chartbook," June 1986, p. 3.

6. Deborah J. Chollet, Employee Benefit Research Institute, "The Erosion of Health Insurance Coverage Among the Non-Elderly Population: Public Policy Issues and Options." Statement before the Committee on Small Business, U.S. House of Representatives, May 6, 1987, p. 1.

7. Ibid., pp. 3–4 and Table 2.

8. Robert Wood Johnson Foundation, "Access to Health Care In the United States: Results of a 1986 Survey." Special Report Number Two, 1987, pp. 6–7.

9. Ibid.

10. See, for example, Robert Wood Johnson Foundation, "Access to Health Care," p. 9, for a discussion of the different estimates reached by different

surveyors and the extent to which such differences can be explained by different surveying techniques:

11. See, for example, Sulvetta and Swartz, "The Uninsured," pp. 6, 7, and 17; and Chollet, supra n. 6 at pp. 5–8.

12. Chollet, "Erosion of Health Insurance Coverage," p. 10.

13. Health-insurance premiums vary widely, depending on age, sex, location, and other factors. $500–1,000/year for individual coverage and $1,500–2,000/year for family coverage are typical prices, but any single person's or family's actual premium could be much lower or much higher.

14. There is technically a fourth choice: no subsidy but a mandate. Because many in the two largest groups, that is, low-income individuals and small employers—upon whom an unsubsidized mandate would be imposed would suffer such severe economic loss as a result, this alternative has not been considered a realistic one by most of the experts and policymakers engaged in the debate over providing the uninsured with health insurance.

15. Sulvetta and Swartz, "The Uninsured," p. 27.

16. Two states have begun to explore this approach. In 1987, Washington enacted a program that offers low-income uninsureds the opportunity to obtain subsidized group insurance. The same year, the Wisconsin legislature enacted—but the governor vetoed—five pilot projects that would have offered uninsureds below 175 percent of the poverty line the opportunity to obtain subsidized individual or group coverage.

17. It is theoretically possible to prohibit those who have already purchased individual insurance from participating in a voluntary subsidy program. This raises, however, both equity and practical problems. The equity problem is this: Why should a low-income person barely above poverty, who previously opted to buy insurance, be denied a subsidy, when a low-income person further above the poverty line, who chose not to buy insurance, is allowed to participate? The practical problem is, How can one effectively deter an individual who has insurance from canceling coverage or simply not renewing it, in order to take advantage of the program? These problems are so enormous that it seems unlikely that such a prohibition would ever be instituted or effectively enforced.

18. The problem of how to deter employers who currently provide coverage from canceling their plans is probably the biggest obstacle that faces a voluntary subsidy program. One possible solution would be to impose a heavy tax on all employers, for example, $1,500 per employee, which would be reduced if the employer were unprofitable or marginally profitable (as determined according to some arbitrary and inevitably imperfect formula) and eliminated if the employer provided all employees with health-insurance benefits that met a certain standard. This approach would, in theory, spare employers who truly cannot afford to pay for their workers' health insurance but deter employers who can afford to pay from canceling coverage by taxing the cancellation at a rate that roughly approximates the health-insurance costs they were previously incurring. It is doubtful, however, whether such a scheme would be effective. The means open to an employer for evading it by juggling expenses and income so as to appear unprofitable on paper are too easy, and the cost of enforcing it would be substantial. More to the point, a "voluntary"

program that depends heavily on a sanction designed to compel employers to provide health insurance no longer deserves to be called voluntary.

19. It would, of course, decline nearly to zero, if all uninsured persons, regardless of income, were required to obtain health-insurance coverage. Should high-income uninsureds also be required to buy insurance or should they be allowed to self-insure? That is, should the mandate to buy health insurance be universal or not? The problems that lack of insurance causes—exposure to economic catastrophe, lower utilization of health services, and cost shifting to the insured—are less serious in the case of high-income uninsureds, and thus the argument for compelling them to buy insurance loses much of its force. On the other hand, these problems will persist to some extent even for a high-income group. A high-income family that has a child in a neonatal intensive-care unit for four months, for instance, will incur costs so enormous that even its greater income and assets may be insufficient to prohibit insolvency, cost shifting to others, or both. There is also the objection that requirements imposed on citizens by the state should, both as an ethical and legal matter, fall on all citizens, regardless of income. On balance, if a requirement is to be imposed at all, the argument in favor of its imposition on all persons seems the strongest. If all were made subject to the requirement, the principal effect would be on the number of uninsureds; the rest of the pros and cons would remain essentially the same.

20. Patricia M. Danzon and Frank A. Sloan, "Covering the Uninsured: How Much Would It Cost?" Nashville, TN: Vanderbilt Institute for Public Policy Studies, 1987, pp. 7–12.

# 12
## The Cost of Justice

Eliminating poverty will cost a lot of money, but the cost is less than you think.

At the same time that the Census Bureau measures how many poor there are in the United States, it also calculates the poor's "income deficit."

> Income deficit is the difference between the total income of families and unrelated individuals below the poverty level, and their respective poverty thresholds. In computing the income deficit, families reporting a net income loss are assigned zero dollars and for such cases the deficit is equal to the poverty threshold. The measure provides an estimate of the amount which would be required to raise the incomes of all poor families and unrelated individuals to their respective poverty thresholds. The income deficit is thus a measure of the degree of impoverishment of a family or unrelated individual.[1]

Table 10 sets forth the Census Bureau's findings as to how much money (in constant 1984 dollars) it would have taken during the last quarter-century to raise the U.S. poor to the poverty line:[2]

The trend in the income deficit tells a disturbing story. From 1960 to 1969 the income deficit declined rapidly, and from 1969 to 1974 it continued the downward trend at a slower pace. The smallest income deficit occurred in 1974: $27.936 billion (in constant 1984 dollars). From that nadir, the income deficit has climbed back to near its original 1960 level of $48.632 billion. In 1983, the income deficit actually exceeded the 1960 level by several hundred million dollars. For 1984 through 1986, the income deficit sank back to the $46–47 billion range,

**Table 10**
**Aggregate Income Deficit, 1960–86**

(constant 1984 dollars)

Aggregate Deficit

(billions)

| Year | Unrelated Individuals | Families | Total |
|------|------|------|------|
| 1960 | $13.303 | $35.329 | $48.632 |
| 1965 | $11.441 | $26.773 | $38.214 |
| 1968 | $10.148 | $19.264 | $29.412 |
| 1969 | $10.913 | $18.142 | $29.055 |
| 1970 | $10.957 | $19.980 | $30.937 |
| 1971 | $11.191 | $19.671 | $30.862 |
| 1972 | $10.957 | $18.908 | $29.865 |
| 1973 | $10.192 | $17.796 | $27.988 |
| 1974 | $ 9.101 | $18.835 | $27.936 |
| 1975 | $10.566 | $20.478 | $31.044 |
| 1976 | $11.225 | $19.286 | $30.511 |
| 1977 | $10.620 | $19.814 | $30.434 |
| 1978 | $11.142 | $19.917 | $31.059 |
| 1979 | $12.278 | $21.076 | $33.354 |
| 1980 | $13.097 | $24.354 | $37.451 |
| 1981 | $14.801 | $27.467 | $42.268 |
| 1982 | $14.678 | $31.497 | $46.175 |
| 1983 | $15.797 | $33.159 | $48.956 |
| 1984 | $15.029 | $31.311 | $46.340 |
| 1985 | $15.352 | $30.817 | $46.169 |
| 1986 | $16.164 | $30.463 | $46.627 |

where it seems to have become stuck. While the percentage of U.S. poor has thus declined from over 22 percent in 1960 to under 14 percent in 1986, and while the number of poor persons has also declined somewhat from nearly 40 billion to under 33 million over that same period, the cost of raising the poor to the poverty line remains virtually unchanged a quarter of a century later. In nominal 1986 dollars, 1986 being the last year for which data were available when this book was being written, the income deficit stood at $49.211 billion.[3]

Whether constant or nominal dollars are used, these annual aggregate income deficits seem enormous. Their magnitude cannot be well understood, however, until they are placed in some kind of perspective. There is no obviously "correct" perspective for viewing such figures, but one framework that might be useful would be to compare each year's income deficit with that year's federal budget. How much would

**Table 11**
**Aggregate Income Deficit versus Federal Budget Outlays, 1960–86**

(constant 1984 dollars)

| Year | Income Deficit (billions) | Federal Outlays (billions) | Deficit as Percentage Of Outlays |
|------|---------------------------|----------------------------|----------------------------------|
| 1960 | $48.632 | $285.109 | 17.06 |
| 1965 | $38.214 | $334.572 | 11.42 |
| 1968 | $29.412 | $465.223 | 6.32 |
| 1969 | $29.055 | $448.858 | 6.47 |
| 1970 | $30.937 | $449.335 | 6.89 |
| 1971 | $30.862 | $455.047 | 6.78 |
| 1972 | $29.865 | $481.470 | 6.20 |
| 1973 | $27.988 | $467.943 | 5.98 |
| 1974 | $27.936 | $457.495 | 6.11 |
| 1975 | $31.044 | $524.801 | 5.92 |
| 1976 | $30.511 | $551.565 | 5.53 |
| 1977 | $30.434 | $563.027 | 5.41 |
| 1978 | $31.059 | $587.363 | 5.29 |
| 1979 | $33.354 | $577.275 | 5.78 |
| 1980 | $37.451 | $600.645 | 6.24 |
| 1981 | $42.268 | $620.070 | 6.82 |
| 1982 | $46.175 | $639.444 | 7.22 |
| 1983 | $48.956 | $689.373 | 7.10 |
| 1984 | $46.340 | $685.968 | 6.76 |
| 1985 | $46.169 | $743.064 | 6.21 |
| 1986 | $46.627 | $763.974 | 6.10 |

raising the poor up to the poverty line in various years during the last quarter-century have cost, compared to the outlays of the federal government during the same years? Table 11—again using constant 1984 dollars for both the income deficit and federal outlays—provides the comparison.[4]

The income deficit as a percentage of federal outlays, after declining greatly from 1960 to 1968, has remained a fairly constant (5–7 percent) proportion of on-budget federal expenditures ever since. The cost of eliminating poverty would be an even lower percentage of federal expenditures if Social Security—which is here treated as off-budget—and other off-budget federal expenditures (which in 1986 totaled $173.360 billion in constant 1984 dollars and represented nearly 23 percent of on-budget outlays) were taken into account.

Another way to place the aggregate income deficit in perspective is to compare it with the cost of other major federal programs. How much does raising the poor up to the poverty line compare with the cost of

**Table 12**
**Aggregate Income Deficit versus Other Federal Direct and Tax Expenditures, 1986**

(actual 1986 dollars)

| Item | Amount (billions) | Amount as Percentage of Income deficit |
|------|------------------|----------------------------------------|
| Income Deficit | $49.211 | 100 |
| AFDC | 9.375 | 19 |
| Food Stamps | 12.397 | 25 |
| Medicaid | 24.903 | 51 |
| Low-income housing | 11.367 | 23 |
| Social Security | | |
|     Disability Insurance | 19.565 | 40 |
|     Retirement Insurance | 134.145 | 273 |
|     Survivors Insurance | 39.997 | 81 |
|     All | 193.707 | 394 |
| Medicare | | |
|     Hospital Insurance (Part A) | 49.000 | 100 |
|     Medical Insurance (Part B) | 25.146 | 51 |
|     All | 74.146 | 151 |
| Commodity price supports | 25.841 | 53 |
| Tax expenditures: | | |
|     --Deduction of home mortgage interest and property taxes | 39.265 | 80 |
|     --Deduction of other non-business taxes | 23.965 | 49 |
|     --Deduction of charitable contributions | 15.175 | 31 |
| National defense | 265.636 | 540 |
| Interest on national debt | 190.166 | 386 |

providing the elderly a minimal pension (Social Security) or health insurance (Medicare), the cost of supporting agricultural prices (crop subsidies), or the cost of subsidizing home ownership (home interest and property tax deduction)? Table 12 compares the cost of eliminating poverty in 1986 with the direct expenditures and "tax expenditures" (i.e., foregone revenue) made by the federal government in Fiscal Year 1986 for a number of well-known programs.[5]

The purpose of comparing the aggregate income deficit with the total federal budget and some of its key components is not to demonstrate that eliminating poverty can be accomplished cheaply. An inexpensive solution, regrettably, is not possible. Rather, the purpose of the comparison is to demonstrate that, while the cost of eliminating poverty is great, it is not as enormous as some may think. It would cost substantially less to eliminate poverty than it now costs to run the Medicare program. Eliminating poverty would cost far less than Social Security, defense spending, or the interest on the national debt. In short, while the cost of raising every American to the poverty line is huge, it is not unthinkable. The U.S. government already incurs comparable or greater expenditures for some of its current programs.

So far in this chapter, the official income deficit and the cost of eliminating poverty have been used interchangeably. While it may theoretically be possible to spend no more than the income deficit in order to eliminate poverty, in the world of government programs the cost of eliminating poverty will be the sum of the income deficit plus the cost of the administrative mechanisms chosen to accomplish the task. Depending on the policies chosen as the means of eliminating poverty, the cost of those administrative mechanisms will vary.

It has been recommended here that eliminating the poverty of those who cannot work, or whose age exempts them from work, should be accomplished simply by increasing or augmenting their SSI or Social Security payments. Such a simple cash-transfer program should not impose significant administrative costs.

As for those who are poor because they can work but cannot find jobs, it has been recommended here that they be offered community-service jobs. This component of eliminating poverty will be the most administratively complex and will therefore generate the largest administrative costs. Much of the work that needs to be done can be accomplished at no cost to the federal government. For instance, community organizations' initial development of useful community-service projects, an activity that will require a great deal of work, need not cost the federal government anything. Eventually, however, after such projects are proposed for funding, they must be reviewed with a fair degree of care; the better projects must be selected; and the projects that receive funds must be monitored and held accountable. Private organizations, local governments, state governments, and federal agencies can be asked to absorb some of the associated administrative costs within their current budgets, but the federal government will probably be obliged to increase spending to administer properly a well-run community-service-jobs program.

Finally, as regards the poor who already work, it is likely that administrative costs can be kept to a bare minimum. The mechanisms for operating the federal Earned Income Tax Credit are already in place. Modifying the EITC so that it provides larger families a higher credit will impose some minor administrative costs on the U.S. Department of the Treasury. Making advanced payment of a modified EITC "mandatory"—that is, requiring all employees who are eligible to apply for it, or requiring all employers (regardless of employees' application) to provide it—would also generate some minor administrative costs. All in all, however, the EITC can be retooled as a comprehensive wage-supplement program at relatively little cost.

If, as in 1986, the income deficit remains at approximately $49 billion, it would be reasonable to conclude that the total cost of eliminating poverty in the United States—including the cost of the money that goes directly to the poor in the form of cash transfers, wages, and wage supplements, plus the cost of administration—could be held to $50 billion. An extra $1 billion for administration, a sum roughly equal to 10 percent of total AFDC payments made to states by the federal government, seems more than generous.

As the preceding chapter suggested, while increasing the income of the poor up to the poverty line will allow the once-poor, like other nonpoor low-income people, to meet most of their basic needs without additional help from government, the low-income population's income will not be sufficient in most cases to allow them to meet two special needs: day care and health insurance. If it is assumed, as recommended in the last chapter, that all persons below 175 percent of the poverty line are offered programs that permit them, based on their ability to pay, to purchase day care and health insurance, what will be the extra cost to government? Compared to the calculation of the total (direct and administrative) cost of eliminating poverty, the calculation of the cost of day-care and health-insurance subsidies is far more complex. A host of potential assumptions must be considered and weighed. Depending on the assumptions chosen, the cost estimates may vary enormously.

Can eligible persons be reasonably asked to contribute 5 percent, 10 percent, or 15 percent of their income toward the cost of day care and health insurance? Or must a reasonable contribution be a sliding percentage of income—for example, 1 percent for persons between 100 percent and 125 percent of the poverty line, 5 percent for persons between 125 percent and 150 percent of the poverty line, and so forth? Should not only income but assets be counted in deciding how much low-income individuals should be asked to contribute to the purchase of their own day care and health insurance? What should the income cut-off be—175 percent of the poverty line as suggested here? 200 percent of the poverty line? or some point in between? Finally, what assumption should be made about the price of day care and health insurance? Should regional price differences be taken into account or should a single national set of prices be established? These and myriad other questions must be answered in order to develop meaningful cost projections.

At this point, therefore, the most that can be said is that, in addition to spending roughly $50 billion to eliminate poverty itself, the federal government may have to spend up to another $25 billion to subsidize the low-income population's purchase of adequate day care and health insurance. The total cost of both eliminating poverty in the United States and affording all of the low-income population the ability to take care of their children properly and obtain adequate health care may therefore be on the order of $75 billion.

The preceding calculation assumes that the cash payments that impoverished SSI and AFDC recipients now get from the states—$2.496 billion in the case of state SSI supplementation payments and $7.254 billion comprising the states' share of AFDC benefit payments—would continue to be paid by the states.[6] Only if poor people continued to get those sums can the income deficit be assumed to stand at about $49 billion, and will it be possible to raise the poor to the poverty line for $50 billion. The survival of state SSI supplementation and state involvement in an AFDC program, however, are contrary to the argument advanced in this book. Consistent with the notion presented here that the current set of welfare programs should be abolished and replaced by a nationally uniform three-part program for directly eliminating poverty by providing cash, community-service jobs, and wage supplements—and consistent with the concept (assumed implicitly thus far, but to be discussed explicitly later in this chapter) that the financial responsibility for such a three-part program for eliminating poverty should be vested in the federal government—state SSI and AFDC expenditures ought to be terminated and the roughly $10 billion in question ought then to be provided to the same poor people by means of the new cash, jobs, and wage-supplement programs financed by Washington. This transfer of fiscal responsibility would raise the federal cost of eliminating poverty from $50 to $60 billion, and it would raise the total federal cost of eliminating poverty plus providing low-income persons with subsidized day care and health insurance from $75 to $85 billion.

It is important to understand that these extremely crude estimates— $50 billion to eliminate poverty prior to a phase-out of state SSI supplementation and AFDC participation, $60 billion to eliminate poverty after those state expenditures are absorbed by the federal government, $25 billion for subsidized day care and health insurance, $85 billion total—represent *gross* federal expenditures. They do not constitute estimates for *net* federal spending, that is, the actual extra cost to the federal government. Eliminating poverty, providing low-income people with day care, and ensuring that everyone has health insurance will permit both state and federal governments to repeal a great many current programs that deal with the symptoms of poverty. The net federal cost of eliminating poverty is the cost that remains after subtracting from the gross federal cost of directly eliminating poverty (plus providing low-income persons with subsidized day care and health insurance) the amounts that need no longer be spent to deal with poverty's symptoms.

In some cases, the elimination of poverty will automatically cancel these symptom-oriented programs, since they require beneficiaries to be below the poverty line in order to function. In other cases, eliminating poverty will not automatically cancel the programs, but it will undermine the initial rationale of a program's existence.[7] In such cases, of course, termination of the program will require policymakers actually to decide that, since the historical underpinning of the program has disappeared, the program should likewise disappear. Since many such programs have by now built up powerful constituencies, it can, of course, be expected that, notwithstanding the lack of a continuing need for certain programs, their champions will continue to advocate their existence, and some of them will unavoidably survive. If poverty were eliminated and appropriate day care and health insurance provided, however, they could all justifiably be repealed. If that occurred, the *net* cost of eliminating poverty would be far less than $85 billion.

Exactly which current federal programs, representing how many billions of dollars, could be terminated? AFDC and its $9.374 billion worth of grants to states would, of course, be eliminated, but that sum would have to be plowed back into the cash payments, community-service jobs, and wage supplements provided to poor people, simply to permit poverty to be eliminated, day care subsidized, and health care provided—all for an additional $85 billion. Repealing AFDC and reinvesting the money is simply a wash; it offers no possibility for reducing the net federal cost. What we are looking for are poverty-related programs whose termination, unlike AFDC's, might pay for the $85 billion. Table 13 presents a menu of opportunities as of federal Fiscal Year 1986.[8]

Let us assume, just to have a good round number, that the federal programs that respond to poverty's symptoms total $75 billion. If all these programs were repealed, the net cost of eliminating poverty and providing subsidized day care and health insurance could thus be limited to perhaps $10 billion: $85 billion gross cost, minus $75 billion in symptom-oriented programs, equals $10 billion that still needs to be found.

Numerous questions and objections can, of course, be raised about the approach suggested here for paying for the elimination of poverty and the provision to low-income people of subsidized day care and health insurance. It is not possible to answer them all here, but it may be useful to consider the more important ones before taking up the toughest fiscal question: After most of the $85 billion price tag is paid by repealing $75 billion (or some lesser amount) worth of symptom-

**Table 13**
**Federal Poverty-Related Programs, FY 1986**

| Department & Program | Expenditures |
|---|---|
| | (billions) |
| Department of Agriculture | |
|     Child Nutrition Programs | 3.631 |
|     Commodity Distributions | 1.632 |
|     Food Donations | 0.205 |
|     Food Stamps | 12.397 |
|     Special Milk Program | 0.014 |
|     Special Supplemental Food Program (WIC) | 1.575 |
|     Temporary Emergency Food Assistance | 0.049 |
| Department of Commerce | |
|     Economic Development Assistance Programs | 0.237 |
| Department of Education | |
|     Compensatory Education for Disadvantaged | 3.390 |
|     Education for the Handicapped | 1.596 |
|     Special Programs and Populations | 0.507 |
| Department of Health and Social Services | |
|     Alcohol, Drug Abuse, &Mental Health | 0.494 |
|     Community Services | 0.374 |
|     Family Social Services | 0.843 |
|     Human Development Services | 1.838 |
|     Low-Income Home Energy Assistance | 2.006 |
|     Medicaid | 24.903 |
|     Social Services Block Grant | 2.702 |
| Department of Housing and Urban Development | |
|     Community Development | 3.326 |
|     Low Rent Housing Operating Assistance | 1.181 |
|     Public Housing | 2.712 |
|     Section 8 Payments | 7.430 |
|     Urban Development Action Grants | 0.461 |
| Department of Labor | |
|     Job Training Partnership Act | 3.019 |
| TOTAL | $76.522 |

oriented programs, where does the remaining $10 billion (or larger amount) come from?

What happens to indigent nursing-home recipients if Medicaid is repealed? Although AFDC recipients (dependent children under 21 and their parents) account for nearly 70 percent of all Medicaid recipients, the aged, blind, and disabled account for almost 75 percent of current Medicaid payments. Like the AFDC recipients whose health-care needs are almost entirely acute and preventive, the aged, blind, and disabled enrolled in Medicaid also have substantial acute- and preventive-care needs, and therefore on behalf of both groups Medicaid programs allocate well over 50 percent of their payments to hospitals, doctors, pharmacies, family-planning centers, early-screening programs, and other health-care providers. These acute- and preventive-care payments, which now total over $21 billion, would be taken over by the new subsidized health-insurance plan discussed in the prior chapter, and because the low-income participants in that program would pay premiums based on their financial ability, the cost to the government would be less than $21 billion. The nearly 45 percent of current Medicaid expenditures, adding up to over $16 billion, which pay the nursing-home bills of primarily aged and disabled persons who live in skilled- and intermediate-care facilities, would not be taken over by the new health-insurance plan. How is this need—this responsibility—to be met?[9]

The answer is that, because of the elimination of state SSI supplementation (state cost in federal Fiscal Year 1986, $2.5 billion), because of the elimination of state responsibility for an AFDC program that has been repealed (state cost in federal FY 1986, $8.2 billion in benefits and administration), and most important, because of the repeal of Medicaid itself (state cost in federal FY 1986, $19.7 billion), the states will have over $30 billion in unencumbered money at their disposal to provide their citizens with nursing-home care. It should also be noted that, thanks to the elimination of poverty nursing-home recipients will be able to contribute more to the cost of their own nursing-home care. Subsidizing low-income persons' stays in long-term-care settings may therefore cost the states less than the $16 billion (in federal FY 1986 dollars) it now costs. The $30 billion in "freed up" SSI supplementation, AFDC, and Medicaid funds should not only be sufficient to permit the states to meet the long-term-care needs of their citizens (or, rather, to meet those needs in the same inadequate way they are currently being met) but would provide the states with enough extra revenue to allocate funds to new purposes or lower taxes.

What about all the other needs—for nutrition, housing, social services, mental-health services, alcohol- and drug-abuse treatment, disadvantaged education, and so forth—that are addressed by the federal programs slated for elimination? How will they be met? Part of the answer is that, with poverty eliminated, most of those needs will disappear. Nonpoor low-income people will generally have enough cash to meet their own demands for protein and other nutrition. They will generally have enough cash to rent adequate housing. Their need to be cared for by middle-class caretakers will diminish enormously.

It is unrealistic to expect, of course, that a low-income population—raised, yes, above the poverty line, but not raised very much above the poverty line—will not continue to have some real needs in the areas of nutrition, housing, education, social services, and so forth. The remaining part of the answer is that, with poverty eliminated, local and state government can properly be entrusted with the responsibility for meeting the nonpoor low-income population's needs that remain. How is this so?

Once poverty is eliminated, the fiscal burden on local and state government will greatly diminish, and their fiscal capacity to meet that burden will greatly improve. Compared to the massive social needs of a poor *plus* near-poor low-income population, the residual social needs of a nonpoor (only) low-income population will be far fewer. Local and state governments' ability to foot the bill for these residual needs will also improve, since they will be collecting significantly more tax revenue from the once-poor (most likely through increased property and sales taxes) in addition to whatever they would normally collect from the rest of their populations. Furthermore, as just noted, some of the $30 billion "freed up" to the states by the elimination of state SSI supplementation and the repeal of AFDC and Medicaid, after the bulk of that sum is reallocated to provide long-term-care subsidies, may also be added to the states' coffers. Given the substantially reduced level of need and the substantially increased capacity to meet it, it is reasonable to expect that local and state governments can be entrusted to do the job.

We now come to the toughest question. After the $85 billion federal cost of eliminating poverty and providing subsidized day care and health insurance is largely met by eliminating up to $75 billion in federal symptom-oriented programs, where will the remaining $10 billion or more come from? The answer must be, by eliminating federal programs of lower priority, or by raising federal taxes, or some combination. In the end, poverty in this country probably cannot be eliminated (and the associated problems of adequate day care and health insurance cannot be dealt with) unless resources outside the poverty sector are tapped. Regardless of how many symptom-oriented programs should be eliminated on the merits—even if the great political support that some of them enjoy posed no obstacle to their repeal—it must be recognized clearly that to eliminate poverty directly and provide low-income people with appropriate day care and health insurance, revenues generated outside the poverty sector will most likely be required. This is not the place to pursue a detailed discussion of all the alternatives for generating such funds, but the broad choices should be made clear.

- Existing federal direct-expenditure programs of lower priority (however that is defined) could be eliminated.

- Existing federal tax-expenditure programs of lower priority (however that is determined) could be repealed.

- New tax revenues could be raised.

There are, regrettably, only so many ways to come up with money. Except for printing it, they all involve taking dollars from something or somebody else. The question then becomes, From what or whom should the cash be taken?

Proponents of that most elusive of concepts, "sound public policy," would generally agree that, whenever any worthwhile government program must be funded, the preferable route would be to defund some unworthwhile government program. Some obvious candidates come to mind. Commodity price-support programs, which cost $25.8 billion in federal FY 1986, that year provided two-thirds of U.S. farmers with nothing, gave one-fifteenth of farmers (with annual sales of over $100,000) almost 70 percent of the money, and represented an average payment of more than $16,000 per farm family.[10] The $39.3 billion "outlay equivalent" in FY 1986, resulting from the deduction for mortgage payments and property taxes, provides subsidies to millions of high-income people—with the subsidy increasing as their income increases—who surely need no subsidy to buy a home. There are many, many more of these direct-expenditure or tax-expenditure programs, which, usually in the name of promoting the national defense or helping the ordinary middle-class family, channel billions to well-to-do individuals and corporations who need and deserve no help. While the Tax Reform Act of 1986 got rid of a lot of them, many more still remain buried in the federal budget or tax code. There is hardly universal agreement about the worthlessness of these programs, however, and in any case they command great political support. Yet, if poverty is to be eliminated in the United States, the modification or repeal of these questionable programs will have to be faced. The money has to come from somewhere. There is no escape from confronting the choices.

Let us now turn—really for the first time—to the issue of the different roles of state and federal governments. Among the other reasons for doing so, an examination of this issue may lead to a solution to the funding problem.

Throughout this book, it has been assumed—and, in the last chapter, it was made explicit—that the programmatic and fiscal responsibility for eliminating poverty, as well as providing day care and health insurance, lies with the federal government. This assumption rests in part on the not unreasonable conviction that the states will never undertake so expensive a task (both because state policymakers believe they cannot afford it and because, even if they thought they could afford it, they believe they should not move ahead unilaterally in a matter that makes their states "magnets" for poor people), and therefore only the federal government can. The assumption of federal primacy made in this book also rests on a particular view about the relative responsibility of the state and federal governments in our constitutional system. It would be well at this point to articulate that view, since it provides a potential alternative solution to the funding problem.

The history of the United States since its independence has been in large measure the history of sorting out the relationship between the states and the federal government. The turmoil that followed the American Revolution made it clear to most contemporary observers (or, at least, to most in the political elite) that states had too much power in certain areas and that the central government, operating under the Articles of Confederation, was too weak in certain areas. The Constitutional Convention of 1787 was, in effect, a grand effort to redefine, or realign, or sort out which level of government should do what.

We are accustomed to think of the accomplishments of the convention that did not involve "sorting out" as the most important features of the U.S. Constitution. The design of a system of checks and balances (i.e., the distribution of legislative, executive, and judicial powers among three branches of government); the creation of different sources of federal power by authorizing districts of equal population to choose the House of Representatives, states to choose the Senate, and a national electoral college to choose the president; and, based on the convention's unstated promise but left to the first Congress to achieve, a people's bill of rights against arbitrary federal power—these achievements stand out as the great features of the Constitution. The thirteen state constitutions, however, already embodied these concepts of government when the convention met. There was broad agreement on their merits. They needed only to be borrowed, reshaped, and adapted to a new context when they were incorporated in the U.S. Constitution.

The problem that the states had not internally solved (and could not internally solve)—in fact, the principal problem that led to the calling of the convention—was the proper division of responsibilities between the state governments and the national government. It was widely agreed that most of the things that government can do should be left to the states. Yet it was also widely held that certain powers that the states were then exercising, for example, regulation of interstate commerce, had to be shifted to the national government. And it was generally felt that certain of the powers that the national government exercised, for example, conduct of foreign policy, needed to be greatly strengthened.

Yet how, exactly, should the new balance be struck between the historical preeminence of the individual states and the need for a stronger national government? Precisely which functions should be prohibited to the states, and which functions should be indisputably vested in the national government? How, to avoid future controversy, should the new division of responsibility be worded? These are sorting-out questions. If we have overlooked the fact that the greatest challenge facing the convention was how to sort out the respective roles of state and federal government, it is perhaps because the sorting-out decisions that the convention made and embodied in the Constitution were relatively less controversial for the founders (probably because so many of them agreed on the outcome) or perhaps because the consensus reached is now so familiar to us.

For better or worse, the authors of the Constitution ended up defining the national government's powers very broadly. During the last century, and particularly since Franklin Roosevelt's first presidential term (1933–37), it has become clear that there are few functions of government that the federal government cannot legitimately exercise under the Interstate Commerce Clause, the General Welfare Clause, and its taxing authority. So, at least, the Supreme Court has ruled with increasing frequency. We now take it for granted that if the federal government wants to engage in a particular kind of domestic activity, it almost certainly has the power to do so.

Seldom, however, have the states been denied authority to run their own programs parallel to programs that the broad language of the Constitution permits the federal government to operate. The conflict— or, more accurately, the overlap—between the powers left to state government and those vested in the federal government is the heart of the sorting-out problem we face today, that is, the failure to sort out the state and federal governments' respective responsibilities on any rational basis.

Since under the Constitution states were left with broad authority to deal with a host of problems and undertake thousands of possible forms of government activity, they have increasingly responded to public pressure to address those problems by enacting thousands of laws and setting up hundreds of programs. From crime to education to health to transportation, states have used their retained authority to regulate and spend. Yet, because the Constitution has been broadly construed to permit the federal government to act in virtually all of the same areas, it has also increasingly responded to public pressure by addressing the same wide range of problems by enacting laws and setting up programs of its own. From crime to education to health to transportation, the federal government has used its own authority to regulate and spend.

The result is a crazy quilt of state and federal programs—a random patchwork—in which both state and federal governments are enacting, administering, and financing, side by side, dozens of programs in the same areas. To the public, it's bewildering. Who's in charge of what? Who is responsible—and thus, who is accountable—for which decisions, which failures, and which successes? There are sometimes answers to these questions, but the average citizen cannot penetrate the maze of overlapping state and federal laws and programs to find the answers. For that matter, state legislators, governors, members of Congress, and presidents of the United States often have difficulty in penetrating the thicket.

As the simultaneous expansion of both state and federal programs produced an increasingly complex crazy quilt of overlapping and sometimes conflicting policies, laws, regulations, and programs, voices of protest began to be raised. Why is it not possible to develop a simpler division of responsibilities between the state and federal governments? Why can the sorting out of duties not be more coherent and rational? The critics of the status quo did not question—as in the 1930s or 1960s—the right of the federal government to do what it is was doing. Nor did the critics of the late 1970s and early 1980s, such as Arizona Governor Bruce Babbitt, Senator Pete Domenici, and Representative David Stockman (later director of the Office of Management and Budget) revive the old argument that various activities of the federal government should not be engaged in because such activities were unnecessary.[11]

Rather, the new critics of the status quo maintained that, notwithstanding the right of both levels of government to carry out virtually every kind of program, an effort should be made to distinguish the functional areas of government that were most suitable for state government from those most suitable for the federal government. Then, based on this classification, the functions that are most fitting for state government to handle should be carried out only by state government, and those functions most fitting for the federal government to handle should be carried out only by the federal government. In short, rather than each level of government doing (almost) everything, let us simplify the overall structure by having states do 100 percent of some things and the federal government do 100 percent of the rest.[12]

The advocates of this realignment of state and federal responsibilities did not always agree on exactly how the roles of state government and the federal government should be sorted out. When the theory got down to details, questions as to which specific program should be handed over to which level of government became tough to answer. Nonetheless, the critics did manage to achieve a surprising degree of consensus that the sorting out should occur in a particular way. Specifically, state government should assume responsibility for most service programs (e.g., police and fire protection, education, transportation, social services, etc.) and the corresponding federal service programs repealed; the federal government should assume full responsibility for income-security programs (e.g., cash assistance) and income-substitute programs (e.g., Medicaid).[13]

Why this particular realignment? Most of those favoring the services-to-the-states/income-to-the-feds solution have not spelled out explicitly or in great detail why they think this particular form of sorting out makes the most sense. To the extent that the proponents have outlined their reasons for the service/income division of labor, however, they fairly consistently set forth or implied the following lines of thought.

First, problems whose dimensions are not significantly affected by the federal government's management of the national economy should be left to the states. At the same time, problems whose magnitude is a direct effect of federal economic policy should be handled by the federal government. In colloquial terms, this argument might be expressed as follows: if you didn't break it, you didn't buy it—but if you broke it, you bought it.

Since service programs—for example, what kind of education policy to have or what kind of transportation system to build—are not directly linked to the vigor of the national economy, it is reasonable to expect that on the whole, the states can effectively handle these problems, regardless of whether the nation's economy is doing poorly or well. The critical policy issues that must be resolved and the costs of providing the services are linked far more to local factors (growth in the school-age population, preference for highways or mass transit) than to whether the federal government's economic, fiscal, and monetary policies are failing or working. There is, therefore, no compelling need to help states to meet their service needs with federal dollars in order to hold them harmless against the vagaries of federal economic policy.

On the other hand, the problems addressed by income and income-substitute programs, such as poverty and unemployment, are intimately connected to the success of the national economy. States can neither effectively address the key policy issues raised by such problems nor finance solutions for them, because the problems themselves fluctuate greatly with the condition of the national economy and the success of national policies. Individuals whose need for income and work is shaped by the failure or success of national economic policies should look for help from the makers of those policies—the federal government.

Second, proponents of the service/income assignment of responsibility believe that problems whose solution is not perceived as costing an unreasonable amount, and whose cost of solving does not vary greatly from state to state, should be left to the states. In contrast, problems whose cost is perceived as crushing, and whose cost of solving varies widely from state to state, should be handled by the federal government. In colloquial terms, if it's small and even, let the states do it, if it's big and uneven, give it to the feds.

Service programs, while costly, are not generally viewed by either state or federal policymakers as so costly that individual states, regardless of their fiscal capacity, cannot be expected to bear the expense. States bore almost all of the cost of police and fire protection, education, transportation, social services, and so forth before the 1960s; since then they have continued to bear most of the cost. It would not be unreasonable, therefore, to ask them to absorb the entire cost.

Income or income-substitute programs, on the other hand, are perceived by policymakers as extremely costly. Poverty and unemployment in the United States remain widespread. Yet most people, including the policymakers, are unwilling to let the poor—poor children in particular—live in utter destitution. The fiscal effect of meeting the commitment to help the poor, however, is perceived to be an enormous one. Furthermore, poverty and unemployment are unevenly distributed among the states. In 1982, for instance, Mississippi's poverty rate was 23 percent. That of Kansas was less than half as big, at 11 percent. Connecticut's was nearly one-third as big, at 8 percent. The poverty rate in 1982 ranged from a high of nearly 25 percent in West Virginia to a low of under 8 percent in Nevada.[14] The variations in state unemployment rates are nearly as dramatic. In 1984 Alabama's unemployment rate was 11.1 percent; New York's was 7.2 percent; and North Dakota's was 4.4 percent. The unemployment rate in 1984 ranged from a high of 15.0 percent in West Virginia (again) to a low of 4.3 percent in New Hampshire.[15] Yet the capacity of states to deal with poverty is also unevenly—and disproportionately—distributed. Many of the states with the highest poverty rates have the least capacity to raise revenues. Many states with relatively less poverty stand in the best position to raise revenues. In 1984, for instance, the high-poverty state of Mississippi had the lowest per capita personal income, $8,777. The low-poverty state of Connecticut had one of the highest per capita incomes, $16,566, nearly twice as much.[16] Because of both the huge perceived state cost of dealing with poverty and unemployment and the mismatch between the scope of the problem in each state and the state's comparative capacity to finance solutions, it makes sense to allocate the burden of income-related programs (whether cash-transfer programs, community-service-jobs programs, wage-supplement programs, or income-substitute programs) to the federal government.

The third consideration in assigning responsibility is that if a problem is left to the states to resolve, the solutions will vary (perhaps substantially) from state to state. If the problem is given to the federal government to solve, the solution will be nationwide and thus uniform. If a problem's different solution in individual states produces no adverse side effects, it should be left to the states. In contrast, if a problem's different solution in the various states produces harmful, unintended consequences, but a national solution eliminates those consequences, it should be assigned to the federal government. In colloquial terms, If variation doesn't hurt, let the states do it; if variation hurts, give it to the feds.

Differences from state to state in the design of service programs generally have no significant unwanted side effects. Citizens will usually not move from Minnesota to Wisconsin, for instance, because the elementary schools in Wisconsin are better or the roads in Wisconsin are in better repair. Businesses also will seldom relocate across state boundaries for such reasons. Finally, differences in state service programs do not typically encourage state legislatures or governors to lower (or raise) the standards that govern their own service programs.

Differences from state to state in income or income-substitute programs, however, do have perverse effects. They induce citizens and governments to act differently than would normally be the case—differently, in some cases, than citizens and governments would prefer to act. While it may be that only a few citizens actually cross state boundaries to get higher welfare or Medicaid benefits, and while it also may be that few recipients remain in a high benefit state primarily because of its higher welfare or Medicaid benefits, there is ample anecdotal evidence and some empirical evidence to suggest that benefit differentials do produce at least a weak "magnet effect."

While differences in state income and income-substitute programs only indirectly influence business location and expansion decisions, their primary—albeit minimal—impact on poor and unemployed people's choice of residence has an important secondary effect on state legislatures and governors. State officials can point to a variety of reasons for holding down AFDC and other welfare benefits, but one reason that consistently emerges is their desire either to maintain their "favorably" low benefits compared to other states or to avoid making their "unfavorably" high benefits even higher, so as to, respectively, avoid becoming a magnet state or avoid becoming an even more powerful magnet state. Differences from state to state in income and income-substitute programs trigger a kind of perverse competition among the states to see who can help the poor the least.

To neutralize these perverse incentives and consequences, the only solutions are for the federal government (1) to allow states to continue to administer income and income-substitute programs, but mandate consistent state benefit levels and other standards, or (2) to take over direct administrative responsibility for income and income-substitute programs and adopt uniform national standards. In either case, a federal takeover has occurred.

If a sorting-out of state and federal responsibility along these lines happened, it would provide a rational and coherent way of finding the extra $10 billion or more that would have to be raised—after repealing up to $75 billion worth of federal programs that address poverty's symptoms—to pay for an $85 billion federal program of directly eliminating poverty and providing low-income persons with subsidized day care and health insurance. In addition to repealing the symptom-oriented programs, Congress could eliminate $10 billion or more worth of service-program funding to states in areas such as transportation and education, as a *quid pro quo* for the federal government's enactment of its new $85 billion program of income transfers (i.e., simple cash payments, community-service-job wage payments, and wage-supplement payments) and income-substitute transfers (i.e., day-care and health-insurance subsidies). It would not be necessary to eliminate all service grants to states—just enough to come up with the dollars needed to pay for the new $85 billion program without raising taxes.

How realistic is such a sorting out? Given the political power of the groups that supported the enactment of federal service programs in the first place and that continue to sustain them in the face of $100–200 billion federal budget deficits, cashing in even a few of them to pay for a new program with no constituency would be extremely difficult. Sorting out state and federal responsibilites along the lines discussed here, nonetheless, represents a choice that ought to be seriously considered, for the only other choice available for funding the elimination of poverty in the United States and providing the low-income population with subsidized day care and health insurance may be to raise taxes.

Sherlock Holmes once tells Watson, "When you have eliminated the impossible, whatever remains, however improbable, must be the truth."[17] So it is with meeting the cost of justice. Various possibilities for generating $85 billion in federal funds exist. Redundant programs can be repealed. Programs that address poverty's symptoms can be repealed. Programs whose purposes are incompatible with sound public policy can be repealed. Programs that provide services that ought to be provided by the states, in return for a federal takeover of income-related responsibilities, can be repealed. There is plenty of money in these programs, taken together, to come up with $85 billion. Powerful interest groups, however, as well as a fear of the large unknown, may make it politically impossible to generate more than a portion of the needed revenue. Then, to paraphrase Sherlock Holmes, the one remaining method for raising federal revenues, however unattractive, must be pursued: Increase tax rates. It is indeed an unattractive choice, but if all other fund-raising methods fail, it is the only way to eliminate poverty (and achieve the critical related goals of providing affordable day care and health insurance) in the United States.

Justice is not cheap. It commands a price, and the price is high.

Paying the price is largely a matter of political will. Do we want to eliminate poverty enough to be willing to impose the price on those individuals and constituencies whom we consider to have a lesser claim on our common resources? Or, to the extent that we lack the political will to eliminate poverty by disinvesting in claims of lower priority, do we still want to eliminate poverty enough to be willing to impose the price on ourselves by raising new resources through new taxes? These are uncomfortable questions, but they are unavoidable. Justice in this country will remain a dream until we face up to them.

## NOTES

1. Bureau of the Census, U.S. Department of Commerce, "Characteristics of the Population Below the Poverty Level: 1984," Series P–60, No. 152, June 1986, p. 122.

2. Ibid., p. 22; idem, "Money Income and Poverty Status of Families and Persons in the United States: 1985," Series P–60, No. 154, August 1986, pp. 32, 34; and idem, "Money Income and Poverty Status of Families and Persons in the United States: 1986," Series P–60, No. 157, July 1987, pp. 35, 38.

3. Bureau of the Census, "Money Income and Poverty Status...1986," p. 35.

4. Office of Management and Budget, "Budget of the United States Government: Fiscal Year 1988," January 5, 1987, pp. 5–28 and 5–29. Outlays are limited to so-called on-budget outlays and exclude transactions of the Social Security Trust Funds. Outlays for the fiscal-year transition quarter of July 1, 1976 through September 30, 1976 are excluded.

5. See Bureau of the Census, "Federal Expenditures by State for Fiscal Year 1986," March 1987, for data on AFDC (p. 9); Food Stamps (pp. 3 and 20); Medicaid (p. 8), low-income housing programs (includes, pp. 10 and 18, public housing; low-rent-housing operating assistance, and housing payments under Section 8); Social Security (p. 19); and Medicare (p. 19). See Office of Management and Budget, "Budget...Fiscal Year 1988," for data on commodity price supports (pp. 2–14, 4–37), national defense (p. 4–71), and interest on the national debt (p. 4–157). See Office of Management and Budget, "Special Analyses: Budget of the United States Government: Fiscal Year 1988," for data on tax expenditures (pp. G–38–G–41). The tax-expenditure data used are calculated to be the "outlay equivalent"; separate calculations of revenue loss are approximately the same.

6. State SSI supplementation payments and AFDC benefit payments are for federal Fiscal Year 1986. See U.S. Congress, House, Committee on Ways and Means, "Background Material and Data on Programs within the Jurisdiction of the Committee on Ways and Means," March 6, 1987, pp. 424, 523.

7. Poverty is here considered the initial rationale of a program's existence if either one of two conditions is the case: (1) the elimination of poverty was set forth in the legislation that created the program (or in the legislative history accompanying the creation of the program) as one of the program's primary

purposes; or (2) if poverty had not existed in the United States to any significant extent at the time of the program's enactment, it is highly unlikely that Congress would have authorized or funded the program. Both criteria are likely to be controversial, especially to those nonpoor individuals who benefit from or have charge of the operation of such programs and whose jobs or income would be threatened by their repeal. These criteria are also not likely to be acceptable to those interest groups, state and federal bureaucrats, and members of Congress who created or have jurisdiction over the programs in question, since their power and status would be threatened by the programs' repeal. Notwithstanding the objections of such self-interested constituencies, these criteria are valid. If poverty or one of its symptoms was either the problem a program was designed to solve or a necessary underlying cause of the program's initial creation, then the elimination of poverty should mean that there is no longer any rational basis for continuing the program.

8. Bureau of the Census, "Federal Expenditures by State," pp. 3–4, 6, 8–11, 13, 18, 20.

9. Committee on Ways and Means, "Background Material," p. 310. Data are for federal Fiscal Year 1985. Total Medicaid recipients were 21.808 million; of these, dependent children under 21 accounted for 9.752 million and adults in families with dependent children for 5.518 million; aged accounted for 3.062 million, blind for 0.80 million, and disabled for 2.936 million; "other" accounted for 1.214 million. In FY 1985, Medicaid payments to providers totaled $37.508 billion, as opposed to $41.150 in total program costs. Of these payments, $10.645 billion (28.4 percent) went to hospitals for inpatient care; $1.789 billion (4.8 percent) for outpatient hospital care; $2.346 billion (6.3 percent) to physicians; $2.316 (6.2 percent) for prescribed drugs; $1.120 (3.0 percent) for home health care; $5.073 (13.5 percent) to skilled-nursing facilities; $11.245 (30.0 percent) to intermediate-care facilities; and the balance for dental, clinic, lab and X-ray, family planning, early and periodic screening, rural health clinics, and other providers.

10. See Office of Management and Budget, "Budget...Fiscal Year 1988," p. 2–14.

11. See Bruce Babbitt, "States Rights for Liberals," *New Republic,* January 24, 1981, Vol. 184, No. 4, p. 21; Pete V. Domenici, "Do the Feds Have to Do Everything," *Wall Street Journal,* February 11, 1976, P. 21; and David A. Stockman, "The Social Pork Barrel," *The Public Interest,* Spring 1975, No. 39, p. 30. See, also President's Commission for a National Agenda, "A National Agenda for the Eighties," 1980; and Advisory Commission on Intergovernmental Relations, "The Federal Role in the Federal System: The Dynamics of Growth," December 1980. Finally, see the policy papers of the National Conference of State Legislatures and National Governors Association issued in 1981–82.

12. Ibid.

13. Ibid.

14. Sheldon Danziger, Institute for Research on Poverty, University of Wisconsin-Madison, "Recent Increases in Poverty: A Comparison of Wisconsin and the U.S.," University of Wisconsin-Madison, November 1983.

15. Committee on Ways and Means, "Background Material," pp. 667–78.

16. Ibid.

17. Arthur Conan Doyle, "The Sign of Four," in *The Complete Sherlock Holmes* (Garden City, NY: Doubleday), p. 111.

# Conclusion: Five Choices

Returning from a Third World country to the United States, one cannot help but be struck by how manageable this country's problems seem. Unlike the poverty that confronts, say, Ethiopia or India or Mexico, the poverty that challenges America seems so easily eradicable. Comparatively few, here, are impoverished. The great majority enjoy a decent standard of living. True wealth is widespread. The citizenry, through their elected legislators, made a commitment nearly a quarter of a century ago to wage war on poverty. The commitment has resulted in the expenditure of hundreds of billions of dollars, and now amounts to somewhere between $50–100 billion in federal spending each year (depending on what one counts as a "front" in the war). Yet poverty remains, fluctuating between 10 and 15 percent of the population, falling with good times, rising with bad times, but never disappearing. Whatever we have been doing for a quarter of a century to get rid of poverty clearly has not worked.

The central thesis of this book is that our failure to eliminate poverty is due primarily to a false premise we have embraced about the causes of poverty. Specifically, we have falsely assumed—conservatives and liberals alike, technical experts and public policymakers alike—that there was something about either the poor themselves (their motivation to work, or their level of education and training), or our attitude toward the poor (our tolerance of their laziness, our racial and sexual discrimination), or the costs the poor must pay in order to work (day care, loss of Medicaid) that needed to be modified in order to get them into the good jobs, providing a nonpoverty income and solid fringe benefits, which the U.S. economy makes available to all. Eliminate one or more of these internal or external barriers, our assumption has been, and the poor will go forth confidently into the labor market, get good jobs, and stop being poor.

In fact, while a more highly motivated, better educated and trained, and less discriminated-against poor population that can afford day care and health insurance would certainly be a good thing, modifying the internal and external obstacles that affect the poor will never get them out of poverty as long as the U.S. job market remains what it is today. As Katharine Abraham's research and other data make clear, the job market is characterized both by a substantial surplus of unemployed jobseekers compared to available jobs and by a huge percentage of low-wage jobs. While it is possible that demographic trends may reduce the unfavorable ratio of unemployed jobseekers to available jobs, the direction of the economy suggests that the percentage of low-wage jobs may well increase as we approach and enter the twenty-first century. The primary cause of poverty in the United States is precisely this shortage of employment and prevalence of low-wage employment. America's poor will never get out of poverty, in the foreseeable future, until these deficiencies in the American job market are corrected.

Once we disenthrall ourselves from the false premises to which we have heretofore clung and accept this revised premise as to why the poor are poor, we face five basic choices. The first and second choices will perpetuate poverty. The third and fourth choices will eliminate poverty, but in an unacceptable manner and at an unacceptable cost. Only the fifth choice will eliminate poverty in a manner that makes sense and at a reasonable cost—if we have the political will to act.

The first choice is to do nothing; continue to enroll a fraction of the poor in the current welfare system, which ensures that virtually all those who receive welfare benefits will remain poor; continue to exclude the majority of the poor from the welfare system, but offer them no alternative help in getting out of poverty, which ensures that a huge group of nonwelfare poor will remain poor.

The second choice is to reform welfare. This can be accomplished in more than one way: by pursuing the conservative agenda of eliminating or reducing AFDC and other antipoverty programs in order to motivate both current and would-be welfare recipients to seek work; by adopting the liberal agenda of providing AFDC recipients and other poor people with education and training, while vigorously attacking racial and sexual discrimination; or by embracing the so-called new consensus that combines conservative work requirements with liberal education and training programs and throws in day-care subsidies and extended Medicaid benefits. In any of these three cases, most of the AFDC recipients who will be affected by reform—who, to begin with, constitute a minority of the poor—will end up roughly where they started: poor.

The non-AFDC poor population, which these reform proposals do not touch and who constitute the majority of the poor, will also end up exactly where they are today: poor. Modifying the barriers that keep AFDC recipients in particular and the poor in general from climbing to more favorable positions in the queue for work is an insufficient method of eliminating poverty, as long as the queue of jobseekers continues to exceed the supply of jobs and as long as such a large percentage of the available jobs pay low wages.

The third basic choice is just to give the poor money. The precise mechanism for accomplishing this—negative income tax or expanded cash-transfer programs—is a detail. The concept is the same: everyone would be guaranteed an income equal to the poverty line, and that guaranteed income would be reduced to the extent that the single individual or family unit earned (or otherwise acquired) income. This choice would indeed eliminate poverty, but its costs would be enormous. On the one hand, it denies the poor the very things for which they, like the rest of us, have a profound psychological and social need: a job, gainful employment, a useful connection with the rest of society. On the other hand, a guaranteed annual income will induce some who are unemployed, some who currently hold low-wage jobs, and even some who hold higher-wage jobs to give up their pursuit of work or the jobs they hold. If society says, "It is legitimate for citizens to get free money for the rest of their lives in lieu of working," millions who would otherwise pursue work or hold jobs (although still probably a minority of the population) will respond. If $50 billion is a reasonable estimate of the current cost of eliminating poverty, a guaranteed annual income equal to the poverty line could have a price tag twice or thrice as large. The cost would, of course, be borne primarily by those who remain at work, through the income taxes they pay, which raises a profound issue of fairness: Why should Joe Jones, who can find a job (and who maybe used to have one), be permitted to stay at home and receive a guaranteed income that is paid for by worker Stan Smith's taxes?

The fourth basic choice is to reallocate the jobs currently provided by the U.S. economy. We could, if we wanted, abandon the notion that hiring decisions should be made by employers. We could then assign every poor individual and every poor family head to a job now held by a person who, if transferred to other employment or displaced altogether, would not end up poor as a result. Single persons making more than $10,000 per year could be reassigned to lower-paying jobs that would still leave them above the poverty line. One of the workers in a two-worker household where each makes more than $15,000 per year could be simply laid off, making her or his job available, while permitting the unit to remain above the poverty line. Persons who have substantial unearned income but who have chosen to work, as well as persons over 65 who are entitled to substantial pensions but who remain in the labor force, could all be compelled to give up their jobs.

In theory, at least, the poor would have plenty of jobs to fill, and low-wage workers would probably have enough middle-wage and high-wage jobs to move up to, if all the "overpaid" or "unnecessary" workers in the United States were thus reallocated to other positions in the economy or laid off entirely. Needless to say, however, such a scheme is neither feasible nor desirable. If implemented quickly, it would bring chaos to the U.S. economy. If implemented over a longer time period, thus allowing for the proper training of millions who would be assigned to jobs that they now simply could not perform, such a scheme would suffer from two enormous drawbacks. First, it would cost billions of dollars to implement (and the cost of training would be borne in part by the workers reassigned or displaced!). Second, it would produce a dramatic reduction in the productivity of the U.S. economy. Many of the poor who get the vacated jobs, despite good training, would be far less productive than the better-trained and vastly more experienced workers they displace.

The worst part of such an approach, however, is its unfairness. There is no justice in eliminating poverty at the price of laying off millions of Americans from jobs they have chosen, want to keep, were hired to do, and are (generally) good at performing. Finally, even if by some miracle it were possible to conclude that all the preceding objections to this scheme either did not matter or could be overcome, the scheme would be so repugnant to the American public that there is a zero percent chance it would ever be implemented.

A modified version of this scheme—assigning the unemployed poor and working poor to *new* good jobs that come open in the economy by (for instance) prohibiting all unemployed single persons from taking high-wage jobs, prohibiting unemployed workers from taking jobs when someone else in the family already has a high-wage job, and prohibiting unemployed persons of independent wealth and unemployed retirees with adequate pensions from taking jobs—deserves a few seconds' thought. It would probably produce substantially less economic chaos. It would also probably impose substantially lower training costs on the taxpayers. It would, perhaps, be less unfair—in the sense that it seems less unjust to withold from someone a good thing that the person does not yet possess than to deprive someone of a good thing that the person already possesses. Nonetheless, even this scaled-down approach of assigning the poor to new good jobs by government fiat would do great harm to the productivity of the U.S. economy, impose enormous costs, and be perceived as unfair by the vast majority. Its political viability, if not nil, is virtually so.

The fifth basic choice, which may well be the only other one available, and which this book advocates, requires three separate (but interrelated) responses to the three tiers of the U.S. poor population. Only the first tier—poor people who cannot work or whom old age exempts from working—would receive a guaranteed annual income. Specifically, their SSI and Social Security paychecks would be supplemented to get them above the poverty line. For the other two tiers, work would be required as a condition for receiving help, and full-time, year-round work would be rewarded with an income above the poverty line. The second tier—consisting of poor people who can work but who cannot find full-time, year-round work—would be offered community-service employment that would provide enough hours of work to plug the gap between their current level of employment and 35 hours of work per week for 52 weeks each year at the minimum wage. The third tier—persons who have dependent children and who already hold jobs (whether community-service jobs or otherwise)—would be given a wage supplement, in the form of an expanded and dependent-adjusted Earned Income Tax Credit, that would be sufficient to get their families above the poverty line. Like the guaranteed annual income, this approach would virtually eliminate poverty in the United States. Unlike the guaranteed annual income, it would give the poor what they want—jobs. The community-service work performed would improve the quality of both urban and rural communities. This three-tiered approach—plus the provision of appropriate day care and health insurance—would require the federal government to spend something on the order of an additional $85 billion. Up to $75 billion of this cost could be offset by eliminating existing programs that would become redundant or that deal with poverty's symptoms, leaving a net federal cost of $10 billion. The $10 billion could be raised either by repealing wasteful or low-priority federal programs, eliminating service programs whose functions could properly be delegated to the states as a *quid pro quo* for the federal takeover of income-related functions, or raising taxes.

Which choice does the U.S. public wish to make? In the end it is truly a matter of choice—our choice. There is no magic about poverty, nor is there any about its elimination. The poor are poor because SSI and Social Security are not designed to eliminate poverty, because there are not enough jobs, and because too many jobs pay too little. Five major options stand before us. Do nothing, which means let the poor stay poor. Tinker with the welfare system, which means let the poor stay poor. Expand the welfare system into a superwelfare system of guaranteed annual incomes, which means that poverty would be eliminated in a manner the poor do not want and at a price that is unnecessarily high. Arbitrarily assign the poor to good jobs in the economy (either displacing current workers or preempting unemployed but nonpoor individuals who would otherwise be hired), which means that poverty would be eliminated in a manner that would damage the U.S. economy, cost an enormous amount of money, and be unfair to the displaced or preempted workers. Or replace the welfare system altogether with a three-tier, work-oriented approach that gets rid of poverty by increasing the disabled and elderly poor's social insurance payments, offering the unemployed poor community-service jobs and supplementing the working poor's wages.

To the extent that poverty continues or disappears in this country as we enter the twenty-first century, it will be neither a matter of accident nor a matter of fate. It will be a matter of choice and will. The options are clear. The methods needed to accomplish the task and the resources required to pay the cost are at our disposal. Tough trade-offs must be made, but they are doable. The decision is ours.

# Select Bibliography

Abraham, Katharine G. "Help-Wanted Advertising, Job Vacancies, and Unemployment." *Brookings Papers on Economic Activity,* Washington, DC: Brookings Institution, 1987.

———. "Structural/Frictional vs. Deficient Demand Unemployment: Some New Evidence." *American Economic Review* 73, No. 4 (September 1983): pp. 708–724.

———. "Too Few Jobs." *Washington Post,* May 25, 1982, p. A–17.

———. "Vacancies, Unemployment and Wage Growth." Ph.D. dissertation, Harvard University, 1982.

Brenner, M. Harvey. "Influence of the Social Environment on Psychopathology: The Historic Perspective." In *Stress and Mental Disorder,* edited by James E. Barrett et al., New York: Raven Press, 1979, pp. 161–177.

———. "Personal Stability and Economic Security." *Social Policy,* Vol. 8, No. 1 (May-June 1977): pp. 2–4.

Chollet, Deborah J. (Employee Benefit Research Institute). "The Erosion of Health Insurance Coverage Among the Nonelderly Population: Public Policy Issues and Options." Statement before the U.S. Congress, House, Committee on Small Business, May 6, 1987.

Congressional Budget Office. "Reducing Poverty Among Children," Washington, D.C., May 1985.

Danziger, Sheldon H., and Weinberg, Daniel H., eds. *Fighting Poverty: What Works and What Doesn't.* Cambridge, MA: Harvard University Press, 1986.

Danzon, Patricia M., and Sloan, Frank A. "Covering the Uninsured: How Much Would It Cost?" Nashville, TN: Vanderbilt Institution for Public Policy Studies, 1987.

Duncan, Greg J. "On the Slippery Slope." *American Demographics,* Vol. 9, No. 5 (May 1987): pp. 30–35.

Goodwin, Leonard. *Do the Poor Want to Work? A Social-Psychological Study in Work Orientations.* Washington, DC: Brookings Institution, 1972.

Harrington, Michael. *The Other America: Poverty in the United States.* New York: Macmillan, 1962.

Himmelfarb, Gertrude. *The Idea of Poverty: England in the Early Industrial Age.* New York: Knopf, 1984.

Krislov, Samuel. "The OEO Lawyers Fail to Constitutionalize a Right to Welfare: A Study in the Uses and Limits of the Judicial Process," 58 Minn. L. Rev. 211 (1973).

Mead, Lawrence M. *Beyond Entitlement: The Social Obligations of Citizenship.* New York: Free Press, 1986.

Murray, Charles. *Losing Ground: American Social Policy, 1950–1980.* New York: Basic Books, 1984.

Orshansky, Mollie. "Children of the Poor." *Social Security Bulletin.* Vol. 6, No. 7 (July 1963): pp. 3–13.

———. "Counting the Poor: Another Look at the Poverty Profile." *Social Security Bulletin.* Vol. 28, No. 1 (January 1965): pp. 3–29.

———. "How Poverty Is Measured." *Monthly Labor Review,* Vol. 92, No. 2, (February 1969): pp. 37–41.

———. "Measuring Poverty." In *The Social Welfare Forum: 1965.* New York: Columbia University Press, 1965, pp. 211–223.

Robert Wood Johnson Foundation. "Access to Health Care in the United States: Results of a 1986 Survey." Special Report Number Two. Princeton, NJ: 1987.

Sulvetta, Margaret B., and Swartz, Katherine. "The Uninsured and Uncompensated Care: A Chartbook." Washington, DC: National Health Policy Forum, June 1986.

Thurow, Lester C. *The Zero-Sum Society: Distribution and the Possibilities for Economic Change.* New York: Basic Books, 1980. Reprinted by Penguin Books, 1984.

U.S. Bureau of the Census. "Characteristics of the Population Below the Poverty Level: 1984," Series P–60, No. 152. Washington, DC, June 1986.

———. "Estimates of Poverty Including the Value of Noncash Benefits: 1985," Technical Paper 56. Washington, DC, September 1986.

———. "Federal Expenditures by State for Fiscal Year 1986." Washington, DC, March 1987.

———. "Money Income and Poverty Status of Families and Persons in the United States: 1985." Series P–60, No. 154. Washington, DC, August 1986.

———. "Money Income and Poverty Status of Families and Persons in the United States: 1986." Series P–60, No. 157. Washington, DC, July 1987.

———. "Receipt of Selected Noncash Benefits: 1985." Series P–60, No. 155. Washington, DC, January 1987.

———. "Who's Minding the Kids? Child Care Arrangements: Winter 1984–85." Series P–70, No. 9. Washington, DC, 1987.

U.S. Bureau of Labor Statistics, "Linking Employment Problems to Economic Status," Bulletin 2222. Washington, DC, March 1985.

———. "Median Weekly Earnings of Wage and Salary Workers Who Usually

Work Full Time by Detailed (3-Digit Census Code) Occupation and Sex: 1986 Annual Averages." Unpublished tabulations. Washington, DC, 1987.

————. "Usual Weekly Earnings of Employed Wage and Salary Workers Who Usually Work Full-Time by Detailed Occupation and Sex: 1986 Annual Averages." Unpublished tabulations. Washington, DC, 1987.

U.S. Congress, House, Committee on Ways and Means. "Background Material and Data on Programs Within the Jurisdiction of the Committee on Ways and Means." 1987 edition (Washington, D.C.: U.S. Government Printing Office, March 6, 1987).

Wilson, William Julius. *The Truly Disadvantaged: The Inner City, the Underclass, and Public Policy*. Chicago: University of Chicago Press, 1987.

# Index

## ABOUT THE AUTHOR

DAVID RAPHAEL RIEMER is currently Director of the Department of Budget and Management Analysis for the City of Milwaukee, Wisconsin.

He previously served as Legal Advisor to Wisconsin Governor Patrick J. Lucey (1975–76); Special Counsel to the Wisconsin Department of Health and Social Services (1976–78); Counsel to the U.S. Senate Subcommittee on Health and Scientific Research, chaired by Senator Edward M. Kennedy (1978–81); Senior Staff Director for Human Resources for the National Conference of State Legislatures (1981–82); and Counsel for Health Care Financing for the Legislative Fiscal Bureau of the Wisconsin State Legislature (1983). In 1984, as a consultant to the Wisconsin Department of Health and Social Services, he prepared the report to the Wisconsin Legislature, "Wisconsin's Uninsured: The Scope of the Problem and Alternative Solutions," which provided the basis for the legislature's enactment in 1985 of a state health insurance program (SHIP). He joined Time Insurance Company, which is headquartered in Milwaukee, as Counsel for Cost Containment in 1985 and was promoted to Director of Managed Health Care Development in 1987. He assumed his current position with the City of Milwaukee in 1988.

Mr. Riemer has served since 1981 on the national board of directors of Congress For a Working America, and from 1985 to 1988 was chair of the board. In 1985, he was appointed a member of the Wisconsin Council on Health Care Coverage for the Uninsured, and in 1986 served as a public member of the Wisconsin Legislature Council's Special Committee on Employment Disincentives. He has spoken at numerous conferences around the country about the uninsured and the comparative merits of different solutions. He has also been active in politics, serving most recently as Issues Coordinator in John Norquist's successful campaign (1986–88) for mayor of Milwaukee.

Mr. Riemer holds an A.B. in History and Literature from Harvard College (1970) and a J.D. from Harvard Law School (1975).